Social Media Warfare
Equal Weapons for All

Social Media Warfare
Equal Weapons for All

By
Michael Erbschloe

CRC Press
Taylor & Francis Group
Boca Raton London New York

CRC Press is an imprint of the
Taylor & Francis Group, an **informa** business

AN AUERBACH BOOK

CRC Press
Taylor & Francis Group
6000 Broken Sound Parkway NW, Suite 300
Boca Raton, FL 33487-2742

Library of Congress Cataloging-in-Publication Data

Names: Erbschloe, Michael, 1951- author.
Title: Social media warfare : equal weapons for all / Michael Erbschloe.
Description: Boca Raton, FL : CRC/Taylor & Francis, [2017] | Includes
bibliographical references.
Identifiers: LCCN 2016052774 | ISBN 9781138036024 (hb : alk. paper)
Subjects: LCSH: Information warfare. | Social media. | Cyberterrorism. |
Cyberspace operations (Military science) | Computer crimes--Social
aspects. | Internet--Moral and ethical aspects. | Privacy, Right of. |
Cyberspace--Security measures. | Irregular warfare.
Classification: LCC U163 .E67 2017 | DDC 355.3/43--dc23
LC record available at https://lccn.loc.gov/2016052774

**Visit the Taylor & Francis Web site at
http://www.taylorandfrancis.com**

**and the CRC Press Web site at
http://www.crcpress.com**

Printed and bound in the United States of America by Sheridan

Contents

Foreword

Writing this book was enlightening in many ways. The breadth of social media warfare tactics used is surprisingly extensive in all sectors including efforts to fight terrorism, combat crime, and provide a forum for special interest groups. What is disturbing is how much social media is used for evil purposes. Much of the rhetoric of evil was omitted from this book because it is disgusting. The volume of hate and oppression in social media is, unfortunately, a reflection of how much evil exists in the world. Although there is much good accomplished using social media, whether it is to support open government, discussion of health and environmental issues, and often just good entertainment, evil people in the world have equal access to social media weapons. That, however, is the nature of free speech, and that speech is protected regardless of an individual's or group's perspectives and philosophies. The World Wide Web and the pre-social media tools took more effort to use than social media applications. Thus, when easy-to-use social media applications arrived at the Internet, so did the deplorable citizenry of the world. Social media was so easy for this deplorable citizenry because proper grammar and correct spelling went by the wayside, as quickly as nasty attitudes and bad manners proliferated like weeds across the new medium. The great commentator, Edward R. Murrow, once said that "The speed of communications is wondrous to behold. It is also true that speed can multiply the distribution of information that we know to be untrue."

Michael Erbschloe

Preface

Social media is no longer just for sharing family vacation and sleeping cat photos. Social media tools and applications are available to everybody with a computer or a smartphone. They are increasingly used as an effective weapon by many people on many sides of different conflicts. Military and civilian organizations of all types will need to become more effective in watching how their foes use social media, defending against ongoing social media attacks, and using social media as a weapon in pursuit of their own goals.

Social media content is driven by the social context in which it is created. The dynamics that drive social media warfare are rooted in the conflict that is inherent between social institutions, governments, corporations, and groups or individuals that are willing to stage an insurgency or protest the social structures and norms that they feel have oppressed them in some way. Social media warfare has also entered the political electoral process and social change movements of all types.

The basic applied theories that guide this analysis are based on a sociological perspective of organization structure and interaction, as well as interactions between social institutions, organizations, and individuals. The central guiding philosophy is rooted in conflict theory and is heavily influenced by the work of C. Wright Mills.

Acknowledgments

I want to thank Richard O'Hanley, publisher at CRC Press, and his publishing team for their support and assistance getting this book from concept into print. Also, I want to thank my sister for her never-ending support of my efforts.

Author

Michael Erbschloe worked for over 30 years performing analyses on the economics of information technology, public policy relating to technology, and technology use in reengineering organization processes. He has authored several books on social and management issues of information technology, most of which covered some aspects of information or corporate security. Michael Erbschloe has also taught at several universities and developed technology-related curriculums. His career has focused on several interrelated areas: technology strategy, analysis, and forecasting; teaching and curriculum development; writing books and articles; speaking at conferences and industry events; publishing and editing; and public policy analysis and program evaluation. He currently works as a consultant on technology and security issues.

Introduction

Social media is no longer just for sharing family vacation and sleeping cat photos. Social media tools and applications are available to everybody with a computer or a smartphone. They have been increasingly used as an effective weapon by many people on many sides of different conflicts. Military as well as civilian organizations of all types will need to become more effective in watching how their foes use social media, defending against ongoing social media attacks, and using social media as a weapon in pursuit of their own goals.

Learning the process of offensive social media attacks for fueling insurgency or social actions takes very little time. Being good at it, on the other hand, does take considerable effort and study, as does any warfare strategy or tactic. It takes time. It also takes planning and dedication. There is no one-stop website that provides all the education and training needed to effectively wage social media warfare or defend an organization during social media conflict. There also is not a single one-size-fits-all social media warfare program that will suddenly make a nation or an organization secure during social media conflicts.

It is necessary to understand that many conflict-oriented social media uses are legal, and governments and law enforcement agencies will and can do little to help the conflicting sides in a social media war. However, when governments are involved in a conflict that has a social media warfare component, they will do all they can to control access to social media tools. But many social media application providers are more than willing to have their tools used by any and all, regardless of which side of the conflict they support. That said, this book provides a structured approach to using social media weapons and protecting an organization from this emerging unconventional warfare strategy.

As the use of social media in conflict situations evolves, many organizations are becoming more vulnerable because they have either naively used social media applications or have no idea how to defend against social media warfare attacks. Organizations have had to address the same challenge when facing cyber threats and have put forth considerable effort to protect against a variety of cyber attack methods. The difference between cyber warfare and social media warfare is that cyber warfare requires a far higher level of technical knowledge and skill. Social media warfare is easier to learn and faster to deploy; but effective social media warfare, like cyber warfare, requires discipline and long-term dedication for successful deployment or defense. Social media warfare tactics also have proven to be rather successful as an unconventional warfare tool.

This book is designed to save managers and social media foot soldiers time that it would otherwise take to research social media warfare approaches and mitigation methods. As a result, this book will better inform managers on setting goals and about defensible actions to take against social media warfare attacks; it also will better enable managers to deal with governments or organizations that may victimize them during social media warfare operations.

To make this book helpful for graduate- or professional-level seminar classes, Seminar Discussion Topics are provided for each chapter. Suggested as well as possible Seminar Group Projects are also provided; each is expected to take no more than thirty minutes for a group to work through and present results.

The chapters are arranged in a manner that provides for the analysis of social media warfare use by different types of organizations or special interest groups. Each group has different offensive and defensive strategies available based on their budgets and skill mix. In addition, many tactics may be applicable across industry sectors or organization type. The content of chapters is discussed below.

Chapter 1: A Framework to Analyze Emerging Social Media Warfare Strategies: Social media warfare has become a study topic in military science, and it will play a bigger role in future conflicts. This chapter introduces the basic concepts and definitions of social media warfare, including the new definition of war, social media warfare study in academic disciplines, social media warfare participants, defensive and offensive social media warfare tactics, the tools of social media warfare, knowledge and skills needed for social media warfare, and how to develop a "lessons learned" process for social media warfare.

Chapter 2: Civilian Government Use of Social Media to Attack, Defend, or Control: Governments face numerous challenges associated with social media warfare because most governments are rather defensive and highly focused on self-preservation; therefore, they are confronted with the possibility of defending their national interest (or at least defending government officials) against social media based or inspired attacks. In many cases governments choose to limit Internet access or punish those citizens who use social media to criticize or question the national government or political leaders. This chapter examines a variety of issues that various types of governments face, and that citizens living under different types of government must deal with as they strive to live free lives. These issues include the growth in Internet use and access to social media, individual freedom and social media warfare, agents of national governments in international relations and internal affairs, cooperation with international agencies, provincial/state and local governments and social media warfare, and citizens speaking out on social media about government.

Chapter 3: Military Applications of Social Media Warfare: Military organizations face great challenges in social media warfare. As with past new threats, there is a learning curve and a training curve. Militaries learn to deal with new threats, and they train current and future troops in how to defend against a technology and how to use the technology as a weapon for their advantage. This chapter covers the challenges that militaries face in dealing with social media warfare, including social media warfare in conflict environments, defending a military force from social media warfare tactics, using social media warfare tactics as offensive weapons, using social media warfare tactics to undermine opposing forces, preventing personnel from undermining force stability when using social media, managing social media warfare operations, training military personnel in social media warfare tactics, and using social media warfare tactics to gain support in non-conflict environments.

Chapter 4: Corporate Efforts to Deploy or Respond to Social Media Warfare Strategies: Corporations, especially large ones, are in a constant state of conflict. Social media warfare is intensifying that conflict. Competition is stiff between corporations, and globalization has opened more avenues for competition and conflict. Corporations have polluted the environment, exploited workers, sold faulty and dangerous products, and alienated social cause groups that feel corporations should be held responsible for the damage they have done. The larger the corporation, the more lawsuits they face every year. This chapter examines how corporations use social media warfare tactics and, in turn, have those tactics used against them. Topics include, the corporate environment and mentality, corporations and defensive/offensive social media warfare tactics, corporate profit building through blended social media warfare tactics, nullifying corporate opponents and critics through blended social media warfare tactics, and how citizens speak out on social media about corporations.

Chapter 5: Special Interest Groups' Use of Social Media as a Weapon: There are hundreds of special interest groups involved in a wide variety of interests ranging from commerce, health, or art, to community development or religion. There are also groups that are involved in political and social causes. This chapter examines well-established special interest groups and the various types of special interest groups, as well as issues related to these groups: health care; guns, hate, and social media warfare; abortion debates and violent acts of extremists; environmentalists and eco-terrorists; lesbian, gay, bisexual and transsexual (LGBT) rights and social media warfare; and religious bias and discrimination in social media warfare.

Chapter 6: Social Media Warfare in the Political Electoral Process: The political electoral process is tumultuous in many countries around the world; it is sometimes characterized by violence and is often laden with ideological conflict and divisiveness. The 2016 presidential election in the United States along with congressional, senatorial, and state-level races were no exception to this pattern of ideological conflict and divisiveness. This chapter examines the role of social media warfare tactics and their use in the 2016 U.S. political electoral process. Topics include convergence, the social media warfare tactics of political candidates, blunders in social media warfare, use of social media warfare by the presidential candidates, campaign staff as a liability in social media warfare, use of social media by candidate supporters, monitoring social media activity and effectiveness, and citizens' sources of information.

Chapter 7: Social Media Warfare for Support of Social Causes: Social causes come and go; some just fade away while others result in the establishment of well-structured special interest groups and various organizations that share the special interest. This chapter examines the use of social media warfare tactics to support social causes (not including the well-established special interests covered in Chapter 5). The social causes examined in this chapter are associated with the Black Lives Matter movement that started in 2014 when, at approximately noon on Saturday, August 9, 2014, an officer of the Ferguson, Missouri Police Department shot and killed Michael Brown, an unarmed 18-year-old African American. Since the killing of Michael Brown, there have been several other incidents where police have shot and killed African Americans. The Black Lives Matter movement was reactive in those cases, and social media warfare tactics were a key factor in the reactions to and protests against all these incidents. This chapter covers issues associated with social media warfare in support of social causes, including Ferguson, Missouri and Michael Brown, Eric Garner and other cases; the issue of police in the United States feeling under siege; and social media warfare to support social causes around the world.

Chapter 8: Mercenaries and Activists of Social Media Warfare: There has long been a place for mercenaries in warfare, and social media warfare is no exception when it comes to the use of mercenaries. Social media warfare mercenaries and activists are a blend of techies, writers, and activists that can be employed or otherwise motivated to support or oppose a cause or organization. This chapter examines the types of social media warfare mercenaries, how to hire or motivate them, and how to utilize their talents in social media warfare. It provides examples of work performed by social media warfare mercenaries. This chapter also examines the topic of social media warfare rangers and activists and their use of social media warfare tactics.

Chapter 9: Social Media as a Weapon to Recruit and Inspire Violent Extremists: The conflict in Syria and Iraq has attracted Western-based extremists who want to engage in violence. This chapter focuses on the terrorist Islamic State of Iraq and the Levant (ISIL), also referred to as the Islamic State of Iraq and Syria (ISIS), and its noted efforts and results in recruiting and inspiring new members. Efforts to stop ISIS success in recruitment and radicalization of devotees are also discussed, including the development of counter narratives and international cooperation to promote grassroots efforts to develop counter narratives, master narratives, and alternative narratives.

Chapter 10: Social Media Warfare for Celebrities and Famous People: Thousands of celebrities and famous people around the world have adopted social media warfare tactics for self-promotion or to support charitable causes. Most of the time, celebrities use social media to promote positive narratives and support causes that are in the public interest. Sometimes, however, celebrities communicate negative narratives and provide an undesirable role model for social behavior. This chapter examines the positive work and outcomes of celebrity use of social media warfare tactics as well as the impact that negative messaging by celebrities can have on society. This includes, non-profit promotional activities of celebrities, positive message promotional activities of celebrities, celebrities and famous people that generate negative messaging, and misleading endorsements using celebrity names and images.

Chapter 11: Child Victims in Social Media Warfare: There are many ways individuals or groups can become victims of social media warfare. The ISIL example discussed in other chapters is certainly an extreme example of what can be done to people using social media warfare. Far removed from that conflict, however, is an ongoing onslaught of attacks on individuals. These can take the form of cyberbullying, slander and exposure campaigns, revenge actions such as revenge pornography, and sexual harassment. This chapter examines some of the ways individuals have been harmed by others through the use of adverse social media warfare tactics as well as how social media warfare tactics were used to fight back against perpetrators. Areas covered include cyberbullying, responding to cyberbullying, the threat of online predators to children, social media warfare to rescue missing and exploited children, and child pornography.

Chapter 12: Adult Victims in Social Media Warfare: Adults, like children, can become victims of social media warfare from several sources of attack. These can take the form of harassment, revenge actions, identity theft, fraudulent transactions, and having their computers or phones hacked. Children can certainly be targets of the same sort of attacks but the major concerns about children including cyberbullying, sexual exploitation, kidnapping, and child pornography are covered in Chapter 11. This chapter examines some of the ways adults have been harmed by other individuals using adverse social media warfare tactics, including revenge porn and sextortion, Internet fraud, and identity theft.

Chapter 13: Law Enforcement Response to Social Media Warfare: Law enforcement agencies and officers are stuck right in the middle of social media warfare. Criminal activity is riddled with social media warfare tactics as are law enforcement's efforts to fight crime. Social protest and civil disobedience is organized quickly using social media and often more quickly than law enforcement can respond. Crimes of fraud and harassment are perpetrated using social media warfare tactics, which creates a challenge for law enforcement to keep abreast of tactics and criminal activity. Another challenge is policing the personal use of social media by law enforcement officers, which at times has been embarrassing and compromising for law enforcement agencies around the world. This chapter examines some of the issues and challenges that law enforcement agencies are addressing in the realm of social media warfare. Topics covered include law enforcement officers' personal use of social media, social media warfare in intelligence and investigative activities, government training of social media warfare intelligence and investigative professionals, and the qualifications, training, and functions of social media warfare analysts.

Chapter 14: Educational Institutions' Response to Social Media Warfare: Social media warfare has an impact on educational institutions at all levels. All schools must develop social media use policies for students, staff, and faculty addressing many issues, including appropriate use, cyberbullying, and students using social media to organize protests against schools. Primary and secondary schools need to teach their students about being secure online, and train their teachers and counselors to better enable them to identify potential issues students have with social media. Colleges and universities have had to develop new curriculums to address the quickly changing world of social media and its impact on governments, criminal justice, business, and social and cultural life. Colleges and universities also have new research opportunities to examine the impact of social media warfare on contemporary society. This chapter examines many of the issues schools face as a result of social media warfare. Topics covered include the impact on curriculums, student life, and educational administration.

Chapter 15: Monitoring Social Media Warfare Threats: Security agencies and criminal justice investigators in the United States and several countries around the world monitor social media under specific circumstances. In addition, political campaigns, corporations, and special interest groups monitor social media regarding issues that threaten them. They also monitor their known adversaries' use of social media. This chapter reviews monitoring trends and tools to monitor social media warfare activities. Areas covered include monitoring social media for security and intelligence purposes, for disaster response purposes, and for law enforcement purposes, and developing monitoring technology for social media warfare and social media monitoring tools.

Chapter 1

A Framework to Analyze Emerging Social Media Warfare Strategies

Warfare and the development and definition of warfare strategies and tactics have long been dominated by military leaders, planners, and field commanders. The principles laid out by Sun Tzu in *The Art of War* have stood the test of time, war after war. Indeed, military science has advanced in part because of need and in part because of the growth and maturity of military academies and warfare colleges that support a structured and disciplined study of warfare strategies and tactics. Social media warfare has become a topic of study in military science and will play a bigger role in future conflicts. This chapter introduces the basic concepts and definitions of social media warfare.

1.1 New Definition of War

Through the centuries, perspectives on war have evolved. By necessity, these perspectives were once dominated by a traditional warfare approach, wherein military forces went face to face against other military forces in a relatively well-defined *theater of war* and with a fairly well-defined *theater strategy*. In the twenty-first century, we are firmly entrenched in the age of *irregular warfare* and *unconventional warfare*, where the theater of war is far less well-defined and theater strategy must be fluid and adaptable, including in and through cyberspace.

Many factors have influenced a shift to the dominance of irregular warfare and unconventional warfare. These include shifting political and social alliances as well as economic conditions that have increased the availability of funding for non-traditional forces. With this new funding, non-traditional forces can obtain a variety of weapons to combine with the age-old skills of improvising affordable and effective weapons to meet combat needs in a particular theater of war. There has also been another very important factor contributing to the shift, a globally accessible means of communications and participation: the Internet and all its offerings of connectivity, social media applications, and tools of cyber warfare.

In many ways, the Internet has made *insurgency* easier to initiate and maintain. The Internet has opened the realm of warfare not only to insurgents fighting against a government, but also to social, cultural, economic, and religious factions around the world wishing to fight and harm each other. The Internet has enabled these factions to intentionally inflict harm on each other without guns and often without face-to-face confrontation. Welcome to the age of *social media warfare*, which provides equal weapons for all.

1.2 Social Media Warfare Study by Academic Disciplines

A review of academic disciplines indicates that several of them will eventually provide research in the area of social media warfare, just as they have on general Internet use and specific uses of social media. Currently, it is clear that military science is well ahead of other disciplines in terms of actual attention being allocated to the impact of social media on warfare and conflict situations. The work emerging from military science will be discussed in Chapter 3: "Military Applications of Social Media Warfare."

Other disciplines can make considerable contributions to the study of the use of the Internet and social media. However, academic disciplines are often slow to initiate research streams in new areas primarily because of a lack of funding for such research. The lack of funding is unfortunate because there is much to be researched. It is unlikely that funding will be increased in the near future given the increasing feeling of disdain for science and academia that the conservative electorate has brought to the legislative process. This attitude has spilled over into many areas resulting in a lack of funding for research topics that conservatives are afraid to address, such as gun violence in the United States.

The conservative dominance of the budget process and the deliberate avoidance of science to help guide policy making have become pervasive. The existence of climate change, for example, is denied by most conservative elected officials who have taken steps backward into a time when creationism was the dominant theory of the beginning of Earth and the origin of the species. But conservatives also have adopted other counterproductive stances, such as cutting off poor families from food stamp programs and refusing to address the rates of suicide and homelessness among military veterans in the United States.

Meanwhile, a review of academic programs listed by the National Center for Education Statistics in its 2000 edition of the *Classification of Instructional Programs* (CIP) shows several academic disciplines that can and will eventually provide more insight into social media warfare. Based on this review of the CIP, the academic disciplines that can contribute to the understanding of social media warfare are

- Mass communication/media studies programs that focus on the analysis and criticism of media institutions—how people experience and understand media content; the roles of media in producing and transforming culture; the social and cultural effects of mass media; and the psychological and behavioral aspects of media messages, interpretation, and utilization.
- Political communication programs that focus on human and media communication in the political process—media effects and image management; political journalism; and the production and distribution of media messages in political settings.
- Social psychology programs that focus on the study of individual behavior in group contexts, group behavior, and associated phenomena—social learning theory, group theory and dynamics; social cognition and inference; attribution theory; attitude formation, criminal behavior, and other social pathologies.
- Sociology programs that focus on the systematic study of human social institutions and social relationships—social theory and social organization and structure; social stratification and hierarchies; dynamics of social change; social deviance and control; and specific social groups, social institutions, and social problems.

The basic applied theories guiding most of this analysis are based on a sociological perspective of organizational structure and interaction as well as interactions between social institutions, organizations, and individuals. The central guiding philosophy is rooted in conflict theory and is heavily influenced by the work of C. Wright Mills.

1.3 Social Media Warfare Participants

The dynamics that drive social media warfare are rooted in the conflict inherent between social institutions, governments, corporations, and groups or individuals that are willing to stage an insurgency or protest the social structures and norms that they feel have oppressed them. But social media warfare has also flooded the political electoral process and social change movements of all types.

There is much debate over the definition of warfare applied to conflicts facilitated or supported by social media. This analysis uses the term *warfare* because the conflicts have gone beyond discourse and debate. Organizations and individuals that participate in social media warfare are intent on harming their opponents in some way and doing so without mercy. These initiating participants do not care about the consequences of their rhetoric, actions, or goals on the world around them. They only want to prevail in achieving dominance in the social realm. The past platforms of discourse and debate that served as a foundation for civil society have deteriorated into a primordial chaos of survival of the fittest. Decorum and civility have been abandoned along the way.

The participants in social media warfare were not created by the Internet or by social media; they have long been there using other means to threaten social order. They have a history of being self-serving and narcissistic; social media has just provided them with a new weapon to instantaneously level their wrath against opponents. In some cases, organizations and individuals are indeed victims of attacks by their opponents and respond by working to neutralize the impact of an attack or to do their opponents as much harm as possible in return. In other cases, participants in social media warfare have viciously attacked their opponents with the desire to do them as much harm as possible to meet short-term goals in long struggles for dominance.

When conflict between organizations, social groups, and individuals has been long-standing and not borne out of social media, the frustration of not gaining dominance by other means has led to participants turning to social media warfare to eventually win their way. The swift pace for attack that social media provides opponents has often resulted in serious backlash; it has actually caused attackers more harm than it has helped them achieve success. Social media is there for all to see and it quickly exposes ill-chosen words to a world that would otherwise not bear witness. Organizations, groups, and individuals that can benefit or be harmed by social media warfare are shown in Table 1.1.

The structure of an organization, its size, purpose, and relationships with other organizations influences how social media warfare strategies are selected and what tactics are employed leading to or during conflict situations. As discussed earlier, this is the age of irregular and unconventional warfare, where strategies must be fluid and adaptable including in and through cyberspace.

1.4 Social Media Warfare Strategies

Warfare strategies are always in place and ready, they are not just pulled out of a box when conflict begins. The nature of any type of warfare requires preparation and readiness. That doctrine has been followed without fail since World War II.

Table 1.1 Types of Organizations in Social Media Warfare

Governmental	Coalitions of nations (military and civilian)
	Nations (national governments)
	Aligned political entities (non-nations)
	Military services (army, air force, naval, space, cyber)
Business and commerce	Industry groups and consortiums
	Corporations
Ideological groups	Religions, sects, and sacred orders
	Special focus and interest groups
Hybrids	Aligned entities of different organization types
Insurgents	Insurgent groups
	Alliances of insurgent groups
	Rogue lone wolves

Preparation and readiness require ongoing activity; adding social media as an element or means of warfare does not reduce the need for ongoing relationship building and force maintenance. It is foolish to think differently, even though many elected officials are ready to cut budgets and reduce military personnel when the threat is not at the front gate. They are not known for their intelligence, just their blustery rhetoric.

New social media warfare strategies are emerging, and with every conflict, no matter how small, lessons are learned about the effectiveness of strategies and tactics. The same thing has happened in the short history of cyber warfare. Traditional warfare, with its merciless slaughter of military forces and civilian populations, has proved to be nothing but destructive and expensive to implement and even more expensive to recover from. One of the most effective deterrents in traditional warfare is maintaining a state of readiness and capability. That state of readiness needs to be so high that the cost to an attacker is even higher in terms of financial and human resources. This strategy may work well when facing the threat of traditional warfare, but insurgents are still capable of inflicting serious damage especially at the far edges of a territory or to the weakest members of an alliance.

Defensive social media warfare strategies can be analyzed in the same light. Alliances are not built in a day and allies are not influenced just once; there must be a level of influence that is constantly maintained. Thus, defensive social media warfare strategies, like any other strategy or tactic, must be nurtured over time.

They are also dependent on maintaining mutual defense alliances and international cooperation to track offenders through cyberspace.

Among aligned entities, awareness, preparation, and training in the use of social media weapons and how social media weapons can be used against them is essential to prevent opponents from gaining a significant advantage in social media. This can be said for virtually every type of organization or types of organizational relationships.

Maintaining influence over aligned entities is an ongoing process, as is gaining leverage vis-à-vis non-aligned entities. Social media warfare is the class in a warfare curriculum that all parties should take to maintain a strong defensive posture. Social media warfare, and how such warfare can be used against alliances or individual entities, must be understood to reduce the possibility of opponents gaining an advantage through their own use of social media. How this relates to military organizations is discussed further in Chapter 3.

Industry groups, consortiums, and corporations face some of the same challenges as government entities when it comes to being prepared for social media warfare. It has taken over 20 years to prepare private sector organizations for cyber warfare attacks, including rogue hackers and insurgent organizations. The philosophy that supports defensive strategies of preparedness and readiness in the governmental realm applies equally to the business realm. This is especially true for critical industry sectors where information sharing is an important factor in successful defensive strategies.

Since the events of September 11, 2001, many governments have supported the implementation of stronger security measures in their country and in allied and trading partner countries. In the United States, the Department of Homeland Security (DHS) has provided leadership in promoting threat analysis and security efforts [1]. The DHS and the Executive Office of the President of the United States have identified 16 critical infrastructure sectors whose assets, systems, and networks are important to sustaining the national interest, including economic stability and sustainability. Presidential Policy Directive/PPD-21 lists the *critical industry sectors* and assigns responsibility for monitoring threats and improving security to specific federal agencies or departments [2]. The sectors and corresponding federal agencies are shown in Table 1.2.

Corporations also face threats outside of the realm of national and infrastructure threats that governments and military organizations do not necessarily face. There are many people and groups that oppose specific types of corporations or specific corporations because of what they do or do not do as a business entity. This puts corporations in a uniquely perilous position and gives them a unique perspective on social media warfare. Corporations may also have enemies that have little if any interest in confronting national governments or alliances of governments. Corporations are especially vulnerable to the damaging slander and harassment social media campaigns that most governments have little interest in addressing and may not violate any national security laws.

Table 1.2   Critical Industry Sectors and Federal Agencies Charged with Security Leadership

Critical Industry Sector	Sector-Specific Agency
Chemical	Department of Homeland Security (DHS)
Commercial facilities	DHS
Communications	DHS
Critical manufacturing	DHS
Dams	DHS
Defense industrial base	Department of Defense (DOD)
Emergency services	DHS
Energy	Department of Energy (DOE)
Financial services	Department of the Treasury
Food and agriculture	Department of Agriculture (USDA) and Department of Health and Human Services (DHHS)
Government facilities	DHS and General Services Administration (GSA)
Healthcare and public health	DHHS
Information technology	DHS
Nuclear reactors, materials, and waste	DHS
Transportation systems	DHS and Department of Transportation (DOT)
Water and wastewater systems	Environmental Protection Agency (EPA)

Industry sectors and companies within the sectors face a long list of ideological groups that oppose just about everything. Animal rights, child labor, imports and exports, equal pay, racial discrimination, sexism, and social responsibility toward the environment are just a few of the issues of interest to these ideological groups. This is covered in more depth in Chapter 4: "Corporate Efforts to Deploy or Respond to Social Media Warfare Strategies."

Groups or movements with an ideological foundation include religious groups, politically motivated groups, or loosely knit collectives drawn together by a shared belief system. In fact, many insurgent groups also maintain cohesion based on philosophical or religious beliefs. Mainstream religious organizations may need both defensive as well as offensive retaliatory social media warfare capabilities. Whereas fringe or radical groups, with little if any physical facilities, may focus their social media warfare strategies more on an offensive capability. The following chapters cover the social media warfare activities of ideological groups:

- Chapter 5: Special Interest Groups' Use of Social Media as a Weapon
- Chapter 6: Social Media Warfare in the Political Electoral Process
- Chapter 7: Social Media Warfare for Support of Social Causes
- Chapter 8: Mercenaries and Activists of Social Media Warfare
- Chapter 9: Social Media as a Weapon to Recruit and Inspire Violent Extremists

There are also a variety of hybrid groups that are difficult to categorize under the previously mentioned types of organizations. They are a mixed alliance of various other types of groups or splinter groups. Finally, self-defined social media wars are commonplace in the world of celebrity and pop culture. These can be vicious and at times damaging to reputations and egos, even though it may be of interest to very few people. Law enforcement or civil litigation may be involved if laws are broken or damage can be proved. There does not seem to be a great deal of strategy applied to such conflicts, but there are several relevant tactics. Chapter 10: "Social Media Warfare for Celebrities and Famous People," covers this type of conflict.

1.5 Defensive Social Media Warfare Tactics

A long list of identifiable defensive tactics is used in social media warfare. Irregular and unconventional warfare leaves open the possibility that a wide variety of tactics will be employed as situations change. The effectiveness of a tactic depends on numerous factors including to what extent individuals in any given conflict situation have access to or use social media applications. Selected defensive tactics are shown in Table 1.3.

Self-validation, or assuring the world of the validity and legitimacy of a position or action taken by an organization or individual, is common practice in virtually all conflict situations. Self-validation serves many purposes. First, it reinforces to members of the initiating organization that they are in the right and that commitment to the cause is good. An example of this is using the "God is on our side" slogan to validate a position or action. Second, employing self-validation reinforces the message to aligned organizations and their members that the initiating organization is right and justified in taking action, and this helps keep allies' comfort level high.

Influencing aligned entities, or working to convince allies of the validity and legitimacy of a position or action taken by an organization or individual, goes a step beyond self-validation. The goal of influencing allies is to have them adopt the

Table 1.3   Defensive Social Media Warfare Tactics

Self validation: Assuring the world of the validity and legitimacy of a position or action.
Influencing aligned entities: Convincing allies of the validity and legitimacy of a position or action.
Reinforcing alliance partners: Showing support of an allies' position or action.
Persuasion of non-aligned entities: Convincing non-allies of the validity and legitimacy of a position or action.
Recruiting and indoctrination: Drawing people into a cause and teaching cause related doctrine.
Relationship building: Establishing cooperative efforts with likeminded people or organizations.
Nullifying opponents: Efforts to discredit opponents.

same position and use the same or similar rhetoric and justifications to convince their own members or population that they are *all* doing the right thing by supporting a cause or action. This helps to deter discord on the part of citizens of a coalition member state or organization.

Reinforcing alliance partners is the process of publicly and noticeably showing support for an allies' position or action. This helps to influence aligned entities as well as non-aligned entities by sending reinforcing signals in support of actions taken by a specific alliance partner or group of alliance partners. In the case of nations, such reinforcement helps to convince a populace that all is as should be and that all the alliance partners are working in conjunction with each other toward the same goal. This helps to deter discord on the part of citizens of cooperating member states.

Persuasion of non-aligned entities is the process of convincing non-allies of the validity and legitimacy of a position or action taken by the initiating entity and all aligned entities involved in a position or action. Persuasion is designed to draw non-aligned entities into a coalition or alliance or at least convince them not to oppose a position or action.

Recruitment and indoctrination is the process of aligning new entities or individuals to a social media warfare cause or any type of cause that has social media warfare components. Drawing people into a cause is only part of the process. In general, new recruits or new alliance partners will need some education on cause-related doctrine and the process and tools through which goals and objectives are being pursued.

Relationship building is the process of establishing and nurturing cooperative efforts with like-minded people or organizations. This is an ongoing process involving existing aligned organizations or individuals as well as non-aligned organizations or individuals that are being courted or controlled in some way. The relationship-building process is never-ending and will always present challenges as social and economic conditions change or evolve.

Nullifying opponents is the process of discrediting opponents in the eyes of alliance partners or non-partners that an alliance, nation, or organization is attempting to influence. Nullifying efforts can reinforce existing positive relationships and help to attract new relationships. The nullification process usually involves debasing or demonizing the ideological or political position of opponents. It can also involve discrediting or invalidating positions taken by opponents based on inaccurate information or data.

1.6 Offensive Social Media Warfare Tactics

There is a long list of identifiable offensive tactics that can be used in social media warfare. In some cases, offensive tactics are basically defensive tactics applied with the purpose of attacking an entity, group, or a cause rather than in their defense. Irregular and unconventional warfare leaves open the possibility that a wide variety of tactics will be employed as situations change. Thus, there is a possibility of employing many different offensive social media warfare tactics. The effectiveness of a tactic depends on many factors including to what extent individuals in any given conflict situation have access to or use social media applications. Selected tactics are shown in Table 1.4.

Deception is the process of using invalid or false information or pretense to convince opponents that a specific position or proposition is true when there is no factual basis for the position. Deception is also the process of trying to influence an opponent or a potential supporter to support a specific position or action based

Table 1.4 Offensive Social Media Warfare Tactics

Deception: False promises and invalid information.
Confusion: Creating and perpetuating uncertainty.
Dividedness: Instigating hatred and suspicion.
Exposure: Unauthorized release of information
Trolling: Post opposing messages to existing posts.
Relationship building: Establishing cooperative efforts with likeminded people or organizations.
Nullify opponents: Efforts to discredit opponents.
Blended threats: Combined activities to accomplish offensive objectives.

on the belief that such support will lead to desired results for the potential supporter. The deceiver attempts to influence the target with a promise of results that the deceiver cannot or does not intend to provide.

Confusion tactics are processes designed to disorient and deceive opponents regarding what is real and not real. In many ways, this is a classic propaganda method that is meant to instill fear, uncertainty, and doubt. It can involve misinformation about what has happened or what is about to happen, and is designed to disorient opposing organizations or individuals and stimulate actions on their part that are counterproductive or even self-destructive.

Divisive tactics involve instigating hatred and suspicion among opponents or the populace of an opposing nation or alliance. Such tactics have been very successful in the rise of fascism and racial and religious hatred. It does come back to the old adage, divide and conquer. It also works incredibly well on populations that feel disenfranchised or downtrodden.

Exposure tactics most often involve the unauthorized release of information that might embarrass or otherwise jeopardize the owner or creator of the exposed information. The most recent examples are the release of U.S. National Security Agency (NSA) material by Eric Snowden and WikiLeaks and the release of information hacked from political party computer systems that are discussed further in later chapters.

Trolling is the process of having *troops* respond to social media posts by commenting on existing posts in an attempt by individuals or in the name of organizations to influence, deceive, or recruit and indoctrinate. The effectiveness of this is yet to be proved, but given the propensity for trolling in social media, it is obvious that there are many who think it is effective. If nothing else, the act of trolling and opposing those with different beliefs may have a motivating effect on these "troops."

Relationship building is the process of establishing and nurturing cooperative efforts with like-minded people or organizations. As an offensive tactic, the goal is usually to persuade alliance partners or non-aligned organizations and individuals that an offensive action was justified.

As in defensive social media warfare opponent nullification processes, offensive nullification efforts are considered first strike or preemptive strike efforts. This means that the target alliance, nation, or organization had not previously tried to nullify the positions or actions of the attackers. Nullifying opponents as an offensive tactic is the process of discrediting opponents in the eyes of alliance partners or non-partners that an alliance, nation, or organization is attempting to influence. Nullifying efforts can reinforce existing positive relationships and help build new relationships. The nullification process usually involves debasing or demonizing the ideological or political views of opponents. It can also involve discrediting or invalidating the positions taken by opponents based on supposed but inaccurate empirical information or data.

Blended threats are combined activities designed to accomplish offensive objectives. This includes deception tactics combined with trolling opponents to help legitimize the deceptive post of an aggressor. In a blended offensive situation, multiple social media platforms can be used along with mixed media methods including texts, photos, or videos. This is the modern approach to classic propaganda campaigns.

1.7 Tools of Social Media Warfare

Hundreds of social media applications have been launched over the last decade. Many are freely available on the Internet, other applications can be purchased and downloaded for smartphone use. The capabilities of social media applications are in a constant state of evolution and any point-in-time comparison is quickly outdated. Trends in social media applications have implications for both defenders and attackers.

There are several types of social media applications and websites. Among the most popular are blogs and blogging support applications; comment applications; content streaming applications; social networking and professional networking websites and applications; and social news. There are numerous social media applications and websites that focus on sharing, including sharing proprietary information, photos, videos, slides, bookmarks, product reviews, and genealogical information. Some applications are designed to serve a global audience but many serve regions, cities, and even smaller communities. The mix is constantly changing and evolving.

Hundreds of specific and branded social media applications have been launched over the last decade. Each is designed to serve one or more of the functions mentioned previously. A sampling of the various social media applications is presented in Tables 1.5 and 1.6.

The sheer number of social media applications creates significant challenges for defenders and defensive strategists and tacticians. The large number of social media applications makes it very difficult to monitor the activity of potential attackers in applications and the content and/or messages created by them using applications. This often puts defenders in a reactive mode and requires that defending troops quickly learn new applications and understand how to monitor and analyze attackers' use of applications. Defenders need to quickly develop countermeasures and tactics to monitor the use of a social media application and if chosen, to minimize its value to attackers or neutralize the impact of the application altogether.

The large number of social media applications creates significant challenges for attackers as well. Although the number of applications provides many opportunities for their use in a conflict situation, it also increases the complexity of using social media applications in general. This often requires that attackers be in a constant state of learning and training; and it requires that attacking troops learn new applications quickly and understand how to maximize their effectiveness. The

Table 1.5   Social Media Applications (A–L)

360.yahoo	Bloson	dogster	fotolog	Groupsite
43things	blurty	dol2day	foursquare	Heello
4talk IM	BrightKite	dontstayin	FriendFeed	Hi5
academia	Brizzly	Dot429	friendster	Hubbub
advogato	buzznet	downelink	Gather	hubpages
asianave	cafemom	elftown	gays	imvu
badoo	care2	Everloop	gazzag	Instagram
bebo	Chi	Evernote	geni	itsjustcoffee
bigadda	Classmates	exploroo	GetGlue	Jaiku
bigtent	Coderwall	Fab	Glogster	Jumptive
biip.no	dailymotion	Facebook	gogoyoko	KirkL
BlackPlanet	Delicious	faceparty	Going	kiwibox
Blip.tv	deviantart	fetlife	goodreads	Last.fm
Blogger	Diddit	fledgewing	Google+	LeFeed
blogster	Digg	Flickr	graduates	LikeALittle
BlogTV	diigo	flixster	GROU.PS	LinkedIn

attacker must quickly organize a cadre of troops with skills in a specific application. Without proper training, attacking troops may compromise information or reveal the location of attacking forces, making a counteroffensive easier to launch against them.

1.8 Knowledge and Skills Needed for Social Media Warfare

Launching effective social media warfare attacks requires knowledge of the target as well as the skills to use social media tools in an offensive manner. General knowledge on a target organization, groups, or individual is readily obtainable through a variety of sources. More intimate cultural or personal knowledge requires more in-depth exposure to the target and perhaps more exposure and experience in the social or cultural context of the target.

Table 1.6   Social Media Applications (L–T)

listography	Ning	Profilder	Snapchat	uStream
livejournal	Noteleaf	Reddit	socialgrid	Utterz
Lunch	ooVoo	ReSearch	Soovox	Viddler
meetin	Orkut	Ruck	Sphinn	Vimeo
MeetMe	oyaye	rudespace	squidoo	Upcoming
meetup	Pandora	ryze	student	wayn
Mixx	Path	Score	SuperFan	WEvolt
mobango	PeerIndex	scribd	Tagged	WordPress
mog	PeopleJar	ScuttlePad	TagWorld	xanga
Mogulus	Picnik	secondlife	Tarpipe	Yelp
multiply	Piczo	Seesmic	Tumblr	YouTube
MyBrandz	Pinterest	SezWho	tigweb	zaadz
MySpace	Plurk	Skid-e-kids	Tribe.net	Zwiggo
Netlog	Posterous	Skitch	Twingly	
Netvibes	Power	skyrock	Twitter	
nexopia	Pownce	slashdot	TypePad	

Once defending forces gain basic skills in the social media application that an attacker is using, they must develop methods to monitor the attacker's use of the application. This can be challenging because of the huge volume of messages and other content that can be quickly created using a social media application. Although if the situation dictates, defending forces can employ enough people to read every social media post or message relating to a specific set of subjects or that come from users with certain profiles.

Defending troops also need to know how a social media application works and establish relationships with service providers and/or developers of the social media application. This knowledge, combined with a collaborative relationship with service providers and/or developers, can provide defenders with a considerable advantage that the attackers do not have, because it is unlikely that attackers will gain insider support from service providers and/or developers. In fact, several social media providers have worked with law enforcement authorities to suspend suspected terrorists' accounts. When defenders understand the functionality of a social media application, they are also able to examine messages and content for actionable intelligence.

ISIS, for example, was given much credit for using social media applications in Middle East conflicts; and their skills were expounded upon by the Western media. This was a masterful sucker punch on the part of the coalition forces fighting ISIS. The use of social media applications by ISIS troops increased and, as it did, it increased the volume of messages and content that provided more and more intelligence information to coalition forces. The lesson here is that the use of social media applications in warfare is a double-edged sword that can harm the attacker as much as it does the defender.

Attacking troops also need to develop skills on how a social media application works. In the case of insurgents' use of social media applications, this presents a considerable challenge to leaders and trainers of these insurgent forces. Basic skills may be easy to learn and teach, but effective use of a social media application in a conflict situation may require advanced skills and methods that take considerable time to learn and put into practice. Without advanced skills, attackers may end up doing themselves more harm than they do defenders.

1.9 Controlling Troops in Social Media Warfare

Both defenders and attackers need to have a disciplined approach toward using social media applications in conflict situations as well as in non-conflict day-to-day use. This includes knowing when and how to use social media applications to ensure that messaging and content do not reveal information that can benefit an adversary. This requires an understanding of what types of vulnerabilities the use of social media applications can create.

Understanding the technology platform used to support social media use such as a smartphone, mobile computing device, or a fixed computing facility is a good start. Smartphones for example, are being used by troops on all sides of conflict situations to communicate with friends and family, and they often use social media applications. This creates several problems.

First, the location of a smartphone, and thus its user, can be identified using various signal tracking technologies. On a more sophisticated level, the StingRay, an international mobile subscriber identity (IMSI-catcher) cellular phone surveillance device (manufactured by the Harris Corporation) can be deployed in war zones just as easily as it can be used in Dade County, Florida, United States. The StingRay has been very effective in helping authorities track down smartphone users and monitor their activity. In addition, many photos that are taken with a smartphone and posted to social media pages have *geotagging* features that reveal the location where the photo was taken and is visible when posted on certain social media platforms, thus providing adversaries with actionable intelligence.

Second, social media application use from fixed computing devices can eventually be traced back to the point of origin, depending on the sophistication of the application and the service provider serving the application. This leaves insurgent attackers more vulnerable because defenders have a better chance of developing cooperative relationships with service providers and applications developers to help obtain location information.

Third, both defensive troops and attacking troops need to be trained in using social media applications for their personal use in order not to compromise operations security. There should also be policies in place by the organizations regarding the use of social media applications. The *U.S. Army Social Media Handbook* provides guidance on how members of the military should use social media applications, and some of the things they should be cautious about when using social media. This is especially relevant when protecting operations security.

The U.S. Army has also warned troops that terrorists have said they are hunting soldiers and their families at home. In fact, the Army has determined that an Al-Qaeda handbook tells member terrorists to seek out information about government personnel, officers, important personalities, and all matters related to them (residence, workplace, leaving and returning times, spouses and children, and places visited) [3]. Such information can be used to retaliate and cause harm to conflict participants.

1.10 Developing a Lessons Learned Process

Conflicts will continue and there will be successes as well as setbacks in all situations. However, what is learned from conflict activities can be used to improve training and the effectiveness of defensive and offensive social media warfare. This is helpful in improving the all-around capabilities of a fighting force. If tactics are effective, they need to be analyzed, recorded, and taught. If tactics are not effective, they also need to be analyzed, recorded, and taught so they can be avoided in future conflicts.

The process of using both positive and negative experiences as a feedback mechanism is an approach of the *Lessons Learned Process* [4], illustrated in Table 1.7.

1.11 Conclusion

Warfare and the development and definition of warfare strategies and tactics have long been dominated by military leaders, planners, and field commanders. Military science has advanced in part because of the growth and maturity of military academies and war colleges. Social media warfare has become a study topic in military science and will play a bigger role in future conflicts. This chapter introduced the basic concepts and definitions of social media warfare. The following important conclusions can be drawn from the material presented in this chapter:

Table 1.7   The Lessons Learned Process

Triggering Events →	Defensive Actions →	Offensive Actions →	Observations of Day-to-Day Operations →
Step 1: →	Collect information from field reports, ↓ event summaries, and observations. ↓		
Step 2: →	↓ Aggregate and analyze information ↓		
Step 3: →	↓ Validate applicability and relevance of lessons ↓		
Step 4: →	↓ Store and archive lessons for future reference ↓		
Step 5: →	Disseminate and share lessons to strategists, tacticians, ↓ planners, and trainers ↓		
Step 6: →	Decide whether to apply lessons learned and how to ↓ apply the lessons learned ↓		
Step 7: →	Develop training courses or modules for ↓ multiple deliver mechanisms ↓		
Step 8: →	Deliver training and collect and analyze training ↓ evaluations from participants ↓		
Step 9: →	Observe, audit, or otherwise evaluate the effectiveness ↓ of training and that lessons were learned ↓		
Step 10: →	Evaluate and document the effectiveness of lessons learned ↓ process as applied to identified training objectives ↓		
Step 11: →	Use evaluation results to help guide future lessons learned projects		

Source: United States General Accountability Office.

Steps 7, 8, and 11 were added by the author.

- In the twenty-first century, we are firmly entrenched in an age of irregular warfare and unconventional warfare, where the theater of war is far less well-defined and theater strategy must be fluid and adaptable, including in and through cyberspace and social media.
- The Internet has made insurgency easier to initiate and maintain; and it has also opened the realm of warfare not only to insurgents fighting against a government, but to conflicts between social, cultural, economic, and religious factions around the world.

- Several academic disciplines will eventually provide research in the area of social media warfare; but currently, military science is clearly well ahead of other disciplines in terms of actual attention allocated to the impact of social media on warfare and conflict situations.
- The dynamics driving social media warfare are rooted in conflict that is inherent between social institutions, governments, corporations, and groups or individuals.
- Social media warfare has entered the political electoral process and social change movements of all types.
- An organization's size, purpose, and its relationships with other organizations will greatly influence how social media warfare strategies and tactics can be effectively deployed.
- Corporations face threats outside of the realm of national and infrastructure threats that governments and military organizations face. Corporations are especially vulnerable to damaging slander and harassment social media campaigns.
- There is a long list of identifiable defensive and offensive tactics that can be used in social media warfare.
- Irregular and unconventional warfare leaves open the possibility that a wide variety of tactics will be employed as situations change, including social media warfare.
- There have been hundreds of social media applications launched over the last decade, and the capabilities of social media applications are in a constant state of evolution.
- The large number of social media applications makes it very difficult to monitor the activity of potential attackers in all applications or the content and/or messages created using applications.
- Launching effective social media warfare attacks requires knowledge of the target as well as the skills to use social media tools in an offensive manner.
- Using social media applications in warfare is a double-edged sword that can harm the attacker as much as it does the defender.
- Both defenders and attackers must have a disciplined approach toward using social media applications in conflict situations, as well as for day-to-day use in non-conflict times.
- Lessons learned from past conflicts can be used to improve training and the effectiveness of defensive and offensive social media warfare.

1.12 Agenda for Action

It has taken far too long to address vulnerabilities in cybersecurity. Research has been done, best practices developed, and products are on the market to reduce and defend against cyber attacks. Clearly, not all have paid heed and the severity of cyber attacks, as well as their economic impact, has increased at an embarrassingly alarming rate. Social media warfare is in its infancy, and it is time to get ahead of it and not flounder as has been done in the face of cyber threats. Good lives are at stake. Action steps should include, but not be limited to, the following areas:

- Establish and support research efforts addressing the threats inherent in social media warfare.
- Establish a special focus research institute addressing social media warfare from a multi-disciplinary perspective.
- Organize symposia where professionals from multiple disciplines can contribute to and participate in on an ongoing basis.
- Establish a multi-disciplinary journal that publishes articles on social media warfare.
- Continue to develop military capabilities, both to defend against social media warfare tactics and to use tactics in an offensive manner.
- Build international and cross-sector relationships to support information sharing regarding social media warfare threats.

1.13 Key Terms

Critical industry sectors are those industries and business sectors that provide essential infrastructure support for economic activity that enables a country to function economically, politically, and socially.

Geotagging is the process of embedding global positioning system (GPS) coordinates in photographs taken using a smartphone or other GPS-capable device.

Insurgency is the organized use of subversion and violence to seize, nullify, or challenge political or economic control of a geographic region or to support isolated pockets of conflict across geographic regions.

Irregular warfare is a violent struggle among and between state and non-state actors for legitimacy and control over territories and relevant populations, with a loosely identifiable theater of war and fluid theater–warfare strategies.

Lessons learned process is a structured method of evaluating incidents or events and determining what individuals or organizations could have done better to deal with the situation, and transforming that lesson into positive actions through employee training, improving procedures, or improving mitigation methods or technology.

Social media warfare is the use of social media applications and related technologies by individuals, groups, or organizations to intentionally inflict harm on others.

Theater of war is generally defined by national and military commanders as the area of air, land, and water that is, or may become, directly involved in the conduct of major operations and campaigns involving combat.

Theater strategy is an overarching construct outlining a combatant commander's vision for integrating and synchronizing military activities and operations with the other instruments of national power to achieve national strategic objectives.

Unconventional warfare involves operatives entering a country covertly and building relationships with local militia to train the militia in a variety of tactics, including subversion, sabotage, and intelligence collection. It also involves unconventional assisted recovery and covert paramilitary operations conducted by other agencies of a government.

1.14 Seminar Discussion Topics

Discussion topics for graduate- or professional-level seminars are

- What experience have seminar participants had in situations where social media warfare strategies or tactics were deployed?
- Who should take the lead in developing social media warfare knowledge and skills?
- What are the obstacles to developing social media warfare knowledge and skills?

1.15 Seminar Group Project

Divide participants into multiple groups with each group taking 10–15 minutes to develop a list of offensive social media warfare tactics. Upon completion, have groups exchange their lists of social media warfare tactics, with groups taking 10–15 minutes to develop defensive measures to effectively counter the offensive tactics. Meet as a group and discuss the offensive tactics selected and the defensive measures to counter the tactics developed by the groups.

References

1. U.S. Department of Homeland Security. October 2015. Critical infrastructure sectors. Accessed May 18, 2016. https://www.dhs.gov/critical-infrastructure-sectors.
2. The White House, Office of the Press Secretary. February 2013. Presidential policy directive—Critical infrastructure security and resilience (Presidential Policy Directive/PPD-21). Accessed May 18, 2016. https://www.whitehouse.gov/the-press-office/2013/02/12/presidential-policy-directive-critical-infrastructure-security-and-resil.
3. U.S. Central Command. FAQ on security for social media. Accessed August 18, 2016. http://www.centcom.mil/visitors-and-personnel/social-media-security.
4. U.S. Government Accountability Office. September 2012. Federal real property security: Interagency Security Committee should implement a lessons-learned process. Accessed August 19, 2016. www.gao.gov/products/GAO-12-901.

Chapter 2

Civilian Government Use of Social Media to Attack, Defend, or Control

Governments, depending on their personality, face numerous challenges with social media warfare. Most governments are rather defensive and highly focused on self-preservation; therefore, they are confronted with the possibility of defending their national interest, or at least their government officials, against social media based or inspired attacks. In many cases, governments choose to limit Internet access or punish citizens who use social media to criticize or question the national government or political leaders. There are also governments that support social media warfare efforts or blended threats, including cyber attacks, as they export and support terrorism. Provincial or state governments also have a stake in social media warfare, as do local or city governments that are dominated by conservative factions and strive to oppress citizens or deprive them of human rights. This chapter examines a variety of issues that various types of governments face and that citizens living under different types of government must deal with as they strive to live free lives.

2.1 Growth in Internet Use and Access to Social Media

According to the 2013 U.S. Census Bureau survey on "Computer and Internet Use in the United States," computer ownership has increased with 78.5% of all households having a desktop or laptop computer and 63.6% having a handheld computer In addition, 74.4% of all households reported Internet use. Computer ownership and Internet use was concentrated among relatively young household-ers, Asian or White households, and those with high incomes, located in metro-politan areas, and relatively high levels of education [1].

Smartphone use was reported by 51.6% of Asian respondents, about 48.0% of white non-Hispanics and blacks, and 45.4% of Hispanics. The usage rates for blacks and Hispanics were similar, with 48.2% of individuals 15 years old and older reporting smartphone use [2].

Internet users in the United States perform a wide a variety social media related tasks on the Internet. These include sending instant messages, taking part in chat rooms or online discussions with other people, using social networking sites such as Facebook or LinkedIn, and using Twitter. Details on Internet usage are shown in Table 2.1.

The growth of Internet usage is a global phenomenon. There are several sources of statistics on Internet usage for much of the world, but there is little empirical data on Internet usage in totalitarian countries like North Korea. Internet usage varies widely around the world. Among Organization of Economic Cooperation and Development (OECD) members, in 2014, 95% of the adult population of Iceland, Norway, Denmark, and Luxembourg accessed the Internet, but just over half of the population in Turkey and less in Mexico did. From 2006 to 2014, total Internet usage rates in OECD member countries increased by 22 percentage points, from 60% to 82%. In addition, some lagging countries began to catch up because of greater availability of mobile broadband. In 2014, half of the OECD's adult population used a mobile or smartphone to connect to the Internet. The OECD also reported that in 2014 over 80% of 65–74-year-olds in Denmark, Iceland, Luxembourg, and Norway reported using the Internet in compared to less than 10% in Mexico and Turkey [3]. In Canada, about 83% of residents used the Internet in 2012, 48% from a handheld device [4].

Citizens of the world's poorest countries are experiencing a surge in mobile telephone use, according to a report by the United Nations Telecommunications Agency, but Internet usage in those nations still lags far behind. During the first decade of the twenty-first century, connectivity in the 48 countries classified as the Least Developed Countries (LDCs) rose by 28%, resulting in increased mobile access to almost 250 million people, but there are still fewer Internet users in the LDCs [5]. Overall, over one billion households in the world have Internet access, but more than half of the world's population still does not use the Internet [6]. More detailed Internet usage statistics can be found at the International Telecommunication Unions website (www.itu.int).

There are about 3.2 billion Internet users worldwide, according to the U. S. Central Intelligence Agency's *World Fact Book*, which also lists the top ten countries by Internet usage (in millions, July 2015 estimate):

Table 2.1   Internet Activities of U.S. Adults, 2011

Activity	Percentage of Adults Performing Activity	Percentage of Internet Users Performing Activity
Buy a product online	55	71
Buy or make a reservation for travel	51	65
Categorize or tag online content like a photo, news story, or blog post	24	33
Create or work on your own online journal or blog	11	14
Do any banking online	47	61
Get news online	59	76
Look for health or medical information online	55	71
Look for news or information about politics	47	61
Look online for info about a job	44	56
Make a donation to a charity online	19	25
Make a phone call online, using a service such as Skype or Vonage	18	24
Pay bills online	42	57
Pay to access content	32	43
Play online games	27	36
Rate a product, service, or person	29	37
Research a product or service online	58	78
Search online for a map or driving directions	60	82
Send instant messages	34	46
Send or read e-mail	68	92
Take part in chat rooms or online discussions with other people	17	22
Use a search engine to find information	71	92

(Continued)

Table 2.1 (Continued)   Internet Activities of U.S. Adults, 2011

Activity	Percentage of Adults Performing Activity	Percentage of Internet Users Performing Activity
Use a social networking site like MySpace, Facebook, or LinkedIn	50	65
Use Twitter	10	13
Visit a local, state, or federal government website	52	67
Watch a video on a video-sharing site	55	71

Source: Statistical Abstract of the United States: 2012 (131st Edition), United States Census Bureau.

1. China 687.9
2. India 325.4
3. United States 239.6
4. Brazil 120.7
5. Japan 118.5
6. Russia 104.6
7. Nigeria 86.1
8. Germany 70.8
9. Mexico 69.9
10. United Kingdom 59.0

2.2 Individual Freedom and Social Media Warfare

Although there has been considerable growth in the use of the Internet and thus access to social media, there are many governments around the world that restrict free speech and Internet access. The 2015 *Country Reports on Human Rights Practices*, published by the U.S. Department of State, Bureau of Democracy, Human Rights, and Labor, provides some details on restrictions of speech and Internet access. The report states that, while many countries do not restrict access to the Internet, some severely restrict access and monitor Internet user activity. Those countries that strive to control the Internet also strive to control all media as much as possible, including broadcast and print, as well as free speech in general. Excerpts from the report show what some countries were doing in 2014 and 2015 to restrict or deny Internet access, along with the country's type of government (in parenthesis):

Afghanistan (presidential Islamic republic): Authorities used pressure, regulations, and threats to silence critics. Freedom of speech was considerably more constrained at the provincial level, where local power brokers exerted significant influence and authority that they often used to intimidate or threaten their critics, both private citizens and journalists. Facebook pages have been shut down for unknown reasons. The Taliban used the Internet and social media (e.g., Twitter) to spread its messages.

Algeria (presidential republic): Individuals were limited in their ability to criticize the government publicly without reprisal. Several activists reported that the slightest misstep in a Facebook update could result in arrest and questioning and it is widely understood that the intelligence services closely monitored the activities of political and human rights activists on social media sites, including Facebook. Internet service providers face criminal penalties for the material and websites they host, especially if subject matters are "incompatible with morality or public opinion" [7].

Angola (presidential republic): The constitution and law provide for freedom of speech and press; however, state dominance of most media outlets and self-censorship by journalists limited the practical application of these rights.

Austria (federal parliamentary republic): Authorities continued to restrict access to websites containing information that violated the law, such as neo-Nazi sites, and restricted access to prohibited websites by trying to shut them and forbidding the country's Internet service providers from providing access to them.

Azerbaijan (presidential republic): There is a clear pattern of repression in Azerbaijan against those expressing dissent or criticism of authorities, primarily human rights defenders, but also journalists, bloggers, and other activists, who may face a variety of criminal charges. Most media practiced self-censorship and avoided topics considered politically sensitive due to fear of government retaliation. Internet service providers are required to be licensed and have formal agreements with the government. There were strong indications that the government monitored the Internet communications of democracy activists. Bahrain (constitutional monarchy): The constitution provides for freedom of speech and press, "provided that the fundamental beliefs of Islamic doctrine are not infringed, the unity of the people is not prejudiced, and discord and sectarianism are not aroused." In practice, the government limited freedom of speech and press through active prosecution of individuals under libel, slander, and national security laws that targeted civilian and professional journalists, and through legislation to limit speech in print and social media. The government restricted Internet freedom and monitored individuals' online activities, including via social media, leading to legal action and punishment of some Internet users. In 2013, the government blocked 70 websites in accordance with laws. In 2012, the government ordered service providers to block Internet users' access to websites officials considered antigovernment, anti-Islamic, or likely to incite sectarian tensions. Many of the blocked websites featured live-streaming audio or video content.

Bangladesh (parliamentary republic): The government may restrict speech deemed to be against the security of the state; against friendly relations with foreign states; and against public order, decency, or morality; or that constitutes contempt of court, defamation, or incitement to an offense. The government restricted some access to the Internet and censored online content, and there were credible reports that the government monitored private online communications. Media reported that during the government-ordered shutdown of Facebook in November and December, government departments and politicians continued to update their pages.

Belarus (presidential republic in name, although in fact a dictatorship): The government interfered with Internet freedom by reportedly monitoring e-mail and Internet chat rooms. While individuals, groups, and publications were generally able to engage in the peaceful expression of views via the Internet, including by e-mail, all who did so risked possible legal and personal repercussions. The government reportedly blocked access to 40 Internet sites. In several instances, cyber attacks of unknown origin temporarily disabled independent news portals and social networking sites.

Brazil (federal presidential republic): A continuing trend was for private individuals and official bodies to take legal action against Internet service providers and providers of online social media platforms, such as Google, Facebook, and Orkut, holding them accountable for content posted to or provided by users of the platform.

Brunei (absolute monarchy or sultanate): The government monitored private e-mail and Internet chat room exchanges believed to be subversive or propagating religious extremism. The government enforced a law that requires Internet service providers and Internet café operators to register, and advised Internet service and content providers to monitor for content contrary to public interest, national harmony, and social morals. The government blocked websites with sexually explicit material, and Internet companies self-censor content and reserve the right to cut off Internet access without prior notice. The government also ran an awareness campaign aimed at warning citizens about the misuse and social ills associated with social media, including the use of social media to criticize Islam, sharia, or the monarchy.

Burma (parliamentary republic): The government reportedly monitored Internet communications under questionable legal authority and used defamation charges to intimidate and detain some individuals using social media to criticize the military. There were instances of authorities intimidating online media outlets and Internet users.

Burundi (presidential republic): The government blocked the use of two or three social media applications on mobile networks for several days following an attempted coup d'état.

Cambodia (parliamentary constitutional monarchy): There were credible reports the government monitored private online communications without appropriate legal authority and announced it would begin enforcing rules requiring all subscriber identity module (SIM) cards to be associated with an identifiable individual. A non-governmental organization (NGO) also alleged, without providing evidence, that the government installed surveillance equipment at Internet service providers to monitor online traffic.

China (includes Tibet, Hong Kong, and Macau) (communist state): Authorities continued to increase efforts to monitor Internet use, control content, restrict information, block access to foreign and domestic websites, encourage self-censorship, and punish those who ran afoul of political sensitivities. According to news sources, more than 14 government ministries participated in these efforts, resulting in the censorship of thousands of domestic and foreign websites, blogs, cell phone text messages, social networking services, online chat rooms, online games, and e-mail. The government also blocked access to selected websites operated by foreign governments, news outlets, health organizations, and educational institutions. The government continued to block almost all access to Google websites, including its mail service, photograph program, map service, and calendar application. Other websites that were blocked during the year included YouTube, Instagram, Facebook, Twitter, Dropbox, SoundCloud, Flickr, and Picasa. Many news sites were blocked, including Reuters, the English-language and Chinese-language websites of the *New York Times*, the *Wall Street Journal*, and Bloomberg. The websites of human rights groups, such as Amnesty International and Human Rights Watch, were also blocked.

Congo, Democratic Republic of the (semi-presidential republic): In the context of large-scale protests, the government suspended access to the Internet and text messaging throughout the country. The government blocked social media sites for several weeks after the protests subsided.

Congo, Republic of the (presidential republic): There were several occasions when the government disrupted Internet access, and there were credible reports that the government monitored private online communications without appropriate legal authority and censored online content by cutting Internet access.

Cuba (communist state): The government restricted or disrupted access to the Internet and censored some online content, and there were credible reports that the government monitored without appropriate legal authority the limited e-mail and Internet chat rooms and browsing that were available.

Djibouti (semi-presidential republic): The government monitored social networks to ensure there were no planned demonstrations or overly critical views of the government.

Ecuador (presidential republic): There were credible reports that the government censored online content and monitored private online communications without appropriate legal authority. The government increasingly monitored Twitter and other social media accounts for perceived threats or alleged insults against the president and government officials.

Egypt (presidential republic): The counterterrorism law criminalizes the use of the Internet to "promote ideas or beliefs that call for terrorist acts" or to "broadcast what is intended to mislead security authorities or influence the course of justice in relation to any terrorist crime." The government attempted to disrupt the communications of terrorist groups operating in northern Sinai by cutting telecommunication networks: mobile services, Internet, and sometimes landlines. This tactic disrupted operations of government facilities and banks. The law requires Internet service providers and mobile operators to allow government access to customer databases, which can allow security forces to obtain information about activities of specific customers and could lead to lack of online anonymity. There were reports that authorities monitored social media and Internet dating sites to identify and arrest lesbian, gay, bisexual, transgender, and intersex (LGBTI) individuals.

Equatorial Guinea (presidential republic): The government restricted and disrupted access to the Internet and censored online content. The government blocked WhatsApp, Facebook, Diario Rombe, and Radio Macuto to prevent communication during student protests. The websites remained blocked for several months, and some remained so at the end of 2015. The government also blocked access to websites maintained by domestic political opposition and exile groups.

Eritrea (presidential republic): It was suspected the government monitored some Internet communications, including e-mail, without obtaining warrants.

Ethiopia (federal parliamentary republic): Authorities harassed, arrested, detained, charged, and prosecuted journalists and other persons whom they perceived as critical of the government, creating an environment where self-censorship negatively affected freedom of speech. The government periodically restricted access to certain content on the Internet and blocked several websites, including blogs, opposition websites, and websites of the Ginbot 7, the Oromo Liberation Front (OLF), and the Ogaden National Liberation Front (ONLF). The government also temporarily blocked news sites such as Al Jazeera and the BBC. Several news blogs and websites run by opposition groups were not accessible. These included Addis Neger, Nazret, Ethiopian Review, CyberEthiopia, Quatero Amharic, Tensae Ethiopia, and the Ethiopian Media Forum. Authorities monitored telephone calls, text messages, and e-mails.

Gambia, The (presidential republic): Internet users reported they could not access the websites of foreign online news blogs such as Freedom Online.

Indonesia (presidential republic): The government prosecuted individuals for free expression under the law on information and electronic transaction law (ITE Law) which outlaws online crime, pornography, gambling, blackmail, lies, threats, and racism, and prohibits citizens from distributing in electronic format any information that is defamatory.

Iran (theocratic republic): The government restricted and disrupted access to the Internet, monitored private online communications, and censored online content. The government collected personally identifiable information in connection with citizens' peaceful expression of political, religious, or ideological opinion or beliefs. The government briefly blocked the online messaging service, Telegram, for "spreading immoral content" [7]. The government also blocked platforms similar to YouTube channels and arrested their administrators. Twitter is officially banned in the country.

Iraq (federal parliamentary republic): There were overt government restrictions on access to the Internet, and there were credible reports that the government monitored e-mail and Internet communications without appropriate legal authority. There were reports that government officials attempted to have pages critical of the government removed from Facebook and Twitter for communications that the government considered "hate speech," although they did not succeed in doing so.

Jordan (parliamentary constitutional monarchy): The law requires the licensing and registration of online news websites, holds editors responsible for readers' comments on their websites, requires that website owners provide the government with the personal data of its users, and mandates that editors in chief be members of the Jordan Press Association. According to journalists, security forces reportedly demanded websites remove some posted articles. The government threatened websites and journalists that criticized the government, while it actively supported those that reported favorably on the government. The government monitored electronic correspondence and Internet chat sites.

Kazakhstan (presidential republic): Observers reported the government blocked or slowed access to opposition websites. Many observers expressed the view that the government planted pro-government propaganda in Internet chat rooms.

Kenya (presidential republic): Authorities monitored websites for violations of hate speech laws.

Korea, Democratic People's Republic of (communist state). Internet access for citizens was limited to high-ranking officials and other designated elites, including select university students. A tightly controlled and regulated Intranet was reportedly available to a slightly larger group of users, including an elite grade school; select research institutions, universities, and factories; and a few individuals. Government employees sometimes had closely monitored access to the Internet and had limited closely monitored access to e-mail accounts.

Korea, Republic of (presidential republic): There were some government restrictions on Internet access, and the government monitored e-mail and Internet chat rooms with wide authority under the law. The government determines whether posts made on social networking sites, such as Twitter and Facebook, or in chat rooms contain content which is defined as harmful or illegal speech. If the government finds prohibited materials, it has the power to warn the user. If the prohibited materials are not removed, the user's account may be blocked.

Kuwait (constitutional monarchy): The government passed a new cybercrime law that bans criticism of Islam, the emir, the judiciary, and neighboring states on Internet-based forums, sites, and publications. The government monitored Internet communications, such as blogs and discussion groups, for defamation and security reasons and continued to block websites considered to "incite terrorism and instability" and required Internet service providers to block websites that "violate [the country's] customs and traditions" [7]. The government prosecuted and punished individuals for the expression of political or religious views via the Internet. Authorities required owners of Internet cafés to obtain the names and civil identification numbers of customers and to submit the information upon request.

Kyrgyz Republic (parliamentary republic): Members of the lesbian, gay, bisexual, transgender, and intersex (LGBTI) community reported that police regularly monitored LGBTI chat rooms and dating sites and arranged meetings with LGBTI users of the sites to extort money from them.

Laos (communist state): The government controlled domestic Internet servers and sporadically monitored Internet usage. During the year, authorities also arrested individuals for online activities, including posting on Facebook photos of alleged police extortion, alleging a governor granted a controversial land concession to a developer, and condemning the government.

Lebanon (parliamentary republic): There was a perception among knowledgeable sources that the government monitored e-mail, Facebook, Twitter, blogs, and Internet chat rooms where individuals and groups engaged in the expression of views. The government reportedly censored some websites to block online gambling, pornography, and religiously provocative material, and other agencies summoned journalists, bloggers, and activists to question them about tweets, Facebook posts, and blog posts critical of political figures.

Libya (in transition): Many bloggers, online journalists, and citizens reported practicing self-censorship due to instability, militia intimidation, and the uncertain political situation. Some activists reported finding what appeared to be "kill lists" targeting civilian dissenters on social media websites affiliated with certain Islamist militias.

Madagascar (semi-presidential republic): In June 2014, the national assembly passed a cybercrime law that includes a provision to prohibit insulting or defaming a government official online. According to Reporters Without Borders, "the law's failure to define what is meant by 'insult' or 'defamation' leaves room for very broad interpretation and major abuses."

Malaysia (federal constitutional monarchy): Authorities monitored the Internet for e-mail messages and blog postings deemed a threat to public security or order. The law requires certain Internet and other network service providers to obtain a license, and permits punishment of the owner of a website or blog for allowing offensive racial, religious, or political content.

Maldives (presidential republic): The Communications Authority of Maldives (CAM) is the regulatory body mandated to enforce Internet content restrictions on sites hosted within the country and to maintain a blacklist of overseas websites. The CAM reported it blocked a few websites that violated domestic laws on anti-Islamism, pornography, child abuse, and other prohibitions. Some other government institutions are mandated to monitor content related to non-Islamic religious discourse, pornography, child abuse, sexual and domestic violence, copyright infringement, and national security.

Mauritius (parliamentary republic): There was anecdotal evidence the government monitored private online communications of some journalists.

Mexico (federal presidential republic): According to Freedom House, the government increased requests to social media companies to remove content. Some civil society organizations alleged that various state and federal agencies sought to monitor private online communications.

Montenegro (parliamentary republic): There were credible reports the government monitored private online communications without appropriate legal authority. NGOs alleged police and intelligence services unlawfully collected data from citizens' mobile phones and Internet usage.

Mozambique (presidential republic): Opposition party members and academics reported government intelligence agents monitored e-mail and used false names to infiltrate social network discussion groups. One site often critical of the government, Verdade, suffered multiple attacks.

Nauru (parliamentary republic): The government sometimes restricted or disrupted access to the Internet. For instance, authorities blocked access to Facebook for a period of time.

Nicaragua (presidential republic): Several NGOs claimed the government monitored their e-mail without appropriate legal authority. Additionally, paid government supporters used social media and website commentary spaces to harass prominent members of civil society, human rights defenders, and a well-known journalist.

Niger (semi-presidential republic): The government blocked Internet access countrywide during January 2015 following protests in several major cities. Sonitel, the government-owned telecommunications company, indefinitely blocked access to certain websites, such as those of terrorist organization Boko Haram, under orders from the High Commission for New Technology and Communication.

Nigeria (federal presidential republic): Sources indicated the government attempted to monitor and suppress Internet and e-mail content, particularly during election periods. According to business executives and network providers, the government has conducted massive surveillance of citizens' telecommunications, and on occasion compelled network operators to release political dissidents' communication data.

Oman (absolute monarchy): The law restricts free speech exercised via the Internet, and the government enforces the restrictions. Authorities monitored the activities of telecommunications service providers and obliged them to block access to numerous websites considered pornographic, or culturally or politically sensitive. Authorities sometimes blocked blogs. Most video–chat technologies, such as Skype, were blocked.

Pakistan (federal parliamentary republic): There were reports that the government restricted Internet access and monitored Internet use, e-mail, and Internet chat rooms. In 2012 the government began a systematic, nationwide content-monitoring and filtering system to restrict or block "unacceptable" content, including material that is un-Islamic, pornographic, or critical of the state or military forces. There also were reports the government attempted to control or block some websites, including sites the government deemed extremist and pro-independence Baloch sites. The government continued to block access to YouTube (begun in 2012) and restricted access to other social media websites.

Peru (presidential republic): The press reported that the National Intelligence Bureau inappropriately gathered information on thousands of politicians, journalists, and businessmen, ostensibly for political purposes.

Qatar (absolute monarchy): In 2014 the government approved a new cybercrime law that severely limits online expression. The law prohibits any online activity that threatens the state, its general order, and its local or international peace. The law requires Internet service providers to block objectionable content based on a request from judicial entities. Internet providers are also obligated to maintain long-term electronic records and traffic data for the government.

Romania (semi-presidential republic): There were reports the government monitored private online communications without appropriate legal authority.

Russia (semi-presidential federation): The government took significant new steps to restrict free expression on the Internet. Threats to Internet freedom included physical attacks on bloggers; politically motivated prosecutions of bloggers for "extremism," libel, or other crimes; blocking of specific sites by national and local service providers; distributed denial-of-service attacks on sites of opposition groups or independent media; monitoring by authorities of all Internet communications; and attempts by national, local, and regional authorities to regulate and criminalize content. The government maintained a federal blacklist of Internet sites. It required Internet service providers to block access to Web pages that it deemed offensive or illegal such as items on the "Federal List of Extremist Materials." During the year authorities blocked or threatened to block some websites and social network pages that either criticized government policy or violated laws on Internet content. The communications regulator also blocked access to Yahoo's video site after the service refused to comply with warnings to block access to an Islamic State video. The regulator also increased its requests to Facebook to block content. The government continued to employ a "system for operational investigative measures," which requires Internet service providers (ISPs) to install, at their own expense, a device that routes all customer traffic to a Federal Security Service (FSB) terminal. The system enables police to track private e-mail communications, identify Internet users, and monitor their Internet activity.

Rwanda (presidential republic): There were numerous reports the government monitored e-mail and Internet chat rooms. Individuals and groups could engage in the peaceful expression of views via the Internet, including by e-mail and social media, but were subject to monitoring. Government-run social media accounts were used to debate and at times intimidate individuals who posted online comments considered critical of the government. The government at times blocked access within the country to several websites critical of its policies.

Saudi Arabia (absolute monarchy): The Ministry of Culture and Information or its agencies must authorize all websites registered and hosted in the country. The General Commission for Audiovisual Media has responsibility for regulating all audio and video content in the country, including satellite channels, film, music, Internet, and mobile applications, independent from the Ministry of Commerce and Industry. In 2011 the government issued regulations for electronic publishing that set rules for Internet-based and other electronic media, including chat rooms, personal blogs, and text messages. Security authorities actively monitored Internet activity, both to enforce societal norms and to monitor recruitment efforts by organizations such as Daesh. Authorities routinely blocked sites containing material perceived as harmful, illegal, offensive, or anti-Islamic. According to Reporters Without Borders, authorities claimed to have cumulatively blocked approximately 400,000 websites.

Serbia (parliamentary republic): There were credible reports that the government monitored private online communications without appropriate legal authority. The law obliges telecommunications operators to retain for one year's data on the source and destination of a communication; the beginning, duration, and end of a communication; the type of communication; terminal equipment identification; and the location of the customer's mobile terminal equipment. While intelligence agencies can access this information without court permission, the law requires a court order to access the contents of these communications.

Seychelles (presidential republic): Opposition activists claimed the government blocked access to their party websites and monitored their postings on social network sites. There also were reports the government monitored e-mails, Internet chat rooms, and blogs.

Singapore (parliamentary republic): Internet service providers are required to ensure that content complies with local laws. The government closely monitored Internet activities, such as social media posts, blogs, and podcasts. Although a government-appointed review panel recommended that the government cease banning 100 specific websites for being pornographic, inciting racial and religious intolerance, or promoting terrorism and extremism, the ban remained in effect.

Somalia (federal parliamentary republic): Al-Shabaab prohibited companies from providing access to the Internet and forced telecommunication companies to shut down data services in Al-Shabaab-controlled areas.

South Africa (parliamentary republic): The law authorizes state monitoring of telecommunication systems including the Internet and e-mail, for national security reasons. The law requires all service providers to register on secure databases the identities, physical addresses, and telephone numbers of customers.

South Sudan (presidential republic): On June 1, 2015, the government expelled Toby Lanzer, the Deputy Special Representative of the UN Secretary-General/ Resident Coordinator and Humanitarian Coordinator of the United Nations

Mission in South Sudan (UNMISS), following remarks he posted on his Twitter account about the economic and political condition of the country.

Sri Lanka (presidential republic): The government placed restrictions on Internet access, including websites it deemed pornographic. Since 2011 websites carrying local news were required to register with the government.

Sudan (presidential republic): The government regulated licensing of telecommunications companies through the National Telecommunications Corporation. The agency blocked some websites and most proxy servers judged offensive to public morality, such as those purveying pornography. Authorities sporadically blocked access to YouTube and "negative" media sites. Reporters Without Borders reported the government established a "Cyber-Jihadist Unit" with a mandate to crack down on "Internet dissidents" in 2011. According to outside reports, the unit monitored social media accounts and electronic communications, especially of those believed to be regime critics.

Suriname (presidential republic): Journalists, members of the political opposition and their supporters, and other independent entities perceived government interference or oversight of e-mail and social media accounts.

Swaziland (absolute monarchy): There were credible reports that the government monitored private online communications without appropriate legal authority. The government press office stated that authorities monitored Internet blogs, the use of social networks such as e-mail, Facebook, Twitter, and Internet chat rooms.

Syria (presidential republic; highly authoritarian regime): According to the 2015 *Freedom on the Net* report, the country remained one of the most dangerous and repressive environments for Internet users in the world. The government controlled and restricted the Internet and monitored e-mail and social media accounts. Individuals and groups could not express views via the Internet, including by e-mail, without prospect of reprisal. The government employed sophisticated technologies and hundreds of computer specialists for filtering and surveillance purposes, such as monitoring e-mail and social media accounts of detainees, activists, and others. Internet blackouts often coincided with security force attacks. The government censored websites related to the opposition, including the websites for local coordination committees as well as media outlets.

The government meanwhile expanded its efforts to use social media, such as Instagram, Twitter, and Facebook, to spread pro-government propaganda and manipulate online content. Government authorities routinely tortured and beat journalists to extract passwords for social media sites; and the Syrian Electronic Army (SEA), a group of pro-government computer hackers, frequently launched cyber attacks on websites to disable them and post pro-government material. Observers also accused the SEA of slowing Internet access to force self-censorship on government critics and diverting e-mail traffic to government servers for surveillance. Media reports have indicated that the SEA hacked the Washington Post's mobile site in May 2015, and the SEA claimed responsibility for hacking a foreign armed force's public website. Daesh forces restricted access to Internet cafés, especially for women, confiscated cell phones and computers, and instituted strict rules for journalists to follow or face punishment. Daesh also increased cyber attacks on journalists and groups documenting human rights abuses.

Tajikistan (presidential republic): Individuals and groups faced extensive government surveillance of Internet activity, including e-mails, and often self-censored their views while posting on the Internet. There were new and continuing government restrictions on access to Internet websites, such as Facebook, YouTube, Google, and Google services.

Tanzania (presidential republic): The government monitored websites and Internet traffic that criticized the government and to combat illegal activities. The law criminalizes the publication of false information, defined as the publication of "information, data or facts presented in a picture, texts, symbol or any other form in a computer system where such information, data or fact is false, deceptive, misleading or inaccurate." Civil society groups expressed concern the act could curtail freedom of expression. For example, after the October 25, 2014, general election, 181 persons working in an opposition election center were detained and eight formally charged with violations of the Cybercrimes Act for compiling election results.

Thailand (constitutional monarchy interim military-run government): The government imposed significant restrictions on Internet freedom, restricting and disrupting access to the Internet, and censoring online content. There was Internet censorship, and the law was used to stifle certain areas of freedom of expression. The government closely monitored and blocked thousands of websites that criticized the monarchy. Many political Web boards and discussion forums chose to self-censor and monitor discussions closely to avoid being blocked, and newspapers disabled or restricted access to their public comment areas.

Turkey (parliamentary republic): Law allows the government to prohibit a website or remove content if there is sufficient suspicion that the site is committing any of eight crimes: insulting the founder of the Turkish Republic, Mustafa Kemal Ataturk; engaging in obscenity, prostitution, or gambling; encouraging suicide, sexual abuse of children, drug abuse, or provision of substances dangerous to health. As of December 2, 2015, EngelliWeb reported there were 106,198 blocked websites, compared with 58,635 in 2014.

Turkmenistan (presidential republic; highly authoritarian): The government continued to monitor citizens' e-mail and Internet activity. Reports indicated that the Ministry of National Security controlled the main access gateway and that several servers belonging to Internet protocol addresses registered to the Ministry of Communications operated software that allowed the government to record Voice over Internet Protocol (VoIP) conversations, turn on cameras and microphones, and log keystrokes. Authorities blocked access to websites they considered sensitive, including YouTube, Twitter, and Facebook, as well as virtual private network connections, including those of diplomatic missions.

Uganda (presidential republic): The government monitored Internet communication in accordance with the Antiterrorism Act, the Regulation of Interception of Communications Bill, and the Computer Misuse Act.

Ukraine (semi-presidential republic): Law enforcement bodies monitored the Internet, at times without appropriate legal authority. Human rights groups that were critical of Russian involvement in the Donbas and Crimea reported that opponents subjected their websites to cyber attacks, such as coordinated denial-of-service incidents and unauthorized attempts to obtain information from computers. Users of social media, particularly Facebook and VKontakte, sometimes had their access temporarily blocked for innocuous or straightforwardly political posts that other users (assumed by many Internet users in the country to be agents of the Russian government) mischaracterized as "hate speech" and flagged as terms of service violations. In one case, a post in support of a blocked user that simply read, "we're with you," led to a block of that Facebook user.

Ukraine (Crimea) (in transition): Russian occupation authorities restricted free expression on the Internet by imposing repressive laws of the Russian Federation. Security services routinely monitored and controlled Internet activity to suppress contrary opinions. According to media accounts, Russian occupation forces interrogated residents of Crimea for posting pro-Ukrainian opinions on Facebook or on blogs.

United Arab Emirates (federation of monarchies): The government restricted access to some websites and monitored chat rooms, instant messaging services, and blogs. Authorities stated they could imprison individuals for misusing the Internet. The country's two Internet service providers, both linked to the government, used a proxy server to block materials deemed inconsistent with the country's values, as defined by the Ministry of Interior. Blocked material included pornographic websites and a wide variety of other sites deemed indecent, including those that dealt with dating and matrimony; lesbian, gay, bisexual, transgender, and intersex (LGBTI) issues; Judaism and atheism; negative critiques of Islam; testimonies of former Muslims who converted to Christianity; posts that explained how to circumvent proxy servers; and some transmissions that originated in Israel. Proxy servers occasionally blocked broad categories of websites. The government also blocked some sites that contained content critical of ruling families. The Telecommunications Regulatory Authority was responsible for creating lists of blocked sites. Service providers did not have the authority to remove sites from blocked lists without government approval. The government also, at least partially, blocked VoIP websites.

Uzbekistan (presidential republic; highly authoritarian): Internet service providers, allegedly at the government's request, routinely blocked access to websites or certain pages of websites that the government considered objectionable. The government blocked several domestic and international news websites and those operated by opposition political parties. The government restricted access to several Internet messenger services, sometimes for several months, requiring a proxy server to access services such as Skype, Viber, and Telegram.

Venezuela (federal presidential republic): The law puts the burden of filtering prohibited electronic messages on service providers and can order service providers to block access to websites that violate these norms and sanctions them with fines for distributing prohibited messages. There were 1008 websites blocked during the year and the government continued to block seven Internet sites that post dollar- and euro-to-Bolivar currency exchange rates differing from the government's official rate. The government used Twitter hashtags to attain "trending" status for official propaganda and had hundreds of employees to manage and disseminate official government accounts. At least 65 official government accounts used Twitter to promote the ruling party. Public Space reported that it suspected the government hacked social networking sites, e-mails, and websites of political figures, civil society activists, writers, journalists, and newspapers, but it did not give specifics.

Vietnam (communist state): The government continued to exercise various forms of control over Internet access. It allowed access to the Internet but only through a limited number of Internet service providers, all of which were fully or substantially state-controlled companies. Despite these controls, Internet access and usage continued to grow. Authorities continued to suppress online political expression through politically motivated arrests and convictions of bloggers as well as through short-term detentions, surveillance, intimidation, and illegal confiscation of computers and cell phones of activists and family members. Political dissidents and bloggers reported the government routinely ordered disconnection of their home Internet service. The government monitored Facebook posts and punished activists who used the Internet to organize protests.

Yemen (in transition): The Houthi-controlled Public Telecommunications Corporation systematically blocked user access to websites and Internet domains it deemed dangerous to the rebel actors' political agenda. According to a study by the University of Toronto's Citizen Lab, Ansar Allah used Internet-filtering technology to censor sources critical of the group and "to manipulate the information environment."

Zambia (presidential republic): The government restricted access to the anti-government online publication, the Zambian Watchdog and other sites critical of the government. Shortly after his appointment as minister of information in February 2015, Chishimba Kambwili threatened to close the Watchdog.

Zimbabwe (semi-presidential republic): The law permits the government to monitor all communications in the country, including Internet transmissions, and the government sometimes restricted access to the Internet. For example, the government blocked Blackberry's Internet services for Zimbabwean-registered Blackberries, including Blackberry's encrypted messaging service that prevented enforcement of the law, allowing the government to intercept and monitor communications.

2.3 A National Government Model for Influencing and Relationship Building

The censorship of social media and oppression of citizens practiced by many governments, as described in the previous section, is based on fear as much as anything else. Fighting crime on the Internet and securing a nation from terrorism is certainly a government's responsibility, but quashing the free exchange of ideas and speech is the work of plain, old, nasty totalitarianism. Governments that practice such behavior and social media tactics do not serve all the people of their nation; they focus on maintaining a social order designed only to serve the elite and powerful at the expense of basic freedoms.

Not all nations take such an approach. The United States has a history of discrimination and oppression of minorities and is still far from perfect in terms of human rights. But it has a very open society and a culture of free speech and exchange of ideas and beliefs. That, of course, comes with a price, and the conservative elite still strives to dictate morals and discriminates against minorities.

Despite the desire of conservative elites to dominate thought and action, the U.S. federal government allows and supports more freedoms than many other countries do, and it has taken a considerably different approach to social media warfare. In terms of social media strategy, the federal government supports and maintains a critical mass of positive, peaceful social media practices tactics:

- Self-validation, to communicate to the world the feeling of and belief in the validity and legitimacy of a freer society. It continues to reinforce to its citizens and allies that it is in the right and has a strong commitment to the cause of freedom.
- Social media practices are designed to influence aligned governments to adopt the same positions and use the same or similar rhetoric that they, as a coalition, are all doing the right thing by supporting similar causes or actions.
- Alliance partners are reinforced and supported when they support common positions and actions. This helps to support the belief, on the part of both aligned entities as well as non-aligned entities, that all alliance partners are working in conjunction with each other toward the same goal.
- Persuasion of non-aligned entities of the validity and legitimacy of the U.S. position or actions is ongoing. This helps draw governments into a global coalition, or at least helps to convince non-aligned governments not to oppose a position or action.
- Recruitment of nations and individuals into a coalition of beliefs and actions is also ongoing; as is the indoctrination, or more softly called, education, into a belief systems and structure. This helps to keep new recruits supporting the cause- related doctrine and the process and tools through which goals and objectives are being pursued.

■ The relationship-building process of establishing and nurturing cooperative efforts with like-minded people or organizations is also ongoing. The relationship-building process is never-ending and does present some challenges as social and economic conditions change or evolve. Social media warfare is one element in an arsenal of tools used to maintain and perpetuate those relationships.

The U.S. federal government has enviable social media enterprises, which surpass those of virtually all entities of any type in the world. The Office of Citizen Services and Innovative Technologies (OCSIT) in the Technology Transformation Service of the U.S. General Services Administration (GSA) plays a leading role in expanding and promoting the use of social media applications by government agencies [8]. The mission of the organization is to

■ Find and share social media and *digital government* resources and capabilities with agencies or government entities throughout the country.
■ Help agencies understand and resolve social media and digital government policy issues.
■ Offer services and tools to help agencies meet digital government goals.
■ Champion DigitalGov solutions.
■ Promote agency DigitalGov efforts.
■ Build relationships with the private and non-profit sectors as well as state and local governments to spread the adoption of digital government methods [8].

The U.S. federal government is pursuing a comprehensive digital government strategy built upon four overarching principles:

■ An *information-centric approach* that manages discrete pieces of open data and content, which can be tagged, shared, secured, mashed up, and presented in a way that is most useful for the consumer of that information.
■ A *shared platform approach* to reduce costs and improve portability of data and content, both within and across agencies, help apply consistent standards, and ensure consistency in how information is created and delivered.
■ A *customer-centric approach* to how the government creates, manages, and presents data through websites, mobile applications, raw data sets, and other modes of delivery, and allows customers to shape, share and consume information, whenever and however they want it.
■ A *platform of security and privacy* that helps to ensure innovation happens in a way that ensures the secure delivery and use of digital services to protect information and privacy [9].

The U.S. federal government also has taken the critical precaution of providing the means for users to confirm the validity of official U.S. government digital platforms. One key step in building a digital government is to assure citizens that they can trust the application used for official engagement and that it is being managed by a legitimate agency and not an unofficial source, phishing scam, or malicious entity. The U.S. Digital Registry serves as the authoritative resource for agencies, citizens, and developers to confirm the official status of social media and public-facing collaboration accounts, mobile apps, and mobile websites. Information in the registry includes the agency, platform, account, language, points of contact, and collaborative tags for each social media application [10].

There are more than 80 social media applications that currently have amended terms of service for official U.S. government use, including Facebook, Flickr, GitHub, Google+, IdeaScale, Instagram, LinkedIn, Pinterest, Scribd, SlideShare, Socrata, Storify, Tumblr, Twitter, UserVoice, Ustream, and YouTube [10].

2.4 Agents of National Governments in International Relations

All national governments maintain some organization structure to interface with and influence other nations or alliances of nations. Social media has become an essential tool in those agency communication efforts. Such agencies employ all the social media warfare tactics of self- validation, influence, reinforcement, persuasion of non-aligned entities, recruitment and indoctrination, and relationship building.

On behalf of the United States, the Broadcasting Board of Governors is specifically designated as the agency whose mission is to inform, engage, and connect people around the world in support of freedom and democracy. The Board oversees the activities of individual broadcasters including the Voice of America (VOA), which operates on several basic principles:

- VOA will serve as a consistently reliable and authoritative source of news. VOA news will be accurate, objective, and comprehensive.
- VOA will represent America, not any single segment of American society, and will therefore present a balanced and comprehensive projection of significant American thought and institutions.
- VOA will present the policies of the United States clearly and effectively, and will also present responsible discussions and opinion on these policies.

VOA operates several broadcasting entities, including Radio Free Europe/ Radio Liberty, Office of Cuba Broadcasting (Radio and TV Martí), Radio Free Asia, and Middle East Broadcasting Networks (Alhurra TV and Radio Sawa). Voice of America delivers news and information in 45 languages to a weekly audience of more than 187 million people around the world.

VOA uses digital, web, and mobile media to engage viewers, listeners, users, and friends. Radio and television broadcast to approximately 3000 affiliates, and satellite transmissions reach countries where free speech is banned or where civil society is under threat. VOA's four mobile social media applications have had more than one million downloads and cater to users on all major mobile platforms. There are over 40 versions of VOA social media applications on Apple iOS, Android and Symbian [11].

The United States interacts with other nations, organizations in those nations, and their populations through over thirty different government agencies. Each agency serves a specific purpose, and all the agencies increasingly rely on social media applications to accomplish their mission of validation, influence, reinforcement, persuasion, recruitment and indoctrination, and relationship building. These agencies include

- Arms Control and International Security
- Bureau of Consular Affairs
- Bureau of International Labor Affairs
- U.S. Commission on International Religious Freedom
- Commission on Security and Cooperation in Europe (Helsinki Commission)
- Court of International Trade
- Defense Intelligence Agency
- Defense Security Cooperation Agency
- Department of Homeland Security (DHS)
- Department of State
- European Command
- Foreign Agricultural Service
- Foreign Claims Settlement Commission
- Global Affairs (State Department)
- Immigration and Customs Enforcement
- Institute of Peace
- Inter-American Foundation
- International Trade Administration (ITA)
- International Trade Commission
- INTERPOL Washington, U.S. National Central Bureau
- Japan-United States Friendship Commission
- Open World Leadership Center
- Overseas Private Investment Corporation
- Peace Corps
- Radio Free Asia (RFA)
- Radio Free Europe/Radio Liberty (RFE/RL)
- Radio and TV Martí
- Saint Lawrence Seaway Development Corporation
- U.S. Trade and Development Agency
- Transportation Security Administration
- Voice of America

2.5 Agents of National Governments in Internal Affairs

National governments also have agencies and agents that work internally to main-tain law and order; they also face social media warfare challenges. In totalitarian nations, many agencies focus on controlling banned discourse and quashing debate and civil disobedience. This is evident in the lack of freedoms that such nations have—most lack an independent judiciary—and in the way agencies harass, question, arrest, and summarily prosecute offenders.

Nations with a greater respect for civil liberties still face some rather nasty social media warfare campaigns from dissidents, but they do so primarily within the laws of a civil society. Just as such nations manage their international relations, internal relations and social order is supported through the use of social media applications and social media warfare strategies and tactics. Law enforcement agencies in most countries are known to patrol social media postings and activity to prevent crime and terrorism. This is covered in Chapter 15, "Monitoring Social Media Warfare Threats," and Chapter 13, "Law Enforcement Response to Social Media Warfare."

Social media has become an essential tool in designated agency communications efforts. Again, such agencies employ all the social media warfare tactics of self-validation, influence, reinforcement, persuasion of non-aligned entities, recruitment and indoctrination, and relationship building.

The U.S. federal government interacts with segments of the population and organizations operating inside its national borders through over fifty different government agencies. Each agency serves a specific purpose and all of them increasingly rely on social media applications to accomplish their missions of validation, influence, reinforcement, persuasion, recruitment and indoctrination, and relationship building. As with agencies involved in international relations, OCSIT plays a leading role in expanding and promoting the use of social media applications by government agencies. These agencies include

- Administration for Children and Families (ACF)
- Administration for Community Living
- Administration for Native Americans
- Administration on Aging (AOA)
- Administration on Developmental Disabilities
- Advisory Council on Historic Preservation
- Agency for Toxic Substances and Disease Registry
- Alcohol and Tobacco Tax and Trade Bureau
- Alcohol, Tobacco, Firearms, and Explosives Bureau
- AmeriCorps
- Antitrust Division
- Archives (National Archives and Records Administration) (NARA)
- Army Corps of Engineers
- Arthritis and Musculoskeletal Interagency Coordinating Committee

- Bureau of Consumer Financial Protection
- Bureau of Indian Affairs
- Bureau of Industry and Security
- Bureau of Land Management
- Bureau of Prisons
- Bureau of Reclamation
- Bureau of the Census
- Centers for Disease Control and Prevention (CDC)
- Centers for Medicare and Medicaid Services (CMS)
- Citizenship and Immigration Services (USCIS)
- Commission of Fine Arts
- Commission on Civil Rights
- Community Oriented Policing Services (COPS)
- Community Planning and Development
- Consumer Financial Protection Bureau
- Consumer Product Safety Commission (CPSC)
- Coordinating Council on Juvenile Justice and Delinquency Prevention
- Customs and Border Protection
- Department of Agriculture (USDA)
- Department of Commerce (DOC)
- Department of Education (ED)
- Department of Energy (DOE)
- Department of Health and Human Services (HHS)
- Department of Homeland Security (DHS)
- Department of Housing and Urban Development (HUD)
- Department of the Interior (DOI)
- Department of Justice (DOJ)
- Department of Labor (DOL)
- Department of Transportation (DOT)
- Department of the Treasury
- Department of Veterans Affairs (VA)
- Drug Enforcement Administration
- Education Resources Information Center (ERIC)
- Election Assistance Commission (EAC)
- Employee Benefits Security Administration (EBSA)
- Employment and Training Administration
- Endangered Species Program
- Environmental Protection Agency (EPA)
- Equal Employment Opportunity Commission (EEOC)
- Fair Housing and Equal Opportunity (FHEO)
- Farm Credit Administration
- Federal Aviation Administration (FAA)
- Federal Bureau of Investigation (FBI)

- Federal Citizen Information Center
- Federal Communications Commission (FCC)
- Federal Deposit Insurance Corporation (FDIC)
- Federal Election Commission
- Federal Emergency Management Agency (FEMA)
- Federal Highway Administration
- Federal Housing Administration (FHA)
- Federal Motor Carrier Safety Administration (FMCSA)
- Federal Railroad Administration (FRA)
- Federal Reserve System
- Federal Trade Commission (FTC)
- Federal Transit Administration (FTA)
- Fish and Wildlife Service (FWS)
- Food and Drug Administration (FDA)
- Forest Service
- Geological Survey (USGS)
- Internal Revenue Service (IRS)
- Marshals Service
- Minority Business Development Agency
- Mississippi River Commission
- National Aeronautics and Space Administration (NASA)
- National Cancer Institute (NCI)
- National Credit Union Administration
- National Endowment for the Arts
- National Endowment for the Humanities
- National Flood Insurance Program (NFIP)
- National Geospatial-Intelligence Agency
- National Guard
- National Health Information Center (NHIC)
- National Highway Traffic Safety Administration
- National Institute of Mental Health (NIMH)
- National Institutes of Health (NIH)
- National Institute of Occupational Safety and Health
- National Institute of Standards and Technology (NIST)
- National Interagency Fire Center
- National Labor Relations Board (NLRB)
- National Oceanic and Atmospheric Administration (NOAA)
- National Park Service
- National Railroad Passenger Corporation (AMTRAK)
- National Science Foundation (NSF)
- National Telecommunications and Information Administration
- National Transportation Safety Board
- National Weather Service

- Nuclear Regulatory Commission (NRC)
- Occupational Safety and Health Administration (OSHA)
- Occupational Safety and Health Review Commission
- Office for Civil Rights, Department of Education
- Office of Elementary and Secondary Education (OESE)
- Office of Fossil Energy
- Office of Refugee Resettlement
- Office of Special Education and Rehabilitative Services (OSERS)
- Pension Benefit Guaranty Corporation (PBGC)
- Postal Service (USPS)
- Railroad Retirement Board (RRB)
- Rural Business and Cooperative Programs
- Securities and Exchange Commission (SEC)
- Selective Service System (SSS)
- Small Business Administration (SBA)
- Smithsonian Institution
- Social Security Administration (SSA)
- Southeastern Power Administration
- Tennessee Valley Authority
- Transportation Security Administration (TSA)
- United States Postal Service
- Western Area Power Administration
- White House
- Women's Bureau (Labor Department)

When federal agencies are working to build relationships with organizations and individual citizens within the United States, their approach to social media content, delivery, and services varies depending on their overall mission. Some agencies provide access to services, others primarily provide access to information. Some agencies serve the general public, while others are more specialized. All federal agencies have posted at least some material on their websites that explain their social media strategies.

The National Archives and Records Administration (NARA), for example, uses social media tools to transform the way the agency serves customers and American citizens. Social media tools help the nation's record keeper to preserve government records and make them more accessible to citizens, researchers, and archivists. The NARA social media strategy is based on six core values:

- Collaboration: Together as one NARA and as partners with the public to accomplish its mission
- Leadership: Out in front among government agencies and cultural institutions
- Initiative: An agency of leaders who are passionate, innovative, and responsible

■ Diversity: Making NARA a great place to work by respecting diversity and all voices
■ Community: Caring about and focusing on the government community, citizen archivists, and each other
■ Openness: Creating an open NARA with authentic voices [12]

Another example is the U.S. Social Security Administration (SSA), which is the leading federal government organization charged with providing financial support for a wide variety of citizens. The social media strategy of the SSA is as complex as any in the world. The SSA is a centralized agency (no bureaus or departments) and has a centralized information technology (IT) environment that supports the automation of major aspects of the agency's core mission. SSA's organizational structure provides clear areas of responsibility for the various aspects of digital services, including hiring, acquisitions, and so on. The agency provides multiple secure delivery channels for its services, including telephone, online, formal data exchanges, Web services (machine to machine), and mobile services. SSA offers many electronic services to third parties, including those in the private and public sector. It also provides government-to-government services and electronic data exchanges with the U.S. military, federal, state, local, and foreign agencies [13].

2.6 Cooperation with International Agencies

Almost all national governments can participate in some form of international cooperation with a wide variety of organizations, many of which are NGOs or organizations that are jointly supported by governments. These organizations have developed social media strategies and participate in a variety of social media warfare tactics, including validation, influence, reinforcement, persuasion, recruitment and indoctrination, and relationship building.

Most of these organizations do not have the level of sophistication that the U.S. federal government has achieved in terms of social media strategies and tactics. Nor do they have the road map for future development that the federal government has put into place. Currently, they also do not have the financial resources to accomplish such work. It is likely that they will improve their social media strategies over time. These types of international organizations include, but are not limited to [14]

■ United Nations organizations
■ Specialized agencies of the United Nations and related organizations
■ International financial institutions
■ Inter-American organizations

- Inter-Asian organizations
- Inter-European organizations
- Inter-African organizations

International financial institutions include

- African Development Bank
- Asian Development Bank
- Bank for International Settlements (BIS)
- European Bank for Reconstruction and Development (EBRD)
- Inter-American Development Bank (IDB)
- International Bank for Reconstruction and Development (IBRD)
- International Center for Settlement of Investment Disputes (ICSID)
- International Finance Corporation (IFC)
- International Monetary Fund (IMF)
- Multilateral Investment Guarantee Agency (MIGA)
- North American Development Bank (NADB)

Other international institutions include

- Center for International Forestry Research (CIFOR)
- Commission for Environmental Cooperation (CEC)
- Commission for Labor Cooperation
- Commission for the Conservation of Antarctic Marine Living Resources (CCAMLR)
- Comprehensive Nuclear-Test-Ban Treaty Organization (CTBTO)
- Convention on International Trade in Endangered Species of Wild Fauna and Flora (CITES)
- COSPAS-SARSAT.INT (International Satellite System for Search and Rescue)
- Global Biodiversity Information Facility (GBIF)
- The Global Fund (to Fight AIDS, Tuberculosis and Malaria) (TGF)
- The Hague Conference on Private International Law (HCOPIL)
- International Agreement Regarding the Maintenance of Certain Lights in the Red Sea
- International Bureau, Permanent Court of Arbitration (PCA)
- International Bureau for the Protection of Industrial Property
- International Bureau for the Publication of Customs Tariffs
- International Bureau of Weights and Measures (BIPM)
- International Center for Agricultural Research in the Dry Areas (ICARDA)
- International Center for the Study of the Preservation and Restoration of Cultural Property (ICCROM)
- International Coffee Organization (ICO)

- International Committee of the Red Cross (ICRC)
- International Cotton Advisory Committee (ICAC)
- International Council for the Exploration of the Sea (ICES)
- International Crops Research Institute for the Semi-Arid Tropics (ICRISAT)
- International Development Law Organization (IDLO)
- International Energy Forum Secretariat (IEFS)
- International Fertilizer Development Center (IFDC)
- International Grains Council (IGC)
- International Human Frontier Science Program Organization (HFSP)
- International Hydrographic Organization (IHO)
- International Institute for Cotton
- International Institute for the Unification of Private Law (UNIDROIT)
- International Mobile Satellite Organization (IMSO)
- International Organization for Legal Metrology (OIML)
- International Organization for Migration (IOM)
- International Organization of Supreme Audit Institutions (INTOSAI)
- International Plant Genetics Resources Institute (IPGRI)
- International Rubber Study Group (IRSG)
- International Science and Technology Center (ISTC)
- International Seed Testing Association (ISTA)
- International Service for National Agriculture Research (ISNAR)
- International Tropical Timber Organization (ITTO)
- International Union of Credit and Investment Insurers (Berne Union)
- International Whaling Commission (IWC)
- Inter-Parliamentary Union (IPU)
- INTERPOL
- Iran-United States Claims Tribunal
- Korean Peninsula Energy Development Organization (KEDO)
- Multinational Force and Observers (MFO)
- North American Commission for Environmental Cooperation (CEC)
- North Pacific Anadromous Fish Commission (NPAFC)
- Organization for the Prohibition of Chemical Weapons (OPCW)
- Organization for Security and Cooperation in Europe (OSCE)
- Pacific Aviation Safety Office (PASO)
- Permanent International Association of Navigation Congresses (PIANC)
- Regional Environmental Center for Central and Eastern Europe (REC)
- Science and Technology Center in Ukraine (STCU)
- Sierra Leone Special Court
- World Customs Organization (WCO)
- The World Heritage Fund
- World Organization for Animal Health (OIE)
- World Trade Organization (WTO)

2.7 Provincial/State Governments and Social Media Warfare

Most countries have some form of provincial or state government structure that leaves much of the day-to-day administration and management of non-federal activities to that level of government. In the United States, most people have more daily contact with their state or local governments than with the federal government. Each state has its own written constitution, and those documents are often far more elaborate than their federal counterpart.

Under the Tenth Amendment to the United States Constitution, all powers not granted to the federal government are reserved for the states and the people. All state governments are modeled after the federal government and consist of three branches: executive, legislative, and judicial. The states have an executive branch that is headed by an elected governor. In most states, the other leaders in the executive branch are also directly elected, including the lieutenant governor, the attorney general, the secretary of state, and auditors and commissioners.

No two state executive organizations are identical. All 50 states have legislatures made up of elected representatives, who consider matters brought forth by the governor or introduced by its members to create legislation that becomes law. The legislature also approves a state's budget and initiates tax legislation and articles of impeachment. State judicial branches are usually led by the state supreme court, which hears appeals from lower-level state courts. Court structures and judicial appointments/elections are determined either by legislation or the state constitution [15].

This sounds good, but in many cases, it is not. Many states focus on regulating morals and are guilty of supporting discriminatory practices against people of color, women, and those with different gender preferences in romantic, family, and sexual relationships. Many states also have long-held policies that stifle voting privileges, disadvantage the poor, discriminate against people who speak languages other than America English and against people that do not follow "mainstream" religions or are not of "mainstream" ancestry. There is an ugly history which many of those in power at the state level either ignore or just pretend never happened. It is the federal government and the United States Constitution that protect the rights and freedoms of individuals against the oppression of state governments that have continuously demonstrated a willingness to violate federal law if they can get away with doing so. The federal government has had to intervene, on behalf of individuals and groups of citizens, many times in the past to end state and local government oppression and exploitation.

States also have various levels of sophistication when it comes to digital government. Although each state is able to participate in a variety of social media warfare tactics, including validation, influence, reinforcement, persuasion, recruitment and indoctrination, and relationship building, few do it very well. It is generally the more populated states with larger budgets that leverage social media warfare tactics.

Much of the activity created by social cause movements and protests occurs in the states, and state and local governments are on the frontline of protecting or harassing demonstrators and picketers. Unfortunately, there is a great deal of mistreatment of protesters by state and local authorities, as was obvious in Ferguson, Missouri, during protests that took place after a police officer shot and killed an unarmed black teenager. These situations are explored more in-depth in Chapter 7: "Social Media Warfare for Support of Social Causes."

Other social causes are also hindered by state governments, including voter rights and abortion rights in states dominated by the conservatives who attempt to impose their archaic social values on others. This was clearly demonstrated over the last few years as states attempted to deprive women of health care and safe abortions. Interestingly, many states have wasted tens of millions of dollars, if not hundreds of millions of dollars, on anti-abortion efforts that have had only modest results. To counter the states, the pro-planned parenthood movement used social media warfare tactics extremely well. From the strife caused by the conservative right, a new unity and awareness of the need for abortion rights blossomed across the nation and around the world. This is also discussed in Chapter 5: "Special Interest Groups' Use of Social Media as a Weapon."

Fortunately for the citizens of the United States, federal law protects people's freedom and rights; if not for this, the states would run all over the citizenry. In addition, organizations like the Southern Poverty Law Center, monitor hate groups and other extremist organizations throughout the country and expose their activities to law enforcement agencies, the media, and the public. The Southern Poverty Law Center also works to teach tolerance and fight injustice, and much of that activity is in response to oppressive laws and police actions at the state and local level. It uses social media warfare strategies to help accomplish these missions.

2.8 Local Governments and Social Media Warfare

The autonomy and power of local governments vary from country to country. Local governments in the United States generally include two tiers: counties, also known as boroughs in Alaska and parishes in Louisiana, and municipalities or cities/towns. In some states, counties are divided into townships. Municipalities can be structured in many ways, as defined by state constitutions, and are called, variously, townships, villages, boroughs, cities, or towns. Various kinds of districts also provide functions in local government outside county or municipal boundaries, such as school districts or fire protection districts.

Municipalities vary greatly in size, from the millions of residents of New York City and Los Angeles to the 200 people who live in Kimmswick, Missouri. Municipalities generally take responsibility for parks and recreation services, police and fire departments, housing services, emergency medical services, municipal courts, transportation services (including public transportation), and public works (streets, sewers, snow removal, signage, and so forth). Whereas the federal government and state governments share power in countless ways, a local government must be granted power by the state. In general, mayors, city councils, and other governing bodies are directly elected by the people [15].

Local governments, like states, also have various levels of sophistication when it comes to digital government. Although each local government can participate in a variety of social media warfare tactics, including validation, influence, reinforcement, persuasion, recruitment and indoctrination, and relationship building, few do it well. It is generally the more populated cities with larger budgets that leverage social media tactics.

Again, much of the activity created by social cause movements and protest occurs in cities, and state and local governments are on the frontline of protecting or often harassing demonstrators and picketers. Unfortunately, at this level too there is a great deal of mistreatment of protesters by local authorities (as seen during protests in Ferguson, Missouri after a police officer shot and killed an unarmed black teenager). These situations are explored more in-depth in Chapter 7.

Another area open to abuse at the local level is the monitoring of student social media activity by local education agencies. These agencies claim to focus social media monitoring efforts on security issues, but, in many cases, have used their monitoring to discriminate against young people who practice non-heterosexual lifestyles. School officials are seldom held accountable for privacy violations and their discriminatory practices, which are used to perpetuate dominance of the elite ruling classes.

2.9 Citizens Speak Out on Social Media about Government

Social media warfare is not just for the big guys. Rather, everyday citizens from around the world like to speak out about what is wrong or right about government, and they do that rather prolifically. Some of the citizen journalists have a considerable fan base of thousands of followers. Perspectives are varied with some being rather bitter and spiteful, while others are rather thoughtful and insightful. A search of social media sites on August 23, 2016, yielded several postings that expressed how people feel about their government. The essence of some of the tags and subject lines found include

- Arch-nemesis of patriarchy and bad governance
- Bad government, bad business, bad environmental results
- Big Government and mainstream party politics are bad
- Big Government Has Many Scandals

- Conservative, Pro-gun! Anti-Obama/Hillary
- Criticizing the government is the way to deal with bad government
- Government is bad for business
- No to bad Government by any Party
- Blame government for bad things in life
- Too much government is bad government
- Government is incompetent and corrupt
- Many people question the need for government
- Time to expose reckless government

2.10 Conclusion

Governments face numerous challenges with social media warfare. Most governments are defensive and focused on self-preservation and choose to limit Internet access or punish those citizens who use social media to criticize or question political leaders. There are also governments that support social media warfare efforts or blended threats, including cyber attacks, as they export and support terrorism. This chapter examined a variety of issues that various types of governments face and that citizens living under different types of government must deal with as they strive to live free lives. Important conclusions can be drawn from the material presented in this chapter:

- Even though there are about 3.2 billion Internet users worldwide and the citizens of the world's poorest countries are experiencing a surge in mobile telephone use, Internet usage in those nations still lags far behind. Internet usage in the 48 countries classified as the Least Developed Countries (LDCs) rose by 28%, resulting in increased access for almost 250 million people.
- Although there has been considerable growth in the use of the Internet, and thus access to social media, there are many governments around the world that restrain free speech and Internet access to continue human rights abuses.
- The United States has a history of discrimination and oppression of minorities and is still far from perfect in terms of human rights even though the country has an open society and a culture of free speech. The conservative elite still works to fight against freedoms as it strives to dictate morals and discriminates against minorities.
- The U.S. federal government has an enviable social media enterprise which surpasses that of virtually all other entities in the world.
- Agencies that represent their nations in a global capacity employ social media warfare tactics of self-validation, influence, reinforcement, persuasion of non-aligned entities, recruitment and indoctrination, and relationship building.

- Nations with a greater respect for civil liberties use social media applications and social media warfare strategies and tactics to help maintain social order; and government agency approaches to social media content, delivery, and services vary depending on their overall mission.
- There are numerous international organizations that nations engage with, and those organizations are slowly adopting a variety of social media strategies.
- Many state governments in the United States focus on regulating morals and are guilty of supporting discriminatory practices against minorities.
- Much of the activity created by social cause movements and protests occurs in states and cities, and state and local governments are on the frontline of either protecting or harassing demonstrators and picketers.
- Unfortunately, in the United States there is a great deal of mistreatment of protesters and dissenters by state and local authorities, as was obvious during protests in Ferguson, Missouri after a police officer shot and killed an unarmed black teenager.

2.11 Agenda for Action

Although social media warfare is in its infancy, many governments around the world have taken aggressive steps to suppress freedoms of speech and press by controlling or monitoring private social media activity. Action steps should include, but not be limited to, the following areas:

- The U.S. Department of State should continue to report annually on human rights abuses and keep reporting on the restrictions that governments put on social media and Internet access, if for no other reason. to remind the world that these gross violations continue.
- The Department of State should include in its annual report human rights violations that occur within the United States, if for no other reason, to show that the United States is willing to admit to such violations and work toward eliminating those violations, especially those made by law enforcement authorities.
- The digital government model of the U.S. federal government should be adopted by governments in other countries.
- The United Nations should take stronger actions against those countries that are quashing free speech and press on the Internet and in social media.
- Local governments and law enforcement in the United States should be held accountable for any violations of privacy in the way they monitor social media.

2.12 Key Terms

Customer-centric approach means that agencies respond to customers' needs and make it easy to find and share information and accomplish important tasks through the delivery of timely data, informative content, simple transactions, and seamless interactions that are easily accessible anytime, anywhere, and from any device.

Digital government is a system of electronically accessible utilities and applications that provide access to government services and information.

Information-centric approach decouples information from its presentation by beginning with the data or content and describing that information clearly, and then exposing it to other computers in a machine-readable format—commonly known as providing web application programming interface (APIs).

Platform of security and privacy means securing how data is stored, processed, or transmitted.

Shared platform approach is the use of a common computer systems or architecture used by all government agencies to reduce inefficiencies created by fragmented procurement and development practices that waste money and results in inconsistent adoption of new technologies and approaches.

2.13 Seminar Discussion Topics

Discussion topics for graduate- or professional-level seminars are

■ What experience have seminar participants had with governments monitoring social media or restricting access to the Internet and social media applications?
■ What mechanisms should be in place for private citizens to report violations of their privacy when using social media?
■ How can social media applications be employed by private citizens or groups to expose violations of their privacy by local law enforcement agencies?

2.14 Seminar Group Project

Divide participants into multiple groups with each group taking 10–15 minutes to examine how the social media warfare tactics of self-validation, influence, reinforcement, persuasion of non-aligned entities, recruitment and indoctrination, and relationship building can be used as defensive social media warfare tactics. Upon completion, have groups exchange their lists of defensive social media warfare tactics, with groups taking 10–15 minutes to develop offensive measures to effectively counter the defensive tactics. Meet as a group and discuss the defensive tactics selected by the groups and the offensive measures to counter the tactics that were developed by the groups.

References

1. The U.S. Census Bureau. November 2014. Computer and Internet use in the United States: 2013. Accessed August 20, 2016. http://www.census.gov/hhes/computer/.
2. The U.S. Census Bureau. June 10, 2013. Census Bureau report details rising Internet use and shows impact of smartphones on digital divide. Accessed August 20, 2016. http://www.census.gov/newsroom/press-releases/2013/cb13-111.html.
3. Organization for Economic Cooperation and Development (OECD). October 18, 2015. Internet users in OECD Science, Technology and Industry Scoreboard 2015: Innovation for Growth and Society. Paris: OECD Publishing. Accessed August 18, 2016. http://www.oecd-ilibrary.org/docserver/download/9215031ec050.pdf?expires =1471701740&id=id&accname=guest&checksum=67C9C2DEE4E66FE4B2DF56 4DE56745BE.
4. Statistics Canada. October 28, 2013. CANSIM Table 358-0154: Canadian Internet use survey, Internet use, by location of use, household income and age group for Canada and regions. Accessed August 20, 2016. from http://www5.statcan.gc.ca/cansim/a26?lang=eng&id=3580154.
5. UN News Centre. May 13, 2011. As mobile miracle transforms poorest nations, Internet use lags behind. Accessed August 20, 2016. http://www.un.org/apps/news/story.asp?NewsID=38376#.V7hjcpXdUsQ.
6. International Telecommunications Union. July 22, 2016. ITU releases 2016 ICT figures. ICT services getting more affordable—But more than half the world's population still not using the Internet. Press release. Accessed August 20, 2016. http://www.itu.int/en/mediacentre/pages/2016-PR30.aspx.
7. U.S. Department of State, Bureau of Democracy, Human Rights, and Labor. 2015 Country Reports on Human Rights Practices.
8. DigitalGov. About DigitalGov. Accessed August 22, 2016. https://www.digitalgov.gov/about/.
9. Executive Office of the President of the United States. Digital government building a 21st century platform to better serve the American people. Accessed August 22, 2016. from https://www.whitehouse.gov/sites/default/files/omb/egov/digital-government/digital-government.html.
10. DigitalGov. U.S. Digital Registry. Accessed August 22, 2016. https://www.digital-gov.gov/services/u-s-digital-registry/.
11. Voice of America (VOA). Broadcasting Board of Governors. Accessed August 22, 2016. https://www.bbg.gov/networks/voa/.
12. U.S. National Archives and Records Administration. December 8, 2010. Social media and digital engagement at the National Archives. Accessed August 22, 2016. http://www.archives.gov/social-media/strategies/.

13. U.S. Social Security Administration. June 9, 2016. Digital government strategy. Accessed August 22, 2016. https://www.ssa.gov/digitalstrategy/.
14. U.S. Department of State. March 31, 2010. List of international organizations approved for detail and transfer of federal employees. Accessed August 22, 2016. http://www.state.gov/p/io/empl/126305.htm.
15. The White House. State & local government. Accessed August 22, 2016. https://www.whitehouse.gov/1600/state-and-local-government.

Chapter 3

Military Applications of Social Media Warfare

Military organizations face tremendous challenges in social media warfare. Or shall we say, military organizations once again are confronted with the impact of new and evolving technology. This, by the way, is inherent to military organizations and, as in the past, with each new technology, militaries must learn how to deal with yet another new threat. As with past new threats, there is a learning curve and a training curve. Militaries learn to deal with new threats and they train current and future troops how to defend against a technology and how to use the technology as a weapon for their advantage [1]. This round, however, may be a little more complicated than past challenges. This chapter covers the challenges that militaries face in dealing with social media warfare.

3.1 Social Media Warfare in Conflict Environments

Unconventional warfare theaters are complex environments where military organizations face a myriad of potential allies and at least as many potential enemies; and it is often difficult to determine who is what. Add the element of social media warfare, and the conflict environment just became more complicated, and operations security more difficult to maintain [2]. Military organizations in unconventional warfare must deal with social media in several ways:

- First, they must be prepared to defend against attacks from opposing forces using social media warfare tactics against them, aligned entities, or local populations.

■ Second, military forces must be prepared to combat opposing forces' use of social media warfare tactics to bolster their own organizing efforts and influence people to oppose what they consider to be enemy forces.

■ Third, military personnel must be skilled in the of use social media warfare tactics against their enemies, including insurgent factions and local populations that support aggressors.

■ Fourth, military organizations need to control the use of social media by their own members, or citizens of their own country, that may accidentally or inadvertently compromise operational security and the overall stability of the fighting force.

■ Finally, a military force must be able to employ defensive and offensive social media warfare tactics, simultaneously and on numerous fronts, to prevail in conflict situations and theaters of war.

Troops on any side of a conflict can use defensive and offensive social media warfare tactics. Defensive social media warfare tactics used in unconventional warfare theaters include self-validation, influence, reinforcement, persuasion of non-aligned entities, recruitment and indoctrination, nullifying opponents, and relationship building. Offensive social media warfare tactics used in unconventional warfare theaters include deception, confusion, divisiveness, exposure, nullifying opponents, trolling, relationship building, and blended tactics.

The simultaneous use of defensive and offensive social media warfare tactics requires a fighting force that can simultaneously work to influence and build relationships with friendly forces, while working to discredit, confuse, and harm opposing forces as much as possible. The process of simultaneously employing defensive and offensive tactics is illustrated in Table 3.1.

Insurgents in recent conflicts, namely the Islamic State of Iraq and Syria (ISIS) in Iraq, learned how to use social media warfare tactics to its advantage and received considerable news coverage about their ability to use social media to inspire, recruit, and indoctrinate fighters and supporters. As ISIS increased its use of social media, opposing coalitions increased their monitoring of ISIS posts of ISIS-inspired social media posts in order to gain intelligence and to reduce the impact of ISIS efforts to inspire, recruit, and indoctrinate.

Coalition governments were able to influence social media application service providers to help in monitoring activity and neutralizing the ability of ISIS to leverage social media. Providers and independent groups shut down hundreds of thousands of accounts and kept doing so as fast as ISIS operatives could get new accounts up and running. The real details on how the coalitions used social media posts to gain actionable information will probably never be known. But one thing is for sure, military forces are now convinced that social media warfare is something that they will be dealing with for a long time.

Table 3.1 Social Media in Conflict Environments

Expeditionary force	← Persuasion of non-aligned entities, relationship building ↓	↓ Recruiting and indoctrination, nullify opponents ↓	← → Social media warfare operations and Social media warfare applications ← →	↑ Deception, confusion, dividedness, trolling ↑	↑ Relationship building ↑	→ Exposure, nullify opponents ↑	Insurgent force
Advisors							Aligned factions
Allied troops							Allied troops
Local loyal troops							Local sympathizing troops
Local loyal government							Local sympathizing government
Local loyal organizations							Local sympathizing organizations
Loyal civilians	← Self validation, influencing, reinforcing ↓						Sympathizing civilians

3.2 Defending a Military Force from Social Media Warfare Tactics

Defensive and counteroffensive social media warfare tactics have become essential to protecting a fighting force. Many defensive tactics are always in play, including self-validation, influencing, and relationship building. These activities have been essential for military success for centuries and now they can be supported or nullified using social media applications. In fact, it is probably far more difficult to deploy these tactics without using social media applications, because they have become so entrenched as modern communication tools. Defensive tactics and their targets are shown in Table 3.2.

The target audiences for defensive social media warfare tactics are shown in the far-left column of Table 3.2; they include the major expeditionary force, advisors, and allied troops as the primary target audience for self-validation tactics. Local loyal troops, governments, organizations, and civilians are the primary target audience for influence, reinforcement, and relationship building tactics. All audiences are targets of recruitment and indoctrination tactics, and the persuasion of non-aligned entities, which all audiences can contribute to, even if ever so slightly and

Table 3.2   Defensive Social Media Tactics in Conflict Environments

Target Audience	Applied Social Media Warfare Tactics		
Expeditionary force	Self validation	Recruiting and indoctrination	Nullifying opponents
Advisors			
Allied troops			
Local loyal troops	Influencing	Persuasion of non-aligned entities	
Local loyal government	Reinforcing		
Local loyal organizations	Relationship building		
Local loyal civilians			

probably more indirectly, by reinforcing the legitimacy of the mission. The basic goals of each tactic are as follows:

■ Self-validation, or assuring the world of the validity and legitimacy of a position or action that an organization or individual takes, is common practice in virtually all conflict situations.

■ Influencing aligned entities, or working to convince allies of the validity and legitimacy of a position or action taken by an organization or individual, goes one step beyond self-validation.

■ Reinforcing alliance partners is the process of publicly and noticeably showing support for an ally's position or action.

■ Persuasion of non-aligned entities is the process of convincing non-allies of the validity and legitimacy of a position or action taken by an initiating entity and all the aligned entities involved in a position or action.

■ Recruitment and indoctrination is the process of aligning new entities or individuals to a social media warfare cause or any type of cause that has social media warfare components.

■ Relationship building is the process of establishing and nurturing cooperative efforts with like-minded people or organizations.

■ Nullifying opponents is the process of discrediting opponents in the eyes of alliance partners or non-partners that an alliance, nation, or organization is attempting to influence.

The nature of defensive social media warfare tactics was discussed in Chapter 1: "A Framework to Analyze Emerging Social Media Warfare Strategies."

3.3 Using Social Media Warfare Tactics as Offensive Weapons

Merely being defensive in a conflict situation involving social media warfare tactics is far from sufficient. Offensive social media warfare tactics can become important tools for destabilizing and undermining an opposing fighting force. Many offensive tactics need to be put into play because, unlike defensive tactics, which can serve many purposes whether in conflict or not, offensive tactics are targeted toward the opposing forces in more specific situations. Offensive tactics and their targets are shown in Table 3.3.

The target audiences for offensive social media warfare tactics are shown in the far-left column of Table 3.3; they include major insurgent forces, advisors, and allied troops as the primary target audience for divisiveness tactics. Local sympathizing troops, governments, organizations, and civilians are the primary target audience for confusion, deception, and relationship building tactics. All audiences are targets for trolling and exposure; all audiences can be impacted, even if ever so slightly and probably more indirectly, by nullifying the legitimacy of the mission. The basic goals of each tactic are as follows:

■ Deception is the process of using invalid or false information or pretense to try to convince opponents that a specific position or proposition is true when there is no factual basis for the position.
■ Confusion tactics are processes designed to disorient and deceive opponents as to what is real and not real. In many ways, it is a classic propaganda method that is meant to create fear, uncertainty, and doubt.

Table 3.3 Offensive Social Media Tactics in Conflict Environments

Target Audience	Applied Social Media Warfare Tactics		
Insurgent force	Dividedness	Trolling	Nullifying opponents
Aligned factions			
Allied troops			
Local sympathizing troops	Confusion		
Local sympathizing government	Deception	Exposure	
Local sympathizing organizations	Relationship building		
Sympathizing civilians			

- Divisiveness tactics involve instigating hatred and suspicion among opponents or the populace of an opposing nation or alliance.
- Exposure tactics most often involve the unauthorized release of information that could embarrass or otherwise jeopardize the owner or creator of the information exposed.
- Trolling is the process of having troops that respond to social media posts with messages that oppose the original posts; they are made by individuals or in the name of organizations that are attempting to influence, deceive, recruit, and indoctrinate.
- Relationship building as an offensive tactic can be geared toward trying to sway insurgent sympathizers to change their loyalties away from the insurgents.
- Nullifying opponents as an offensive tactic is the process of discrediting opponents in the eyes of alliance partners or non-partners that an alliance, nation, or organization is attempting to influence.

The nature of offensive social media warfare tactics was also discussed in Chapter 1.

3.4 Using Social Media Warfare Tactics to Undermine Stability and Abilities of Opposing Forces

Destabilizing an adversary during or before conflict situations arise, is an excellent way to gain an advantage and reduce the cost and time that it takes to end a conflict on satisfactory terms. To accomplish this, requires a mix of tactics or blended threats, which are a set of combined activities designed to accomplish offensive objectives. They include deception tactics combined with trolling opponents to help legitimize a deceptive post made by an aggressor, as well as physical actions ranging from small quick attacks to major offensives. In a blended offensive situation, multiple social media platforms can be used along with mixed media methods, including text, photos, of video. This again, is the modern approach to classic propaganda campaigns.

Destabilization is almost an art form, and impeding an adversary's ability to use social media warfare tactics can lead to near-term chaos and confusion and long-term collapse of communications and offensive social media warfare abilities. In the case of ISIS, coalition forces were able to work with social media application service providers to get accounts shut down. This slowed down ISIS social media warfare efforts. Meanwhile, various combinations of events in the theater set ISIS back and hindered its ability to regroup and reclaim large amounts of territory. The social media warfare capabilities of ISIS never regained their once bragged about status.

Social media warfare tactics blended into certain mixes will always have some impact on a fighting force. The degree to which social media warfare tactics are effective largely depends on what other tactics are employed to destabilize and opponent. The good thing about social media warfare tactics is that they can be executed relatively inexpensively and sustained over a long time.

Social media clusters, or groups of pages and a critical mass of postings, can be fabricated and manipulated. The key to successfully establishing a deceptive entrapment scheme is to make the entire activity look authentic. A reputation can be established for such an online community of social media content, and an entire set of players can be created and staffed as avatars or impersonators from various backgrounds. The process might be a little slow, but it can draw people into an environment of seemingly like-minded people. Entrapment and tagging of visitors and new members can take time but yield much useful information and create confusion among the people that are lured into a community disguised as friendly to the opposition.

A less time-consuming tactic is creating confusion among members of opposing forces. Combining social media content with deceptive stories in other media can make people believe that something has happened or is going to happen. The more people in the opposing force that rely on social media as a source of information or inspiration, the more useful this tactic will be over time.

There are endless combinations of things that can be done with social media applications that contribute to confusion and disorientation among opposing forces and serve to recruit segments of the population whose loyalties are torn. This tactic is not new, and it was used with earlier propaganda technologies and well before social media applications and the Internet came into use. The only limit is imagination, and of course having enough culturally fluent troops to create deception and to communicate with possible defectors or informants from opposing or insurgent forces.

3.5 Preventing Personnel from Undermining Force Stability When Using Social Media

There have been many lessons about people saying too much of the wrong thing in a social media post, and the information in that post being used by an adversary to do harm. It is essential that all people assigned to military responsibilities be trained in using social media applications for their personal use in a manner that does not compromise operations security. There should also be policies in place by military organizations regarding the personal use of social media applications.

The United States Army Social Media Handbook provides guidance on how members of the military should use social media applications and some of the things they should be cautious about when using social media. A *culture of security* should be established in which security pervades every aspect of daily life and the use of social media, not just while deployed. This is especially relevant when protecting operations security. *The United States Army Social Media Handbook* brings to light several important issues:

- The importance of establishing *social media policies* that specify who in an organization is responsible for social media operations and when, why, where, and how social media can be used on behalf of an organization.
- Methods of identifying *security threats*, such as imposter social media accounts, and what to do to avoid these accounts, how and whom to report these accounts.
- How to identify scams, what to do to avoid getting taken in by a scam, and how and whom to report the scams.
- How to maintain security of official U.S. Army social media accounts and pages, including assignment of responsibilities, content management and control, protecting *sensitive information*, monitoring, and *security vigilance*.

It is also very important that military members be well indoctrinated on *security awareness* when it comes to using social media applications for personal use. It is also important to train military family members in how to maintain security when they are using social media applications for *personal use*. This is very relevant to protecting operations security. *The United States Army Social Media Handbook* raises several other important issues:

- Members should not post any information that reveals where they are stationed or where they work.
- Members should not post any information that reveals where they are being reassigned to or any details about where they will work in the future.
- Members should not post any information that reveals what kind of work they do.
- Members should not post any information that reveals anything about their coworkers' locations or job responsibilities.
- Members should be cautious when posting photos because many photos taken with digital devices have *geotagging* features that reveal the location where the photo was taken; this is visible when posted on certain social media platforms, thus providing adversaries with actionable intelligence.

3.6 Managing Social Media Warfare Operations

The most important aspect of managing social media warfare operations is creating a command structure and a division or labor that controls which aspects of social media warfare will be centralized and which will be distributed among various command levels. These include

- Interactions and joint operations among allies and requests for assistance
- Interactions and joint operations with other agencies or branches of military and requests for assistance
- Interactions and joint operations with other local governments and requests for assistance
- Relationships with service providers and requests for assistance
- Relationships with indigenous assets and requests for assistance

There are several military commands and units that could, and perhaps do so on an ongoing basis, benefit from social media warfare and actively participate in social media warfare. The U. S. Cyber Command is a key player in cyberspace, working on behalf of the country and several military units. On June 23, 2009, the secretary of defense directed the commander of U.S. Strategic Command (USSTRATCOM) to establish a sub-unified command, the U.S. Cyber Command (USCYBERCOM); full operational capability (FOC) was achieved on October 31, 2010. The command is located at Fort Meade, Maryland.

According to its website, USCYBERCOM plans, coordinates, integrates, synchronizes, and conducts activities to direct the operations and defense of specified Department of Defense (DOD) information networks. USCYBERCOM also prepares to conduct and, when directed, conducts full-spectrum military cyberspace operations in order to enable actions in all domains and to ensure U.S. and its allies freedom of action in cyberspace and deny the same to adversaries.

USCYBERCOM is designing the cyber force structure, training requirements, and certification standards that will enable the military services to build the cyber force required to execute their assigned missions. The command also works closely with interagency and international partners in executing these missions. USCYBERCOM is a sub-unified combatant command subordinate to USSTRATCOM. Its service elements include Army Cyber Command (ARCYBER), Fleet Cyber Command (FLTCYBER), Air Force Cyber Command (AFCYBER), and Marine Forces Cyber Command (MARFORCYBER). Coast Guard Cyber Command (CGCYBER), although subordinate to the Department of Homeland Security (DHS), has a direct support relationship with USCYBERCOM [3].

The U.S. Army Intelligence and Security Command (INSCOM) also has an active role in social media warfare. INSCOM conducts intelligence, security, and information operations for military commanders and national decision makers. It is headquartered at Fort Belvoir, Virginia, and has 17,500 soldiers, Department of the Army civilians, and contractors who work at 180 locations in 40 countries. INSCOM executes mission command of operational intelligence forces; conducts worldwide multi-discipline and all-source intelligence operations; delivers advanced skills training, linguist support, specialized quick reaction capabilities, and intelligence-related logistics in support of army, joint, and coalition commands and the National Intelligence Community.

INSCOM and the Department of the Army, G-2 established the U.S. Army Operations Group Provisional (AOG) in March 2003 to conduct human intelligence operations. Since that time, AOG has been a productive member of the Department of Defense Human Intelligence (HUMINT) community. AOG conducts operations in all HUMINT disciplines and supports commanders from the tactical to strategic and army levels, including units involved in combat operations in Iraq, Afghanistan, and worldwide. According to the INSCOM website, the major units under the command are

- 1st Information Operations Command (Land) is the only U.S. Army full-spectrum information operations (IO) organization engaged from information operations theory development and training to operational application across the range of military operations.
- 66th Military Intelligence Brigade conducts theater-level, multi-discipline intelligence and security operations and, when directed, deploys prepared forces to conduct joint/combined expeditionary and contingency operations in support of U.S. Army Europe and U.S. European Command.
- 116th Military Intelligence Brigade conducts 24/7 tasking, collection, processing, exploitation, dissemination, and feedback of multiple organic and joint intelligence aerial-intelligence surveillance and reconnaissance (A-ISR) missions collected in overseas contingency areas of operation.
- 207th Military Intelligence Brigade is assigned to U.S. Africa Command with operational control to U.S. Army Africa. It conducts intelligence collection and exploitation in order to disrupt transnational and transregional threats and promote regional stability in Africa.
- 300th Military Intelligence Brigade (Linguist) provides trained and ready linguist and military intelligence soldiers to commanders from brigade through army level.
- 470th Military Intelligence Brigade provides timely and fused multi-discipline intelligence in support of U.S. Army South, U.S. Southern Command, and other national intelligence agencies.
- 500th Military Intelligence Brigade provides multi-disciplined intelligence support for joint and coalition war fighters in the U.S. Army Pacific area of responsibility (AOR).
- 501st Military Intelligence Brigade conducts theater-level, multi-discipline intelligence for joint and combined war fighters from the Republic of Korea.
- 505th Military Intelligence Brigade conducts theater-level, multi-discipline intelligence collection and analysis operations to support U.S. Army North (USARNORTH) preparation for unified land operations, conduct of security cooperation activities, and force protection within the U.S. Northern Command (USNORTHCOM) AOR.
- 513th Military Intelligence Brigade deploys in strength or in tailored elements to conduct multi-discipline intelligence and security operations in

support of army components of U.S. Central Command and theater army commanders.

- 704th Military Intelligence Brigade conducts synchronized full-spectrum signals intelligence, computer network, and information assurance operations directly and through the National Security Agency (NSA) to satisfy national, joint, combined, and army information superiority requirements.

- 706th Military Intelligence Group provides personnel, intelligence assets, and technical support to conduct signals intelligence operations within the National Security Agency/Central Security Service Georgia (NSA/CSS Georgia) and worldwide.

- 780th Military Intelligence Brigade conducts signals intelligence, computer network operations, and enables dynamic computer network defense operations of army and defense networks.

- 902d Military Intelligence Group provides direct and general counterintelligence support to army activities and major commands.

- Army Cryptologic Operations (ACO) serves as the Army G-2 and service cryptologic component (SCC) representative to provide cryptologic leadership, support, guidance, and advice to U.S. Army war fighters and intelligence leaders.

- Army Field Support Center (AFSC) provides specialized operational, administrative, and personnel management support to Department of the Army and other DOD services and agencies.

- Army Operations Group (AOG) conducts human intelligence operations and provides expertise in support of ground component priority intelligence requirements using a full spectrum of human intelligence collection methods.

- Joint Surveillance Target Attack Radar System (JSTARS) provides army aircrew members aboard joint surveillance and target attack radar system (JSTARS) aircraft to support surveillance and targeting operations of army land component and joint or combined task force commanders worldwide.

- National Ground Intelligence Center (NGIC) is the primary producer of ground forces intelligence of the DOD [4].

3.7 Training Military Personnel in Social Media Warfare Tactics

Propaganda is a key element in modern war and has been for centuries. Positive and negative propaganda remain a viable tool for military forces. ISIS propaganda has been an important tool for the insurgency to recruit and indoctrinate. That effort has been at least moderately successful, and it is something that coalition forces have had to address. Just how this was accomplished has yet to be fully revealed.

The history of propaganda is worthy of study by anyone involved in or interested in social media warfare. Authored by Lieutenant Colonel Jesse McIntyre III (U.S. Army, retired), "To Respond or Not to Respond: Addressing Adversarial Propaganda" provides a fascinating history of propaganda in modern warfare. McIntyre notes that German political and military leaders attribute Germany's defeat in World War I, in part, to Allied propaganda efforts. He also notes that history shows that counter propaganda efforts must be executed skillfully to keep them from backfiring [5].

Social media warfare troops will need cyber skills, military intelligence, civilian intelligence skills, language skills, cultural knowledge, and propaganda skills. Developing these skills and knowledge will take considerable training and time. Cyber skills are certainly something that people can be trained in, but intelligence analysis talent takes longer to develop and requires technical knowledge as well as cultural knowledge and multilingual skills. Propaganda skills can also be learned, but not everyone will have a natural propensity to become a propagandist.

Military academies have educated military leaders for a long time. DOD has a website that provides an excellent overview of five military academies in the United States:

- The U.S. Military Academy (Army) in West Point, New York
- The U.S. Naval Academy (Navy/Marine Corps) in Annapolis, Maryland
- The U.S. Air Force Academy (Air Force) in Colorado Springs, Colorado
- The U.S. Coast Guard Academy (Coast Guard) in New London, Connecticut
- The U.S. Merchant Marine Academy in Kings Point, New York [6]

Graduates of these five academies receive a bachelor of science degree and are commissioned as officers in their respective service branch. In all cases, there is a service obligation of a minimum of 5 years. Admissions criteria include, high school academic performance, standardized test scores (SAT or ACT), athletics and extracurricular activities, leadership experience and community involvement, and a congressional letter of recommendation (not required by the Coast Guard Academy) [6].

The senior military colleges (SMCs) have become an effective means of educating officers and offer a combination of higher education and military instruction. SMCs include Texas A&M University, Norwich University, the Virginia Military Institute, the Citadel, Virginia Polytechnic Institute and State University (Virginia Tech), University of North Georgia, and the Mary Baldwin Women's Institute for Leadership. Cadets must participate in the Reserve Officers' Training Corps (ROTC), but only those cadets who receive an ROTC scholarship are required to enter military service following graduation [6].

There are also war colleges for each military branch that address contemporary warfare topics for senior officers. The war colleges are

- U.S. Air Force Command and Staff College (ACSC) (Montgomery, Alabama) focuses on preparing the joint strategic leaders through air, space, and cyberspace education.
- U.S. Army Command and Staff College (CGSC) (Fort Leavenworth, Kansas) provides career officers with a larger context of unified action—multi-service, interagency, and multinational operations. Additionally, prominent local colleges have created numerous cohort programs tailored to meet the schedule needs of CGSC students.
- U.S. Marine Corps Command and Staff College (CSC) (Quantico, Virginia), part of the Marine Corps University, trains joint, multinational, and interagency professionals to overcome diverse twenty-first century security challenges.
- U.S. Navy College of Naval Command and Staff (Newport, Rhode Island) provides education in three core subject areas: strategy and policy, joint maritime operations, and national security decision making.
- Maritime Advanced Warfighting School (MAWS) (Newport, Rhode Island) is a component of the Naval War College (NWC) educational mission to develop strategic and operational leaders with the skills required to plan, execute, and assess combined, joint, and naval operations.
- U.S. Air Force Air War College (AWC) (Montgomery, Alabama) develops senior leaders for strategic-level employment of air, space, and cyberspace forces.
- U.S. Army War College (USAWC) (Carlisle Barracks, Pennsylvania) is the Army's professional development institution, preparing selected military, civilian, and international leaders for the responsibilities of strategic leadership in a joint, interagency, intergovernmental, and multinational environment.
- U.S. Marine Corps War College (MCWAR) (Quantico, Virginia) prepares selected officers and civilians for decision making across a range of military operations in joint, interagency, and multinational environments.
- U.S. Navy College of Naval Warfare (Newport, Rhode Island) offers three core subject areas: national security decision making, strategy and policy, and joint military operations.
- The Eisenhower School, previously known as the Industrial College of the Armed Forces (ICAF) (Washington, DC), is part of the National Defense University (NDU); it provides graduate-level education to senior members of the U.S. armed forces, government civilians, foreign nationals and private industry.
- National War College (Washington, DC) is part of the National Defense University (NDU); its mission is to educate future leaders of the armed

forces, Department of State, and other civilian agencies for high-level policy, command, and staff responsibilities. The curriculum emphasizes joint and interagency perspectives.

■ Joint Advanced War Fighting School (JAWS) (Norfolk, Virginia) produces graduates who can create campaign-quality concepts, plan for the employment of all elements of national power, accelerate transformation, succeed as joint force operational/strategic planners, and be creative, conceptual, adaptive and innovative. Students must be capable of synergistically combining existing and emerging capabilities in time, space, and purpose to accomplish operational or strategic objectives [7].

There are many other schools and training centers for military personnel that could help train military personnel in social media warfare tactics and related topics:

■ The Defense Information School, Ft Meade, Maryland, teaches skills for creating editorial publications, radio programs, and television programs; it produces outstanding public affairs and visual information personnel. It is responsible for growing and sustaining a corps of professional organizational communicators who fulfill the communication needs of the military.

■ Defense Language Institute Foreign Language Center (DLIFLC), located in Monterey, California, it teaches oral and written fluency in foreign languages for use in military intelligence roles that involve listening in on communications or translating in the field. As part of the Army training and doctrine command (TRADOC), the Institute provides resident instruction at the Presidio in Monterey, California in 24 languages, 5 days a week, 7 hours per day, with two to three hours of homework each night. Courses last between 26 and 64 weeks, depending on the difficulty of the language [8].

Military personnel are also trained in several military occupational specialties that may work in social media warfare, including the army military intelligence responsible for all collected intelligence during army missions. Military intelligence officers specialize in specific areas: imagery intelligence, all-source intelligence, counterintelligence, human intelligence, and signals intelligence/electronic warfare. There are also several specialties, such as skilled linguists and interpreters/translators that are needed to be effective in social media warfare [9]. There are over 20,000 media and public affairs specialists in the U.S. military services, with the Army having over 6,000 and the Air Force over 7,000 such specialists [10]. Future training for military social media warfare specialists may include work in field laboratories or red team/blue team competitions designed to develop and sharpen skills.

3.8 Using Social Media Warfare Tactics to Gain Support in Non-Conflict Environments

Military organizations, like governments, maintain constant efforts in self-validation, influence, and relationship building even when there is no ongoing conflict. Military organizations in freer societies work constantly on their relationships with other military organizations, civilian populations where installations are located, and the families of service members [11]. On the other hand, military organizations in far less freer nations work to maintain their relationships with the populace through intimidation, bullying, harassment, and, far too often, more extreme measures.

Again, using the U.S. military services as an example, these service branches put a great deal of effort into social media and have a strong *social media presence*. *The United States Army Social Media Handbook* provides considerable guidance to all levels of the Army on how to best use social media to meet desired validation, relationship building, and communications with all the Army's constituents. There are numerous examples of successful use of social media by army units. One of the most important messages conveyed in the handbook is that the Army wants to use social media to communicate its story and also to listen to what others have to say.

The Army is taking the use of social media very seriously; it sets policy and communicates through specific directives on the use of social media. Key documents include DOD Directive 8550.1, DOD Internet Services and Internet-based Capabilities, and the Secretary of the Army Delegation of Authority Approval of External Communications.

Social media is an integral part of the U.S. Army and DOD operations. The U.S. Army maintains an official directory of its social media presence to serve as a *consolidated registry* and resource for all information regarding official Army presence on public social media sites. All sites listed on the page have been reviewed and approved by the Army's Office of the Chief of Public Affairs and are subject to army policies and guidelines [12].

DOD has created the *Department of Defense Captioning Style Guide*; it provides a standard method of writing captions for DOD imagery. This publication is designed to help all personnel involved in the creation of official DOD imagery to write and edit captions that are accurate, clear, concise, and meet DOD style standards [13]. The DOD has also established an official Social Media Hub, which provides training and guidance to service members using social media (http://dodcio.defense.gov/Social-Media/) [14].

A review of the Army's social media management and guides shows that the Army is well ahead of many organizations when it comes to using and controlling social media applications to support mission goals and objectives. The Army is doing a splendid and superior job using social media than most private companies are; those companies lagging should start taking lessons from the U.S. Army.

3.9 Support for Military Families in Social Media

The U.S. military has used social media warfare to build relationships, validate its mission, and influence society in general. An August 28, 2016 review of social media accounts by non-military organizations or individuals did not reveal much in the way of discord or discontent. The review did show that members of the military and their families have many sources for support and information on the Internet. Some of the sources of support have a considerable fan base with thousands of followers. Stags and subject lines in these sources include

- National Military Family Association
- Military OneSource: resources, referrals, consultations and counseling
- Military Avenue: Supporting the Needs of American Military Families
- Joining Forces Michelle Obama & @DrBiden's initiative to serve military and their families
- Military Homecomings: families reunited with their loved ones
- Operation Homefront: strong, stable, and secure military families
- Boot Campaign: patriotism, veterans' issues, assistance to military
- GEHiresHeroes: Tweets GE news, jobs, and other items of interest to veterans
- VoteVets: 450,000+ veterans, family, supporters working to protect veterans' interests
- GiveanHour: free mental health services for military members and families
- Ops OnceinaLifetime: Once in a Lifetime experiences for military members and families.
- Operation Shower: Hosting baby showers for military families
- Women Veterans ROCK: Coalition of Women Veteran and Advocacy Organizations.
- Veterans Writing: Veterans Writing Project provides no-cost writing seminars for veterans, active service members, and family members

3.10 Conclusions

Military organizations face tremendous challenges in social media warfare. Militaries learn to deal with new threats and train current and future troops in how to defend against a technology and how to use the technology as a weapon of their advantage. The following important conclusions can be drawn from the material presented in this chapter:

- Unconventional warfare theaters are complex environments where military organizations face a myriad of potential allies and at least as many potential enemies; it can often be difficult to determine who is what, and social media warfare can complicate relationships and make operation security more difficult.

■ The simultaneous use of defensive and offensive social media warfare tactics requires a fighting force that can work to influence and build relationships with friendly forces and, at the same time, work to discredit, confuse, and harm opposing forces as much as possible.

■ Coalition governments were able to influence social media application service providers to help in monitoring activity and neutralizing the ability of ISIS to leverage social media.

■ Offensive social media warfare tactics can become important tools in destabilizing and undermining an opposing fighting force. Social media clusters, or groups of pages, and a critical mass of postings can be created and manipulated.

■ It is important that military members be well indoctrinated in *security awareness* when it comes to using social media applications for personal use, and military family members need training in how to maintain security when they are using social media applications.

■ The most important aspect of managing social media warfare operations is creating a command structure and a division of labor that controls which aspects of social media warfare will be centralized and which will be distributed among various command levels.

■ Social media warfare troops will need cyber skills, military intelligence and civilian intelligence skills, language skills, cultural knowledge, and propaganda skills. Developing these skills and knowledge will take considerable training and time.

■ Military organizations, like governments, maintain constant efforts of self-validation, influence, and relationship building, even when there is no ongoing conflict.

3.11 Agenda for Action

Social media use in warfare and non-conflict environments is changing rapidly and military organizations, at least in the United States, are developing social media policies and tactics. Military organizations are particularly vulnerable to social media warfare tactics, and the security of operations may be put at risk in many ways. Action steps should include, but not be limited to, the following areas:

■ Establish and support research efforts addressing the threats to military operations in social media warfare.

■ Include social media warfare issues in all relevant military training and education programs.

- Increase military social media application use, management, and content monitoring; these should be ongoing activities, and lessons learned procedures should be applied to both successes and failures.
- The U.S. Army is doing a splendid and greatly superior job in using social media than most private companies are; a knowledge transfer program should be established to help train organizations in critical industry sectors on social media management and deployment.

3.12 Key Terms

Consolidated registry is a mechanism the U.S. military services use to inventory, approve, and authenticate social media use throughout all levels of the services.

Culture of security is an organization culture in which security pervades every aspect of daily life and in all operational situations.

Geotagging is the process of embedding global positioning system (GPS) coordinates in photographs taken using a smartphone or other GPS-capable devices.

Personal use means using a service or an item only for personal reasons and goals that do not have any relationship to the organization employing the individual using the item or service.

Security awareness is the basic level of understanding of security and recognition of the importance of security.

Security threats are conditions, people, or events that can jeopardize the security of an organization, a facility, any asset belonging to an organization, or the employees of the organization.

Security vigilance is the constant attention given to security during day-to-day operations; it contributes to security by encouraging the reporting of security violations and makes suggestions on how to improve security when weaknesses are observed.

Sensitive information is that information held by or created by an organization that, if revealed to the wrong party, would cause harm to the organization owning or creating the information.

Social media applications are any existing or future networked computer program that facilitates communication between individuals or individuals and groups.

Social media policies specify who in an organization is responsible for social media operations and specify when, why, where, and how social media can be used on behalf of an organization; they provide guidance on the inappropriate use of social media by corporate media staff and employees.

Social media presence is an organization's use of social media accounts and applications to communicate with individuals or groups; it is also the mention, comments, discussions, and display of any material on any social media application that relates to or depicts an organization.

3.13 Seminar Discussion Topics

Discussion topics for graduate- or professional-level seminars:

- What experience have seminar participants had in situations where social media warfare strategies or tactics were deployed?
- What experience have seminar participants had in the creation or management of social media content? What social media applications were utilized?
- What experience have seminar participants had in training social media staff in the creation or management of social media content? What was the target audience for the training?

3.14 Seminar Group Project

Divide participants into multiple groups with each group taking 10–15 minutes to develop a list of dos and don'ts when using social media warfare tactics. Upon completion, have groups exchange their lists with groups taking 10–15 minutes to expand on the dos and don'ts list. Meet as a group and discuss the offensive tactics selected by the groups and the defensive measures to counter the tactics that were developed by the groups.

References

1. Burnore, Nathanael. 2013. Social media applications for unconventional warfare. Master's thesis, U.S. Army Command and General Staff College. Accessed August 24, 2016. www.dtic.mil/dtic/tr/fulltext/u2/a598982.pdf.
2. Ressa, Maria A. 2012. The new battlefield: The Internet and social media. *Combating Terrorism Exchange* 2, No. 4. Accessed August 24, 2016. http://www.nps.edu/Academics/Schools/GSOIS/Departments/DA/Documents/vol%202%20no%20 4%20FINAL%20web.pdf.
3. U.S. Cyber Command. 2015. U.S. Cyber Command factsheet. Accessed August 24, 2016. http://www.stratcom.mil/factsheets/2/Cyber_Command/.
4. The U.S. Army Intelligence and Security Command. Website of the U.S. Army Intelligence and Security Command. Accessed August 24, 2016. https://www.inscom.army.mil/.
5. McIntyre, Jesse, III. 2016. Addressing adversarial propaganda. *Military Review*. Accessed August 26, 2016. usacac.army.mil/CAC2/MilitaryReview/Archives/English/MilitaryReview_20160630_art012.pd.

6. Today's Military. Service academies and senior military colleges. Accessed August 27, 2016, from http://todaysmilitary.com/training/service-academies-and-military-colleges.
7. U.S. Navy. War colleges. Accessed August 27, 2016. http://www.public.navy.mil/bupers-npc/officer/Detailing/rlstaffcorps/supply/Documents/WAR%20COLLEGES.pdf.
8. U.S. Army. Specialized skills training. Accessed August 27, 2016. http://myarmy-benefits.us.army.mil/Home/Benefit_Library/Federal_Benefits_Page/Specialized_Skills_Training.html?serv=149.
9. U.S. Army. Careers and jobs. Accessed 27, 2016. http://www.goarmy.com/careers-and-jobs/officer-careers-and-specialties.html.
10. U.S. Department of Labor, Bureau of Statistics. Military careers. *Occupational Outlook Handbook*. Accessed August 27, 2016. http://www.bls.gov/ooh/Military/Military-Careers.htm.
11. Mayfield, Thomas D., III. 2011. A commander's strategy for social media. *Joint Force Quarterly* 60. Accessed August 24, 2016. www.au.af.mil/au/awc/awcgate/jfq/mayfield_strat_for_soc_media.pdf.
12. U.S. Army. Army social media. Accessed August 28, 2016. https://www.army.mil/media/socialmedia/.
13. Defense Imagery Management Operations Center (DIMOC). 2014. Department of Defense captioning style guide. Accessed August 28, 2016. http://www.dimoc.mil/documents/styleGuide/StyleGuide-141017.pdf.
14. Department of Defense. DOD social media hub. Accessed August 28, 2016. http://dodcio.defense.gov/Social-Media/.

Chapter 4

Corporate Efforts to Deploy or Respond to Social Media Warfare Strategies

---

Corporations, especially large ones, are in a constant state of conflict. Social media warfare is intensifying that conflict. Competition is stiff between corporations, and globalization has opened more avenues for competition and conflict. Corporations also face tax challenges, and as they relocate from country to country they find that their new home may turn into less of a tax haven than expected. On the one hand, regulators and lawmakers work to hold corporations accountable for their many sins; on the other hand, they take campaign contributions from industry groups in exchange for less regulation and the freedom to be corrupt. Corporations have polluted the environment, exploited workers, sold faulty and dangerous products, and alienated social cause groups who feel corporations should be held responsible for the damage they have done. The larger the corporation, the more lawsuits they face every year. This chapter examines how corporations use social media warfare tactics and, in turn, have those tactics used against them.

4.1 Corporate Environment and Mentality

The major goal of corporations is to make money for their owners or stockholders. Over the centuries, corporations have clung to that goal as their sole purpose, and ignored the world around them as well as their impact on that world. That mentality, and the business environment it created, did not work out very well, and in fact in many countries corporate business still represents the most destructive social dynamic.

Many countries are working toward a cleaner environment and improved social conditions for their citizens. On the opposite end of the spectrum is China, the world's largest emerging industrial economy. Corporations in China prefer the old mentality and the environment shows the effects of this; China is home to a majority of the world's most polluted cities and it shows only marginal, if any, respect for worker rights and workplace conditions.

Because corporations in the United States, Europe, and Japan operate under the heavy scrutiny of regulatory forces, which of course they deeply resent, the environment is improving and worker rights and workplace conditions are improving as well. Business investors and politicians in the United States still constantly squawk, whine, moan, and groan about government regulation. They also work to evade citizen demands for great corporate social responsibility, even though embracing that responsibility has proved to be profitable in both the short and long term.

The Guiding Principles on Business and Human Rights endorsed by the United Nations (UN) Human Rights Council on June 16, 2011, with strong support from the United States, are the first global set of guidelines on business and human rights. The Guiding Principles provide an important framework for corporations, states, civil society, and others as they work to strengthen their respective approaches to business and human rights. The principles are organized under a three-pillar framework:

- Protect: States have a duty to protect against human rights abuses by third parties, including business enterprises, through appropriate policies, regulations, and adjudication.
- Respect: Businesses have a responsibility to respect human rights, including acting with due diligence to avoid infringing on the rights of others, and addressing adverse impacts with which they are involved.
- Remedy: There is a need for greater access to remedy for victims of business-related abuse, both judicial and non-judicial [1].

Another major issue that corporations need to deal with is the global movement for improved environmental protection. The International Standards Organization's (ISO) ISO standard 14001 addresses the issues of corporate impact on the environment. It also describes the specification and requirements for an environmental management system (EMS) to reduce negative impact on the environment. As with most macro ISO standards, 14001 calls for constant improvement over time and reducing the negative environmental impact on the part of corporations.

An EMS encourages an organization to continuously improve its environmental performance. The system follows a repeating cycle and the organization first commits to an environmental policy, then uses its policy as a basis for establishing a plan, which sets objectives and targets for improving environmental performance. The next step is implementation. After that, the organization evaluates its environmental performance to see whether the objectives and targets are being met. If targets are not being met, corrective action is taken. The results of this evaluation are then reviewed by top management to see if the EMS is working. Management revisits the environmental policy and sets new targets in a revised plan. The company then implements the revised plan. The cycle repeats, and continuous improvement occurs. The five main stages of an EMS, as defined by the ISO 14001 standard, are as follows:

- Commitment and Policy: Top management commits to environmental improvement and establishes the organization's environmental policy. The policy is the foundation of the EMS.
- Planning: A company first identifies environmental aspects of its operations such as air pollutants or hazardous waste that can have negative impacts on people and/or the environment. Once significant environmental aspects are determined, a company sets objectives and targets.
- Implementation: A company follows through with the action plan using the necessary resources (human, financial, etc.). An important component is employee training and awareness for all employees. Other steps in the implementation stage include documentation, following operating procedures, and setting up internal and external communication lines.
- Evaluation: A company monitors its operations to evaluate whether targets are being met. If not, the company takes corrective action.
- Review: Top management reviews the results of the evaluation to see if the EMS is working. The plan is then revised to optimize the effectiveness of the EMS. The review stage creates a loop of continuous improvement for a company [2].

As global movements to pressure corporations to be better citizens progress, a third area that corporations must deal with is national or local regulation, much of which is aligned with the goals of protecting human rights and the environment. In the United States, corporations must deal with federal government regulations as well as state regulations and state and local laws on how corporations conduct business and manage their operations. There are over 400 federal agencies that, depending on the industry sector, corporations may be regulated by in some fashion, and many have state-level counterparts. The major federal regulatory agencies of the United States are

- Department of Agriculture (USDA)
- Department of Commerce (DOC)
- Department of Defense (DOD)
- Department of Education (ED)
- Department of Energy (DOE)
- Department of Health and Human Services (HHS)
- Department of Homeland Security (DHS)
- Department of Housing and Urban Development (HUD)
- Department of the Interior (DOI)
- Department of Justice (DOJ)
- Department of Labor (DOL)
- Department of State (DOS)
- Department of Transportation (DOT)
- Department of the Treasury (TREAS)
- Alcohol, Tobacco, Firearms, and Explosives Bureau
- Centers for Medicare and Medicaid Services
- Consumer Financial Protection Bureau (CFPB)
- Consumer Product Safety Commission (CPSC)
- Environmental Protection Agency (EPA)
- Equal Employment Opportunity Commission (EEOC)
- Executive Office of the President (EOP)
- Federal Aviation Administration
- Federal Financial Institutions Examination Council (FFIEC)
- Federal Trade Commission (FTC)
- General Services Administration (GSA)
- Internal Revenue Service (IRS)
- Interstate Commerce Commission (ICC)
- National Labor Relations Board (NLRB)
- National Transportation Safety Board (NTSB)
- Nuclear Regulatory Commission (NRC)
- Occupational Safety and Health Administration (OSHA)
- Office of Personnel Management (OPM)
- Security Exchange Commission (SEC)
- Small Business Administration (SBA) [3]

The final corporate battlefront addressed in this book is citizen group and special interest group pressure on companies to engage in *corporate social responsibility* (CSR). The trend toward CSR has been steadily increasing, though its extent varies among industries. CSR exists when companies self-regulate according to sustainable legal standards, ethical principles, and international norms. There are many ways and various degrees of rigor by which sustainability is measured. Systems of rating and endorsement have been established by nations, the UN, states/provinces, industries, professional associations, and environmental groups. Companies often display their ratings and awards in public relations materials to great positive effect. In fact, sometimes a business will seek to boost its public image by advertising itself as greener than it actually is. This is referred to as green washing [4].

The U.S. Department of State has a strong commitment to CSR, which is exemplified by its comprehensive approach to providing support and guidance in areas of responsible corporate conduct. Key areas of focus are labor and supply chains, energy and the environment, anti-corruption, health and social welfare, partnerships and exchanges, and the empowerment of women and girls [5].

4.2 Corporations and Defensive Social Media Warfare Tactics

Corporations face social media warfare threats that other organizations do not necessarily face on the four battlefronts discussed in the previous section. There are many people and groups that oppose specific types of corporations or specific corporations because of what they do or do not do as a business entity. Genetically modified food is an example of what corporations are engaged in that many people around the world oppose.

This puts corporations in a uniquely perilous position and results in them having a unique perspective on social media warfare. Corporations are especially vulnerable to damaging slander and harassment social media campaigns, which most governments have little interest in addressing and which may not violate any national security laws.

Defensive social media warfare tactics, like offensive tactics, have long been a part of corporate arsenals. The most relevant tactics for defending a corporation are

- Self-validation, or assuring the world of the validity and legitimacy of a position or action that a corporation or individual representative takes, is a common practice in virtually all conflict situations.
- Influencing industry groups, or working to convince business partners of the validity and legitimacy of a position or action taken by a corporation or individual representative, goes one step beyond self-validation.
- Reinforcing industry and business partners is the process of publicly and noticeably showing support for an ally's position or action.
- Persuasion of independent entities is the process of convincing non-allies of the validity and legitimacy of a position or action taken by an initiating entity and all the aligned entities involved in a position or action.

- Recruiting and indoctrination involve the process of aligning new companies, special interest groups, or individuals with a company's social media warfare cause.
- Relationship building is the process of establishing and nurturing cooperative efforts with companies or groups that share an interest in the same business sector or who can benefit from a company's actions.
- Nullifying opponents is the process of discrediting opponents in the eyes of industry groups or business partners or non-partners that a company is attempting to influence.

Different defensive social media warfare tactics are more effective with different target audiences. Some tactics will work with multiple audiences but may require an alternative message or content in social media. Defensive social media warfare tactics and their target audiences are shown in Table 4.1. The target audiences for defensive social media warfare tactics in corporate environments are shown in the far-left column of Table 4.1 and include corporate leaders, stock holders, and the overall industry sector of which a company is a member as the primary target audience for self-validation tactics. Local lawmakers, regulators, adversarial organizations, and customers are the primary targets for influencing, reinforcing, and relationship building tactics. All audiences are targets for recruitment and indoctrination tactics and persuasion of aligned and non-aligned organizations or

Table 4.1 Defensive Social Media Tactics in Corporate Environments

Target Audience	Applied Social Media Warfare Tactics		
Corporate leaders	Self-validation	Recruiting and indoctrination into corporate goals Persuasion of aligned and non-aligned entities	Nullifying opponents
Stock holders			
Industry sector			
Lawmakers	Influencing Reinforcing Relationship building		
Regulators			
Adversarial organizations			
Customers			

companies. The tactic of nullifying an opponent helps builds relationships with other organizations or it eliminates an opponent from the battlefield.

4.3 Corporations and Offensive Social Media Warfare Tactics

As with any organization, corporations cannot afford to merely be defensive in a conflict situation with social media warfare tactics in play. Offensive social media warfare tactics can become important tools for neutralizing or undermining adversaries. Many offensive tactics need to be put into play simultaneously because offensive tactics are targeted toward the opposition in specific situations. Offensive tactics are shown in Table 4.2. These offensive tactics also can be used against corporations and can result in considerable damage to reputation and even disruption of operations.

Offensive social media warfare tactics, like defensive tactics, have long been part of the corporate arsenal, but perhaps under a different name. They are also in the arsenals of corporate adversaries who will not hesitate to use them in full force and prolonged conflicts. The most relevant tactics for offensive or counteroffensive actions are

■ Deception is the process of using invalid or false information or pretense to try to convince opponents or other interested parties that a specific position or proposition is true when there is not a factual basis for the position.
■ Confusion tactics are processes designed to disorient and deceive opponents or other interested parties regarding what is real and not real. In many ways, it is a classic propaganda method meant to create fear, uncertainty, and doubt.

Table 4.2 Offensive Social Media Tactics in Corporate Environments

Deception: False promises and invalid information.
Confusion: Creating and perpetuating uncertainty.
Dividedness: Separating opponents.
Exposure: Unauthorized release of information.
Trolling: Post opposing messages to existing posts.
Relationship building: Establishing cooperative efforts with likeminded organizations.
Nullify opponents: Efforts to discredit opponents.
Blended threats: Combined activities to accomplish offensive objectives.

- Divisiveness tactics involve instigating hatred and suspicion among opponents, or recruiting interested as well as non-interested individuals into a cause that aligns with the interests of the corporation.
- Exposure tactics most often involve the unauthorized release of information that might embarrass or otherwise jeopardize the owner or creator of the information exposed, in this case, organizations that may oppose a corporation's actions or positions.
- Trolling is the process of having imposters or neutral parties respond to a social media post by posting responses that oppose the messages of an existing post, which was made by individuals or in the name of organizations that oppose a corporation.
- Nullifying opponents as an offensive tactic is the process of discrediting opponents in the eyes of interested and even non-interested parties. Nullifying efforts can reinforce existing positive relationships and help to attract new relationships.
- Blended threats are combined activities that are designed to accomplish offensive objectives. They might include deception tactics, combined with trolling opponents to help legitimize the deceptive post made by an opposing organization or individual. In a blended offensive situation, multiple social media platforms can be used along with mixed media methods, including texts, photos, or videos. This again, is the modern approach to classic propaganda campaigns.

Many companies, or their owners and high-level executives, have come under fire in social media conflicts over the last several years. Pharmaceutical companies and their executives face unrelenting social media attacks when their price gouging is revealed. Several automakers faced heavy social media attacks for falsifying mileage ratings on their vehicles and when serious safety defects were made public by researchers or regulators.

As social media conflicts intensify, more and more people join in quickly to share their experiences and encourage each other to keep up an attack on a company. Literally overnight, thousands of people can come together in a conflict against a target corporation. As the volume of social media posts increases, broadcast or web media usually picks up the story and might add new information to the conflict and continue to incite people.

4.4 Corporate Image Building through Blended Social Media Warfare Tactics

Corporations work very hard at creating an image they wish to project to business leaders, stock holders, lawmakers, regulators, customers, and the public. These images are developed by the *selective release of information* and disclosure of details about the company. This has always been the case, and now social media has become a weapon in developing and maintaining those images. Information that may reflect poorly on the image of a company is withheld and refuted if presented by other parties.

The social media warfare tactics of self-validation, influence, reinforcing preferred perspectives, persuasion, and relationship building are always kept in play by advertising firms, public relations departments, and marketing staff. In a world where corporations are transparent and honest about all they do, these tactics would provide the world with a more balanced account of a corporate actions. However, there is little transparency and honesty when it comes to corporations' image building. When it comes to what the public sees, corporations seek to control all the information.

The selective release of information by corporate image builders can be, and often has been, laced with deceptive and confusing information designed to perpetuate uncertainty and cast doubt on what adversaries say about a corporation. Endorsements are a tool of corporate image builders. They seek and often pay celebrities or experts to endorse products and provide testimony on the goodness of a company. These endorsements have become social media warfare fodder and are designed to influence and persuade.

There have been several cases—some perhaps urban legends—of corporations employing social media warfare tactics like trolling and having social media monitors make favorable posts and comments to discredit negative social media posts. What it comes down to is that the targets of image-building efforts (business leaders, stock holders, lawmakers, regulators, customers, and the public) need to be constantly aware that what they see, hear, and read about any corporation is a staged and manipulated image that might be very far from reality. Naive investors and customers are often entrapped by the contrived images of a corporation. Naive or corrupt lawmakers and regulators should use caution when citing publicly released corporate information to support their position on a company, especially if that information was released by the company under scrutiny.

4.5 Corporate Profit Building through Blended Social Media Warfare Tactics

Corporations love to grow profits and will use their corporate image to promote product lines or specific products. They will also use deceptive tactics and create confusion among customers regarding what company offers the best product and value. General corporate image-building tactics and content face little scrutiny from regulators. On the other hand, product marketing efforts are subject to truth-in-advertising standards for product information disclosure in the United States. This has all become more significant in the realm of social media because companies can now open shops on Facebook, Google Shopping, and other sites, and regulators have more and more activity to monitor.

In a June 2015 white paper by Jessica Rich (director of the Bureau of Consumer Protection of the Federal Trade Commission (FTC)), entitled, "FTC year in review: Advertising and privacy in the age of influencers, smartcars, and Fitbits," Rich points out that corporations are making many unsubstantiated and false claims about the products that they are marketing. The analysis identifies several areas where deceptive tactics are being employed, including deceptive health claims, deceptive endorsements, and *native advertising* [6]. There are several issues as well as specific cases that the FTC has dealt with in the last few years regarding deceptive tactics:

- A California-based online entertainment network engaged in deceptive advertising by paying influencers to post YouTube videos endorsing Microsoft's Xbox one system and several games. The paid influencers failed to adequately disclose that they were being paid for their seemingly objective opinions [7].
- Warner Brothers, Home Entertainment, Inc. settled FTC charges that it deceived consumers during a marketing campaign for the video game "Middle Earth: Shadow of Mordor," by failing to adequately disclose that it paid online influencers, including the wildly popular PewDiePie, thousands of dollars to post positive gameplay videos on YouTube and social media. Over the course of the campaign, the sponsored videos were viewed more than 5.5 million times [8].
- National retailer Lord & Taylor agreed to settle FTC charges that it deceived consumers by paying for native advertisements, including a seemingly objective article in the online publication *Nylon* and a *Nylon* Instagram post, without disclosing that the posts were paid promotions for the company's clothing [9].
- A California mining company and its president settled FTC claims that they allegedly defrauded customers using an Internet investment pitch that played on fears of a worldwide financial breakdown due to the Y2K computer glitch [10].
- The FTC charged that National Payment Network, Inc. (NPN), headquartered in California, for allegedly violated the FTC Act by deceptively pitching to consumers an auto payment program, both online and through a network of authorized auto dealers, that it claimed would save consumers money. NPN failed to disclose that the significant fees it charged for the service often cancelled out any actual savings; fees averaged $775 on a standard five-year auto loan [11].
- The FTC found that nearly 11% of adults in the United States (an estimated 25.6 million people) paid for fraudulent products and services in 2011. Of the 15 specific scams the FTC asked about, the most-reported frauds involved weight-loss products, prize promotions, unauthorized billing for

buyer's clubs or internet services, and work-at-home programs. One-third of respondents first learned of the fraudulent pitch online [12].

■ The FTC sued 1-800-CONTACTS, the largest online retailer of contact lenses in the United States, alleging that it unlawfully orchestrated and maintained a web of anticompetitive agreements with rival online contact lens sellers that suppresses competition in online search advertising auctions and that restricts truthful and non-misleading internet advertising to consumers on the search results page generated by online search engines such as Google and Bing [13].

■ Lumosity paid $2 million to settle deceptive advertising charges for its "Brain Training" program, which the FTC charged deceived consumers with unfounded claims that Lumosity games can help users perform better at work and in school, and reduce or delay cognitive impairment associated with age and other serious health conditions [14].

■ LifeLock was to pay $100 million to consumers to settle FTC charges that it violated a 2010 order in an action brought by the FTC and 35 state attorneys general that required the company to secure consumers' personal information and prohibits the company from deceptive advertising [14].

In many cases, companies have been formed for the single purpose of defrauding consumers through the use of the Internet to reach a mass audience and without spending a lot of time or money. A website, online message, or spam e-mails can reach large numbers with minimum effort. It's easy for fraudsters to make their messages look real and credible, and it is sometimes hard for investors to tell the difference between fact and fiction [15]. These fraudsters have mastered the social media warfare tactics of deception and confusion, and they work to steal money from individuals as well as companies.

Social media has also opened more opportunities to embed advertising in other content. According to the FTC, a basic truth-in-advertising principle is that it's deceptive to mislead consumers about the commercial nature of content. Advertisements or promotional messages are deceptive if they convey to consumers, expressly or by implication, that they're independent, impartial, or from a source other than the sponsoring advertiser. The FTC requires that

■ Disclosures are clear and prominent on all devices and platforms that consumers may use to view native ads.

■ In assessing effectiveness, disclosures should be considered from the perspective of a reasonable consumer.

■ Disclosures are not effective unless consumers understand them to mean that native ads are commercial advertising.

■ Disclosures should be in plain language that is as straightforward as possible. An advertiser also should make disclosures in the same language as the predominant language in which the ad is presented [16].

4.6 Nullifying Corporate Opponents and Critics through Blended Social Media Warfare Tactics

Corporations increasingly face the need to deal with critics that use social media to attack a company or industry. Certainly, some companies have violated so many laws and ethics that it is almost inevitable that they will be attacked with offensive social media warfare tactics. Other companies might be victims of offensive social media warfare attacks by copy-cat competitors or disgruntled current or former employees. Regardless of the motivation behind an attack or the legitimacy of claims made by critics, corporations are developing strategies to deal with an onslaught of negative social media. Several social media warfare tactics are used to respond to attacks, they include

- Self-validation, influence, and reinforcement tactics are used by corporations after attacks on reputation or corporate actions. A salvo of social media items is released that target stock holders, customers, regulators, and lawmakers. The intent is to reinforce the good reputation of the company.
- Influencing, persuasion, trolling, and confusion tactics are used to cast doubts on the validity of criticisms and the legitimacy of those criticizing. Such social media content is often created by the company through proxies that come to the defense of a company or industry group.
- Divisiveness tactics are used to create distance and animosity between different critics that may be attacking a company for the same or similar reasons.
- Exposure tactics are used to reveal information about attackers that discredits them as individuals or organizations and creates doubt about the validity of their positions against the company. This can also be effectively done through proxies.
- Relationship building and recruitment and indoctrination tactics are used to develop positive relationships with existing friends or to gain new supporters for the company that is the target of criticisms and attacks.

4.7 Controlling How Employees Use Social Media

Although social media can be relatively easy to adopt, it brings with it long-term costs and an increased overhead. Companies need to control how social media tools are used and who gets to use the tools on behalf of a company. Corporate staff cannot just begin using a social media tool and then release content without monitoring what happens. Before using a specific tool, social media staff need to evaluate how much control built-in features provide and decide if that is sufficient to protect their company from the tool's misuse by both insiders and outsiders. Staff can evaluate social media tools by questioning what types of controls and security are available for the tool and what resources are required to securely use the tool. This can be accomplished by asking and answering a series of questions:

- Who in the company will be responsible for managing the use of the social media tool?
- Who in the company will establish policies and procedures necessary for governing the use of the social media tool?
- How secure can the tool be made from hacking and to prevent it being hijacked?
- How much control will management have over how the tool is used?
- How can control of the account be regained if it is misappropriated?
- How will staff be able to tell if something malicious has happened to the account?
- How will management know if the tool is being improperly used?
- Who will be able to post to the social media account and how can that be controlled?
- Who in the company will be responsible for the day-to-day monitoring of the account, including postings or comments?
- Who in the company will be responsible for training employees on the appropriate use of the social media tool?
- When should management evaluate the results gained from using the social media tool and how will that been accomplished?

As a logical first step, specific staff should be designated responsibility over the use and control of social media tools. But before staff goes too far into the realm of social media, management should develop policies regarding the use of social media tools that are officially used by and represent the company. In addition, before jumping in too far, management should establish some basic policies that are designed to protect the company from inappropriate use of the tools by corporate staff. Social media policies should address how and who uses social media and what constitutes appropriate use by determining

- The social media tools that are authorized for use in the company
- The types of content and examples of services to which the policies apply
- When and why it is appropriate to use social media tools
- When and why it is NOT appropriate to use social media tools
- What constitutes (acceptable/non-acceptable) non-official/personal use of social media and social networking by employees

It may be difficult to cover every potential use or abuse of social media by employees. This may be especially true when it comes to the non-official and personal use of social media by employees. Establishing guiding principles for

Table 4.3   Sample Guiding Principles for Social Media Use

The following principles should guide employee use of social media in a
non-official/personal capacity:

■ Be aware of revealing your company affiliation in online social networks.
  If you identify yourself as a company employee or have a public facing
  position for which your company association is known to the general
  public, ensure your profile and related content (even if it is of a personal
  and not an official nature) is consistent with how you wish to present
  yourself as a professional.
■ Employees should have no expectation of privacy when using social
  media tools.
■ When in doubt, stop. Don't post until you're free of doubt. Be certain that
  your post would be considered protected speech for First Amendment
  purposes. Also, add a disclaimer to your social networking profile, personal
  blog, or other online presences that clearly states that the opinions or views
  expressed are yours alone and do not represent the views of the company.
■ In a publicly accessible forum, do not discuss any company-related
  information that is not already considered public information. The discussion
  of sensitive, proprietary, or classified information is strictly prohibited. This
  rule applies even in circumstances where password or other privacy controls
  are implemented. Failure to comply may result in disciplinary action.

non-official and personal use of social media use can be helpful in covering unfore-
seen circumstances. A sample set of guiding principles [17] are listed in Table 4.3.

It is also advisable that employees know who in the corporation is designated to
manage and use social media on behalf of the company; and all employees should
be informed that they, unless specifically designated to do so, should not use social
media representing the company. In addition, the use of social media by executives
and managers should be controlled and monitored to assure that proprietary information is not being posted and that they properly identify themselves if speaking
for the company. Executives are some of the worse people a company needs to deal
with when it comes to using social media. In many past cases, the executives have
let their personal feelings influence what they post in social media and the company staff spends time and money cleaning up after the mishaps of the executives.

4.8 Citizens Speak Out on Social
Media about Corporations

As they do about governments, rather normal, everyday citizens from around the
world like to speak out about what is wrong or right with corporations and corporate behavior. They do so as prolifically as they do about governments. Some citizen
journalists have a considerable fan base with thousands of followers. An informal

survey of social media posts conducted on September 1, 2016, revealed what many people feel or think about corporations. Perspectives are varied with some being rather bitter and spiteful while others are rather thoughtful and insightful. This is the essence of some of the tags and subject lines found:

- Bad Corporation!: The many ways that corporations repeatedly screw people
- Bad Corporate Tweets: Work on your social media game
- Bad Corporate Hashtags: Mocks stupid corporate hashtags
- The wave of public anger over being screwed by corporations
- We Hate Wal-mart: It is accused of dishonorable and illegal acts
- We all hate Wal-Mart: Tells us our real-life stories!
- Cashier at Wal-Mart hates his job
- I am for Animal Rights, Hate MONSANTO
- Hate Monsanto with passion
- Corporate War Crimes: Legal issues on allegations of corporate violations of human rights
- Corporate Crime Wave: Stop poisoning us with GMO's
- Expose and prosecute corporate crimes and help victims
- End Child Labor: Millions of children engaged in child labor and do hazardous jobs
- GoodWeave: Working to stop child labor in the carpet industry
- Coalition to stop worst forms of child labor and child slavery
- Problems with palm oil production: Destroying rainforest, endangering wildlife, displacing indigenous people
- The Equal Pay Coalition: Fighting to close the gender pay gap
- Fans raising money to gain equal pay for female pro athletes

4.9 Conclusions

Companies are in constant conflict with a variety of potential adversaries. Competition is stiff between corporations and globalization has opened more avenues for competition and conflict. Social media warfare can be helpful for a company but it also can be equally problematic and something to be avoided. The following important conclusions that can be drawn from the material presented in this chapter:

- Corporations are under pressure to ensure that they respect human rights in everything they do and everywhere they do anything.
- Corporations are also under pressure to deal with the global movement toward improved environmental protection.
- Many citizen groups and special interest groups are working to make companies more socially responsible. The trend toward CSR has been steadily growing, though its extent varies among industries.

■ Corporations are especially vulnerable to damaging slander and harassment social media campaigns.
■ Corporations increasingly face the need to deal with critics that use social media to attack a company or industry.
■ Many companies or their owners and high-level executives have come under fire in social media conflicts over the last several years.
■ As social media conflicts intensify, more and more people join in quickly to share their experiences and help rally each other to keep up an attack on a company.
■ Companies need to control how social media tools are used and who gets to use the tools on behalf of a company.

4.10 Agenda for Action

Corporations are basically surrounded by people and organizations that want to influence what a company does or does not do. Thus, corporations are in a unique position to experience social media warfare as a defensive as well as an offensive activity. Action steps should include, but not be limited to, the following areas:

■ Through industry groups or consortiums, corporations should develop policies and procedures to deal with unprovoked social media warfare attacks.
■ Corporations should develop formal procedures to monitor social media content that is critical of the company, reveals proprietary information, or threatens company employees or facilities.
■ Corporations should continue to train staff and executives how to use social media applications in a manner that does not embarrass the company, regardless of whether they are using social media in a professional or a personal capacity.

4.11 Key Terms

Corporate social responsibility (CSR) is a perspective as well as a set of conditions that demonstrates to what extent corporations are being responsible for their actions, and what efforts they take to mitigate the negative consequences of those actions on the environment and the people that are impacted.

Native advertising is the use of formats that make advertising or promotional messages look like objective content.

Selective release of information is the deliberate release of information designed to create a positive image and the withholding of information that may tarnish the desired image a corporation is trying to build.

4.12 Seminar Discussion Topics

Discussion topics for graduate- or professional-level seminars:

- What experience have seminar participants had in situations where a company was being attacked using social media warfare strategies? How did the company react?
- What experience have seminar participants had in situations where they were being attacked using social media warfare strategies? How did they react?
- What experience have seminar participants had in companies that monitor social media content that is critical of the company, reveals proprietary information, or threatens company employees or facilities? How was monitoring managed?

4.13 Seminar Group Project

Divide participants into multiple groups with each group taking 10–15 minutes to develop a strategy to deal with unprovoked social media warfare attacks on a company. Meet as a class and discuss the various methods the groups developed to deal with unprovoked social media warfare attacks on a company.

References

1. U.S. Department of State. 2012. UN guiding principles on business and human rights. Accessed August 28, 2016. https://www.dhs.gov/critical-infrastructure-sectors.
2. U.S. Environmental Protection Agency. Learn about environmental management systems. Accessed August 28, 2016. https://www.epa.gov/ems/learn-about-environmental-management-systems#ISO-14001.
3. U.S. National Archives and Records Administration. *Federal Register.* Accessed August 28, 2016. https://www.federalregister.gov/agencies.
4. U.S. Library of Congress. Corporate social responsibility. Accessed August 28, 2016. https://www.loc.gov/rr/business/green/corporate.html.
5. U.S. Department of State. 2013. Corporate social responsibility and the U.S. Department of State. Accessed August 28, 2016. http://iipdigital.usembassy.gov/st/english/pamphlet/2013/07/20130711278465.html#axzz4IkWRLvG2.
6. Rich, Jessica. 2015. FTC year in review: Advertising and privacy in the age of influencers, smartcars, and Fitbits. Accessed August 29, 2016. https://www.ftc.gov/public-statements/2016/06/ftc-year-review-advertising-privacy-age-influencers-smartcars-fitbits.
7. U.S. Federal Trade Commission. 2016. FTC approves final order prohibiting Machinima, Inc. from misrepresenting that paid endorsers in influencer campaigns are independent reviewers. Press Release. Accessed August 30, 2016. https://www.ftc.gov/news-events/press-releases/ 2016/03/ftc-approves-final-order-prohibiting-machinima-inc.

8. U.S. Federal Trade Commission. 2016. Warner Bros. settles FTC charges it failed to adequately disclose it paid online influencers to post gameplay videos. Press Release. Accessed August 30, 2016, from https://www.ftc.gov/news-events/press-releases/2016/07/warner-bros-settles-ftc-charges-it-failed-adequately-disclose-it.

9. U.S. Federal Trade Commission. 2016. Lord & Taylor settles FTC charges it deceived consumers through paid article in an online fashion magazine and paid Instagram posts by 50 'fashion influencers.' Press Release. Accessed August 30, 2016, from https://www.ftc.gov/news-events/press-releases/2016/03/lord-taylor-settles-ftc-charges-it-deceived-consumers-through.

10. U.S. Federal Trade Commission. 1999. California mining company settles FTC charges that it defrauded investors through Internet pitch. Press Release. Accessed August 30, 2016. https://www.ftc.gov/news-events/press-releases/1999/11/california-mining-company-settles-ftc-charges-it-defrauded.

11. U.S. Federal Trade Commission. 2016. FTC, multiple law enforcement partners announce crackdown on deception, fraud in auto sales, financing and leasing. Press Release. Accessed August 30, 2016. https://www.ftc.gov/news-events/press-releases/2003/05/ftc-and-states-unite-fight-fundraising-fraud.

12. Small, Bridget. 2013. Fraud harms 25.6 million people: Anyone you know? *Business* (blog). Accessed August 30, 2016. https://www.ftc.gov/news-events/blogs/business-blog/2013/04/fraud-harms-256-million-people-anyone-you-know.

13. U.S. Federal Trade Commission. 2016. FTC charges that 1-800-CONTACTS harms competition in online search advertising auctions and restricts truthful advertising to consumers. *FTC International Monthly*. Accessed 30, 2016. https://www.ftc.gov/policy/international/ftc-international-monthly/august-2016.

14. U.S. Federal Trade Commission. 2016. FTC International Monthly. Accessed August 30, 2016. https://www.ftc.gov/policy/international/ftc-international-monthly/january-2016.

15. U.S. Securities and Exchange Commission. Investor publications Internet: Fraud. Accessed August 30, 2016. http://www.sec.gov/investor/pubs/cyberfraud.htm.

16. U.S. Federal Trade Commission. Native advertising: A guide for businesses. Accessed August 30, 2016. https://www.ftc.gov/tips-advice/business-center/guidance/native-advertising-guide-businesses.

17. U.S. Department of the Interior. 2015. Social media policy. Accessed September 1, 2016. https://www.doi.gov/notices/Social-Media-Policy.

Chapter 5

Special Interest Groups' Use of Social Media as a Weapon

There are hundreds of special interest groups that are involved in a wide variety of interests, ranging from commerce and health, to art, community development, and religion. There are also groups that are involved in political and social causes. This chapter examines well-established special interest groups with a specific area of interest. Other groups that emerge and form during times of social upheaval and engage in time-specific activities are discussed in Chapter 7: "Social Media Warfare for Support of Social Causes." Special interest groups that are involved in politics and the electoral process are discussed in Chapter 6: "Social Media Warfare in the Political Electoral Process."

5.1 Types of Special Interest Groups

There are two major types of special interest groups. First, is the stand-alone group formed to pursue a specific interest or to work in a defined realm for social action, social change, or influence of the public and government and private sector decision makers. Second, are special interest groups that are a part of an industry sector or part of a larger organization; these subgroups have a more narrow field of endeavor but are still related to the overall goals of the larger organization. This chapter focuses primarily on stand-alone special interest groups that are part of

Table 5.1 Different Focuses of Special Interest Groups

Abortion	Healthcare
Affirmative action	Human rights
Animal rights	Immigration
Campaign finance reform	Industry specific groups
Drug addiction and treatment	Labor—Workers rights
Education	Military veterans
Environment	Religious organizations
Fraternal organizations	Taxes taxation
Gun control—Gun rights	Voter rights
Hate groups	Women's' issues
LGBT rights	World trade

an industry sector or have a specific interest; it does not focus on the subgroups of larger organizations. Special interest groups have many areas of focus. Table 5.1 provides popular examples of special interest group activity.

These very powerful groups are actively involved in social media warfare and expend considerable energy on self-validation, recruitment and indoctrination, influence, and relationship building. These groups generally have large budgets and professional staff that work in lobbying, education programs, fund-raising, and communications. Some of the most powerful special interest groups in the United States are listed in Table 5.2.

There are hundreds of smaller and less powerful special interest groups and charities that are involved in numerous issues. Smaller organizations do not have as large a staff or the budget to support one. Volunteers are essential for the smaller special interest group and supply much of the labor needed to keep organizations afloat. Social media warfare tactics help the small groups self-validate, recruit, and

Table 5.2 Powerful Special Interest Groups in the United States

American Association of Retired Persons
American Israel Public Affairs Committee
American Medical Association
Americans for Prosperity
National Abortion and Reproductive Rights Action League
National Association for the Advancement of Colored People
National Rifle Association
U.S. Chamber of Commerce

indoctrinate; but these groups have few resources to do much more. Several special interest groups have very little in the way of a formal organization structure, but they do have considerable grassroots support behind the social cause promoted by a few small organizations.

What drives attacks against or by special interest groups is the perspective they have on issues that they support or oppose. The offline profile of radical special interest groups drives their online actions and approach to social media warfare. The largest, as well as many smaller, organizations focus efforts on inducing members or supporters to lobbying and pressure elected officials. The smaller groups often motivate a grassroots constituency to take physical action along with social media warfare tactics. This results in a rather unique approach for each of the different groups. There are several social media warfare tactics that are frequently used by special interest groups and those that oppose the groups:

- Self-validation supports the validity and legitimacy of an organization and the subject of special interest.
- Influencing aligned entities aims to have them adopt the same position and use the same or similar rhetoric and justifications for the position or issue supported by a large organization or by a few smaller organizations with a grassroots following.
- Reinforcing alliance partners shows support for an ally's position on an issue.
- Persuasion of non-aligned entities is working to convince non-allies of the validity and legitimacy of a position on an issue.
- Recruitment and indoctrination is the process of aligning new entities or individuals to a position on an issue, and getting them to adopt the same rhetoric on the topic. Relationship building is the process of establishing and nurturing cooperative efforts with like-minded people or organizations.
- Nullifying opponents is the process of discrediting an opponent's position on an issue.
- Deception is the process of using invalid or false information or pretense to counter an opponent's position on an issue.
- Confusion is designed to disorient and deceive opponents or neutral parties about the facts or perspectives on an issue.
- Divisiveness involves instigating hatred and suspicion among opponents regarding an issue.
- Exposure involves the release of information that can embarrass or otherwise jeopardize the legitimacy of an opponent's position on an issue.
- Trolling is leaving posts online in opposition to existing posts, made by individuals or in the name of an organization or a position on an issue.
- Blended threats are combined activities that are designed to counter an opponent's position on an issue or legitimize a supporter's position; they involve multiple social media tools.

5.2 Healthcare Special Interest Groups and Social Media Warfare

Healthcare is an industry sector comprised of several specialized component organizations that contribute to the overall functioning of the sector. The component organizations each have a different role in healthcare goods and services. Care givers, doctors, clinics, and hospitals are the focal point of activity, supported by suppliers and service organizations, many of which are funded through health insurance programs or charitable contributions. Each of these sector sub-components might comprise a special interest.

Adjunct to the care givers are the research organizations that develop methods of treatment and provide education and training in specific fields, such as cancer and arthritis or other specific diseases. These organizations in turn, are supported through donations from specialized charities, foundations, or government agencies, each of which can be narrowly focused enough to be considered a special interest.

Healthcare has been a focus of many special interest groups in the United States and around the world since the end of World War II. As important as healthcare is to modern societies, it is an issue that is laden with conflict given interface with religion and conservative values vis-à-vis contraception, abortion, and prevention of sexually transmitted disease. There are, however, several healthcare special interest groups that manage to stay above the fray and avoid conflict in their pursuit of improved health and disease eradication.

There are many organizations that use social media warfare strategies in a constructive manner in pursuit of their goals. Examples of these organizations are listed in Table 5.3.

Table 5.3 Large Healthcare Organizations in the United States

American Cancer Society
American Diabetes Association
American Heart Association
American Lung Association
Cleveland Clinic Foundation
Cystic Fibrosis Foundation
Doctors without Borders
Leukemia and Lymphoma Society
March of Dimes Birth Defects Foundation
Mayo Foundation
Muscular Dystrophy Association
Patient Access Network Foundation
Project Hope
Shriner's Hospitals for Children
St. Jude Children's Research Hospital
United Way

These organizations serving special health interests use social media warfare tactics but do not get involved in skirmishes regarding their position or their work. They certainly pursue self-validation, influence, recruitment and indoctrination, and relationship building tactics. There are also several U.S. federal government agencies that support healthcare research and education. Government healthcare organizations use similar social media warfare tactics as other government agencies. These are some of the government agencies and special interest organizations that support the healthcare sector:

- Agency for Healthcare Research and Quality (AHRQ)
- Agency for Toxic Substances and Disease Registry
- Arthritis and Musculoskeletal Interagency Coordinating Committee
- Centers for Disease Control and Prevention (CDC)
- Centers for Medicare and Medicaid Services (CMS)
- Department of Health and Human Services (HHS)
- Department of Veterans Affairs (VA)
- Health Resources and Services Administration
- National Cancer Institute (NCI)
- National Health Information Center (NHIC)
- National Institute of Mental Health (NIMH)
- National Institutes of Health (NIH)
- Substance Abuse and Mental Health Services Administration (SAMHSA)
- The Office of Disease Prevention and Health Promotion

5.3 Hate and Social Media Warfare

The healthcare sector is comprised of several well-organized special interest groups. There are several special interests that do not have such a high level of organization but rely heavily on grassroots support to promote their perspective toward a special interest. Hate as a special interest is one such example. Certainly, there are well-organized hate groups, but there is no central organization that directs hate activity. Unfortunately, hate is something that self-perpetuates without the need for a central command.

The United States, like all countries, faces a myriad of social problems and challenges. Unfortunately, hate is one of the biggest problems that has plagued the United States for the last century. The U.S. Federal Bureau of Investigation (FBI) Uniform Crime Reporting Program collects data about single-bias and multiple-bias hate crimes. A single-bias incident is defined as an incident in which one or more offense types are motivated by the same bias. As of 2013, a multiple-bias incident has been defined as an incident in which one or more offense types are motivated by two or more biases. Highlights of the 2014 hate crime statistics include

- In 2014, there were 5462 single-bias incidents that involved 6385 offenses, 6681 victims, and 5176 known offenders. The 17 multiple-bias incidents reported in 2014 involved 33 offenses, 46 victims, and 16 offenders.
- Analysis of the 5462 single-bias incidents reported in 2014 revealed that 47.0% were racially motivated; 18.6% resulted from sexual orientation bias; 18.6% were motivated by religious bias; 11.9% stemmed from ethnicity bias; 1.8% were motivated by gender-identity bias; 1.5% were prompted by disability bias; and 0.6% (33 incidents) resulted from gender bias.
- In 2014, law enforcement agencies reported that 3081 single-bias hate crime offenses were racially motivated. Of these offenses, 63.5% were motivated by anti-black or African American bias; 22.8% stemmed from anti-white bias; 5.5% resulted from anti-Asian bias; 4.6% were motivated by anti-American Indian or Alaska Native bias; 3.6% were a result of bias against groups of individuals consisting of more than one race (anti-multiple races, group); and 0.1% (4 offenses) were motivated by anti-Native Hawaiian or other Pacific Islander bias.
- In 2014, law enforcement agencies reported 1178 hate crime offenses based on sexual orientation bias. Of these offenses 58.0% were classified as anti-gay (male) bias; 23.6% were prompted by an anti-lesbian, gay, bisexual, or transgender (mixed group) bias; 14.3% were classified as anti-lesbian bias; 2.6% were classified as anti-bisexual bias; and 1.5% were the result of an anti-heterosexual bias.
- In 2014, hate crimes motivated by religious bias accounted for 1092 offenses reported by law enforcement. A breakdown of the bias motivation of religious-biased offenses showed that 58.2% were anti-Jewish; 16.3% were anti-Islamic (Muslim); 6.1% were anti-Catholic; 4.7% were anti-multiple religions, group; 2.6% were anti-Protestant; 1.2% were anti-Atheism/Agnosticism; and 11.0% were anti-other (unspecified) religion.
- Of the single-bias incidents in 2014, 790 offenses were committed based on the offenders' biases toward the perceived ethnicity of the victims. Of these offenses, 52.4% were anti-not Hispanic or Latino bias; and 47.6% were anti-Hispanic.
- Of the 6418 reported hate crime offenses in 2014, 27.2% were intimidation; 26.4% were destruction/damage/vandalism; 23.6% were simple assault; 12.0% were aggravated assault; and the remaining offenses included additional crimes against persons and property.

Hate continued to thrive in the United States and in June 2015, a self-declared white supremacist named Dylann Roof, shot and killed nine churchgoers, all African American, at their Charleston, South Carolina, church. The Emanuel African Methodist Episcopal Church is the oldest black church in the Southern United States. In June 2016, Omar Mateen, an American-born man who had allegedly pledged allegiance to the Islamic State of Iraq and Syria (ISIS), gunned down 49 people at a gay nightclub in Orlando, Florida. These offenders had no relationship with each other except that they chose to act upon their hatred.

The South Carolina incident prompted new calls to remove the Confederate flag from public buildings in the United States. Many people see the Confederate flag as a symbol of hate and a reminder of the period in which the United States supported slavery. The subsequent removal of the flag from several locations was cheered by those citizens who want to move past hatred and to a more equitable society. On the other hand, there are many people that do not want to move forward and organized, through social media warfare tactics, to protest and resist the removal of their sacred hate symbol. Confederate flag sales boomed on many websites, while other ecommerce websites had enough respect to remove and ban the sale of Confederate flags and other Confederate items.

People that commit hate crimes seem to like to talk about the crimes or their motivations. Many have had social media pages and have left a wide variety of social media posts. Upon apprehension of hate crime perpetrators, law enforcement agencies routinely look at their social media pages and posts. Often, what is found is disgusting.

Some hate crime perpetrators work alone because they are so socially maladjusted that they do not have many friends. However, many haters like to be members of groups. The Southern Poverty Law Center tracked over 800 hate groups operating in the United States in 2016. The Center provides a map of where these hate groups operate so that citizens can see how many hate groups exist in their area [2].

In addition to the Southern Poverty Law Center, many other groups use social media warfare tactics to fight hate crimes. These groups use social media warfare tactics to recruit and indoctrinate citizens in an anti-hate agenda and to build relationships between organizations, communities, and individuals to combat hate. Organizations fighting hate include the following:

- American-Arab Anti-Discrimination Committee
- American Association of University Women
- Anti-Defamation League
- Asian American Justice Center
- Hindu American Foundation
- Human Rights Campaign
- The Leadership Conference on Civil and Human Rights
- National Association for the Advancement of Colored People
- National Center for Transgender Equality
- National Council of Jewish Women
- National Disability Rights Network
- National Gay and Lesbian Task Force
- National Organization for Women
- Sikh American Legal Defense and Education Fund
- The Sikh Coalition [3]

Mainstream social media application providers and website managers work with law enforcement to fight against hate, and they have policies that generally disallow hate speech, threats, and dangerous material from being posted. Pages and posts that support terrorist activities or organized crime are deleted and accounts are suspended. Any content posted that encourages crimes against people or property are often removed. Hate speech is deleted from many websites and social media streams that include content directly attacking people based on race, ethnicity, religion, sexual orientation, and so on. Social media providers largely rely on reports from social media users to identify organizations and people dedicated to promoting hate on websites or in social media. They also employ a variety of social media monitoring tools to identify and eliminate hate content.

However, mainstream social media is not the only communications tool available on the Internet. The alternative right (Alt-Right) has its own web space. Its websites may come and go quickly, but the Internet and social media applications are used by the alternative right to spread far-right ideologies, form groups, and support communication between individuals whose primary perspective is one of white supremacy. They also believe in racial purity and that their white privilege conflicts with modern social conditions and perspectives, such as political correctness and human rights for all people. In the United States, the alternative right and many radical right-wing groups feel that immigration and racial equality is a threat to white power and the dominance in society that they would like to maintain. Many of them feel that God is on their side and use that to promote their perspective. Social media warfare tactics used by hate groups include the following:

- Self-validation to support the validity and legitimacy of a hate group's position
- Influencing like-minded hate groups to adopt a position and use the same or similar rhetoric and justifications for an issue
- Reinforcing hate group partners' position on an issue
- Recruiting and indoctrinating new members to a hate group
- Relationship building with other hate groups
- Deception regarding a hate group's target or targets
- Divisiveness to instigate hatred toward a target group
- Trolling social media posts and debating the viewpoint of a poster

Hate groups still manage to get plenty of posts and pages on mainstream social media sites. Like many social media writers, the haters are rather prolific. Some of these hater journalists have a considerable fan base and many followers. Their perspectives vary, some are bitter and spiteful, others are advocate anti-social behavior. An informal survey of hate related social media posts conducted in early September 2016 found numerous hate posts on popular mainstream social media sites. The "n-word" has been removed from posts listed in this book, but this is the essence of some of the tags and subject lines found on social media sites:

- Ultra Right! Radicalized National Socialist! Anti-Multiculturalism! White Power!
- White Pride! White Lives! Have a white history month. Uppity Negroes STFU/Damn Porch Monkeys
- White Power: save white people from being a dying breed. Fuck n-word and Indians! And everyone who is not white
- For The White Race! The White Race Only! Fuck n-word And Fuck Kikes!

The same informal survey showed that it is easy to find anti-Muslim posts just about anywhere on the Internet, and they can be as nasty as those listed earlier. The essence of these tags and subject lines is presented here (misspellings have been corrected, specifically, Muslum was changed to Muslim).

- No Anti American Muslim Animals in Our Country. No Political Correct Crap!
- The Muslim-In-Chief keeps ISIS going. They know Obama is Anti-American
- Scary military veterans post pro-Trump anti-immigrant, anti-Muslim, pro-guns and white nationalist tweets
- Anti-America Muslim Activity Should Be Stopped By Force!
- No more foreigners. No more Muslims
- I'M ANTI MUSLIM…..I'M ANTI OBAMA
- Wipe That Muslim Smile Off your Face, Satan!

5.4 Guns, Hate, and Social Media Warfare

There are several other special interests that do not have a high level of organization but rely heavily on grassroots support to perpetuate a perspective on an issue. Guns are an example of such a special interest. There are certainly well-organized gun advocacy groups, but there is no central organization that directs all activity. Unfortunately, the love of guns is another example of something that self-perpetuates without the need for a central command.

There are an estimated 300 million guns in the United States and almost one in three Americans own at least one gun. The owners of these weapons are most likely white, married men aged 55 and older. Gun ownership in America is considered normal by many people; others view gun ownership, especially of automatic weapons, as a social problem that leads to violence and crime. People in the United States frequently use guns to harm each other; in 2013, gun violence killed 33,636 people and injured 84,258 others in the United States [4]. Gun ownership is increasing in the United States with robust gun sales year after year.

The primary mission of the National Rifle Association (NRA) is to protect the right to own guns in the United States, and it does a very good job of this. The NRA actively lobbies the U.S. Congress and contributes considerable sums of money to the reelection campaigns of congressional members who vote the way the NRA wants them to vote. The NRA is also active in state-level politics and exerts considerable influence in most states.

When gun ownership issues arise in websites, blogs, or social media pages, there is often a flurry of activity. This happens frequently after a mass shooting in the United States. Mass shootings are happening in the United States at an alarming and increasing frequency. Social media warfare tactics are used by both gun ownership advocates and by advocates for greater control of guns, especially automatic weapons. Both sides use self-validation tactics and a variety of approaches to influence opinions and actions and to recruit and indoctrinate people. Both sides also troll opposing social media posts and post adversarial comments in return.

There is a strong relationship between hate and gun ownership in the United States. This relationship is manifested in acts of violence by domestic terrorists. Domestic terrorism cases often involve firearms, arson, or explosives; crimes of fraud; and threats and hoaxes. Domestic terrorism includes acts within the territorial United States that are dangerous to human life, violate federal or state criminal laws, have no actual connection to international terrorists, and appear to be intended to intimidate or coerce a civilian population, influence domestic government policy through intimidation or coercion, or affect the conduct of the government by mass destruction, assassination or kidnapping. Current domestic terrorism threats include animal rights extremists, eco-terrorists, anarchists, anti-government extremists such as sovereign citizens and unauthorized militias, black separatists, white supremacists, anti-abortion extremists, and other unaffiliated disaffected Americans, including lone wolfs [5].

Special interest terrorism differs from traditional right-wing and left-wing terrorism in that extremist special interest groups seek to resolve specific issues, rather than effect widespread political change. Special interest extremists continue to conduct acts of politically motivated violence to force segments of society, including the public, to change attitudes toward issues considered important to their causes. These groups are at the extreme fringe of animal rights, pro-life, environmental, anti-nuclear, and other movements.

Some special interest extremists, most notably within the animal rights and environmental movements, increasingly have turned to vandalism and terrorist activity in attempts to further their causes [6]. These groups use social media warfare tactics to recruit and indoctrinate people and when possible use social media to expose the undesirable activities of their targets. Social media warfare tactics used by supporters of gun rights include

- Self-validation to support the validity and legitimacy of a gun rights supporters' position.
- Influencing like-minded gun rights groups to adopt a position. use the same or similar rhetoric and justifications on an issue. and rally around the Second Amendment to the U.S. Constitution.

- Reinforcing gun rights group partners' position on an issue.
- Recruitment and indoctrination of new members to a gun rights group.
- Deception of the facts about guns and gun rights.
- Trolling social media posts and debating the anti-gun viewpoint of the poster.

An informal survey of social media posts on gun rights conducted on September 2, 2016 revealed that it is easy to find pro-gun posts just about anywhere on the Internet and that they can be scary, and very often lack any sensible thought. The following list shows the essence of these posts:

- Leftists have no limit to how far they will go to take our guns
- Ban radical Islamists! Not our guns
- Guns don't kill people but Islamic terrorists do
- Radical Democrat Party trying to strip citizens of their natural rights of gun ownership
- If a radical Muslim kills people why blames guns?
- Donate to the NRA and support a radical right-wing fear-mongering organization
- Democrats push talk of radical gun control while Americans stockpile for civil war

5.5 Abortion Debates and Violent Acts of Extremists

Abortion rights are the subject of debate in many countries around the world and religion is often at the center of the debate on a women's right to an abortion. Abortion has been legal in the United States since the 1973 Supreme Court ruling on *Roe v Wade*. This ruling opened the door to safe abortions in the United States. However, debate on abortion continued and it eventually deteriorated into violent acts by extremists against abortion providers and those seeking an abortion. The rise of the political right in state legislatures across the country turned the debate on abortion into years of manipulative and obstructionist legislation passed by conservative white male legislators who believe they know what is best for women. Another argument is that white male-dominated legislatures prefer to deliberately thwart the economic and political independence of women as much as they possibly can and under any circumstance.

Some anti-abortion extremists believe that violence and bloodshed are justified in support of their views on abortion. These violent extremists have turned to murder, bombings, assault, vandalism, kidnapping, and arson. They have also made death threats, and sent hate mail and suspicious packages. Violent anti-abortion extremists have targeted women's reproductive clinics and the healthcare professionals and staff who work in these facilities, including doctors, nurses, receptionists, and even security guards. In a 2009 case, for example, a Kansas doctor who performed abortion services was shot and killed in his local church by an anti-abortion extremist. Those who use violence to defend abortion rights have murdered, threatened, and attacked those who oppose abortion [7].

From 2014 to 2015 the debate on abortion intensified as anti-abortionists released some extremely edited videos that they claimed proved Planned Parenthood was selling aborted baby parts. That sparked congressional hearings as well as state-level investigations by a variety of agencies into the practices of Planned Parenthood clinics. Although no credible evidence was found of any wrongdoing by Planned Parenthood, conservative white male-dominated state legislatures passed a plethora of bills to block Planned Parenthood from receiving public funding for abortion.

Conservatives used a variety of social media warfare tactics ranging from self-validation and relationship building to fostering confusion by releasing unsubstantiated assertions and conclusions about abortion. In this battle, liberal or abortion rights advocates outgunned the conservatives in social media many times over. In fact, a ground swell of support arose for Planned Parenthood and women started opening up about their experiences with abortion and sharing stories about those experiences on social media. Tens of thousands of social media posts were made in support of Planned Parenthood and in support of abortion rights. Conservatives tried to troll the posts but were greatly outnumbered and often chased out of chats and post threads. Anti-abortion groups used several of the following social media warfare tactics:

- Self-validation to support the validity and legitimacy of the anti-abortion group's position.
- Influencing like-minded anti-abortion groups to adopt a position and use the same or similar rhetoric and justifications to oppose abortion rights.
- Reinforcing anti-abortion group partners' position on the issues.
- Recruitment and indoctrination of new members to an anti-abortion mentality or group.
- Relationship building with other anti-abortion groups.
- Deception of the facts about abortion or why the group opposes abortion rights.
- Divisiveness to instigate hatred toward abortion rights advocates.
- Trolling social media posts and debating the viewpoint of the poster.

The abortion debate is alive and well in social media posts. Sometimes nonsensical, sometimes inciting violence, these types of posts can be found in many places on the Internet. The following represents the essence of social media posts found in an informal survey conducted on September 2, 2016:

- 20% of women's health clinics in the United States have experienced severe anti-abortion violence.
- Anti-abortion and anti-PP, and cutting domestic violence funding?

- Anti-abortion and homophobic violence often justified by Christian beliefs.
- Anti-abortion groups have become cults!
- Anti-abortion people at school trying to teach people, please make them leave.
- Anti-abortion terrorists have a violent ideology, not a mental illness.
- Anti-abortion violence in this country adds up to 11 murders and 26 attempted murders.
- Inflammatory anti-abortion speech goes hand-in-hand with clinic violence.
- Republicans seek plan to fight Zika and push their anti-abortion agenda at the same time.
- Repubs put anti abortion and confederate flag bullshit in Zika bill.

5.6 Environmentalists and Eco-Terrorists

Back in the 1960s, a new environmental protection movement emerged voicing concerns about industrial pollution, endangered species, clean water, and clean air. Much of what the United States now has in place regarding environmental protection was highly influenced by that movement. This includes environmental protection curriculums in schools, the emergence of a very large recycling industry, and federal, state, and local laws on handling waste material and obsolete technology. The Internet and social media became tools for environmentalist to self-validate, recruit and indoctrinate, and influence the public and decision makers.

Not surprisingly, business and industry have strongly resisted improved or stronger environmental protection measures, and the U.S. Environmental Protection Agency has been labeled as an enemy of business. This enemy status has been constantly reinforced by business and industry through their lobbying efforts in the U.S. Congress as well as state legislatures across the country. Business and industry contribute heavily to election campaigns at the national and state levels and have essentially purchased the votes and support of elected representatives of the people. Business and industry have also been to federal courts to oppose regulations to protect the environment. The private sector is clearly more concerned about profits than maintaining a sustainable environment.

As in the case of many special interests and social causes that emerged out of the 1960s, not all environmental protection and other advocacy has been pursued peacefully. Animal rights and environmental extremists, operating under the umbrella of the Animal Liberation Front (ALF) and Earth Liberation Front (ELF) used a variety of tactics against their targets, including arson, sabotage, vandalism, theft of research animals, and the occasional use of explosive devices.

Serious incidents of animal rights/eco-terrorism decreased in 2004, a fact that can be attributed to a series of law enforcement successes that likely deterred large-scale arsons and property destruction. Following a rash of serious animal rights/eco-terrorism incidents, including $50 million worth of arson damage in San Diego and two bombing incidents in the San Francisco area, law enforcement made progress in their battle against eco-terrorist activity. Nevertheless, the FBI expects that animal rights extremism and eco-terrorism will continue to threaten certain segments of government and private industry, specifically in the areas of animal research and residential/commercial development [8].

Social media warfare tactics are used by all sides of the environmental protection debate. Business and industry self-validate and work to influence policy makers while building relationships to oppose regulation. Pro-environment forces work to recruit and indoctrinate citizens into the cause and have ridiculed elected officials and exposed the nasty habits of business and industry. Eco-terrorists and those who advocate violence to protect the environment focus on a small selection of social media warfare tactics:

- Self-validation or supporting the validity and legitimacy of an eco-terrorist group's position
- Reinforcing eco-terrorists' partners' position on issues
- Recruiting and indoctrinating new members
- Deception of the facts about an eco-terrorist group's target or targets

The environmental debate and responses to eco-terrorist activity is alive and well in social media posts. An informal survey of the Internet, conducted on September 2, 2016, revealed that these types of posts are found in many places on the Internet. The following represents. the essence of these posts:

- Eco-terrorists love dirt and snow more than they love people
- Eco-terrorists spike logs to hurt lumber mills
- Evil rich corporations are the real Eco-terrorists destroying habitat!
- Greens are mostly benign, but some are real eco-terrorists
- The FBI investigates eco-terrorists because they do harm, unlike oil companies!
- The real eco-terrorists are the climate change deniers!
- Violent eco-terrorists should be sent to jail
- Why try to appease ignorant, un-educated eco-terrorists?

5.7 Lesbian, Gay, Bisexual, and Transsexual Rights and Social Media Warfare

Lesbian, gay, bisexual, and transsexual (LGBT) rights represent another special interest that does not have one central leading organization but rather several national-level organizations and state and local level counterparts. Social media warfare has played a major role in overcoming the social customs that for so long supported the oppression of LGBT citizens in the United States and many other countries in the world. The struggle is not over as there are still many countries that oppress LGBT citizens.

The pathway to equal LGBT rights in the United States and most countries in the world has been long and laden with violence against LGBT people as well as institutionalized discrimination and oppression of LGBT citizens. The Supreme Court of the United States made major decisions in 2013 that furthered equality for lesbian, gay, bisexual, and transgender (LGBT) Americans. In one case, the Supreme Court overturned the Defense of Marriage Act (DOMA), a law passed by the U.S. Congress in 1996. At that time, some states recognized same-sex marriage, but others did not. Under DOMA, even if a same-sex couple was married in a state that allowed such unions, the couple could not receive federal marriage benefits, including tax benefits, or be recognized as married by the U.S. federal government. In 2013, the Supreme Court ruled that DOMA violated the Constitution because it denied equal protection under the law to same-sex couples. Since that landmark ruling, U.S. federal courts have overturned the remaining state laws prohibited same-sex marriage.

Accepting attitudes toward homosexuality and gender expression have grown slowly over decades. The police raid of the Stonewall Inn, in New York City in June of 1969 and the riots that followed were a turning point in the drive for LGBT rights. Hundreds of protesters rose up, inspiring activist groups to form. The Stonewall riots are commemorated with gay pride parades in many cities around the world in June of each year. Much has happened during the last decade to improve LGBT rights:

- Ending the "don't ask don't tell" policy toward LGBT members of the armed forces of the United States
- Improved hate crime prosecution and protection for all citizens in the United States
- Expanded healthcare access for LGBT citizens
- Ensuring equality for LGBT U.S. federal government employees and those who are employed by government contractors
- Efforts to prevent bullying of LGBT students
- Efforts to end workplace discrimination

However, getting this far in improving the legal rights and legal protections of LGBT citizens was not easy, and it is not yet over. Resistance to the expansion of LGBT rights came from two major sources. First, were the religious organizations; second were the plain, old, homophobic, fascist conservatives. Religious objections were based on an interpretation of the Christian Bible or similar doctrine of other religions. Religious objectors have stated that homosexuality is against their god, and they continue to condemn LGBT citizens. Religious objectors and homophobes have perpetuated many false stereotypes and lies about LGBT people.

Conservative politicians still promise their supporters that they will work to end equal marriage rights and other rights that the LGBT community has worked so hard to gain. Religious leaders have also not given up, and the still preach discrimination against and exclusion of LGBT citizens. Corporations on the other hand, are ready to leave this debate behind and move into the future because so many of their employees and customers are LGBT.

Churches, religious leaders, conservative politicians, homophobic people, and anti-human rights organizations have worked in concert for decades to battle expanded LGBT rights. Although they currently make less noise, they are fully prepared to resume the fight. Anti-LGBT forces and their ground troops have worked in unison, with a consistent message and consistent animosity toward LGBT people. Even though the Catholic Church was found to have numerous pedophiles in its ranks, much of the organization still denies LGBT rights and continues to discriminate. Anti-LGBT activists have used about every social media tactic they could muster to stop the advancement of LGBT rights:

- Self-validation, influencing aligned entities, and reinforcing alliance partners is the mainstay of conservative anti-LGBT special interest groups' social media warfare tactics; they constantly reiterate their doctrine of homosexuality being against god.
- Recruitment and indoctrination are also tools used by the conservative, anti-LGBT special interest groups; they help to bring in people who are uncertain about what to believe about homosexuality.
- Persuasion and relationship building tactics have also aided conservative, anti-LGBT special interest groups, as they worked to get anti-LGBT legislation passed in Congress and at the state level. Much of the discriminatory legislation has been overturned.
- Deception, divisiveness, and confusion are favorite social media warfare tactics of conservative, anti-LGBT special interest groups; they have spread volumes of false and misleading information about LGBT people, which helped to create panic and confusion among the populace.

Pro-LGBT rhetoric can be found in many social media posts. These types of posts can be found in many places on the Internet. An informal survey of social media posts conducted on September 2, 2016, clearly shows that some attitudes have changed while others remain steadfastly the same. The essence of these social media posts is revealed in the following:

- Anti-LGBT pastor charged with child molestation, go figure!
- Don't forget the U.S. has a presidential candidate running on an anti-LGBT platform

- Double murder is likely anti-LGBT hate crime in Missouri
- Let's close anti-LGBT hate churches
- No points for those celebrating the civil rights movement while pushing anti-LGBT
- Time to stop legalizing Anti-LGBT discrimination

5.8 Religious Bias and Discrimination and Social Media Warfare

Beyond the efforts of the conservative right to deny LGBT citizens equal rights, there are several ongoing conflicts in the religious arena that involve social media warfare tactics. The United States and many other countries have a long history of religious discrimination and, in some cases, segregation. There is a long history of religious discrimination around the world, which country is under study determines which religion was discriminated against: in one place or another a religion has been the target of discrimination. Muslims, Mormons, and Jewish people have experienced considerable discrimination in the United States. Many have also experienced religious bias–based violence as well as institutionalized barriers to full participation in a society.

In the twenty-first century, religious bias and discrimination has once again risen on a wave of fascism that is gripping countries in Europe as well as the United States. Many observers have commented that the trend toward fascism and religious discrimination is reminiscent of the rise of Nazi fascism prior to World War II. The rhetoric is similar and the attitudes of many citizens toward Muslims and Jewish people are, unfortunately, crystallizing into hatred.

Politicians in the 2016 elections in the United States played on this hatred and paranoia and have irresponsibly fueled the fires of religious bias and hatred. The political rhetoric reinforces the attitudes and actions of hate groups, and it helps their members validate their perspectives and their hate. Hate rhetoric can also inspire hate-based crimes as discussed in Section 5.3.

Religious bias almost always leads to efforts to scapegoat religious minorities and blame them for the social problems or economic conditions that a nation faces. The blame game becomes contagious and is fueled by the rhetoric of politicians and hate-group leaders who use social media warfare tactics to spread confusion designed to disorient and deceive people about religious bias and divisiveness, which instigates even more hatred and suspicion among the populace.

Although there are special interest leaders that feel that they will benefit from the social unrest, which is based on religious bias, the populace only partially unites behind them. Leaders, however, can continue to influence individuals and groups to induce them to adopt the same position and use the same or similar rhetoric and justifications for religious bias. Efforts are made to recruit and indoctrinate to persuade individuals to formally join the ranks of those who fuel religious bias, especially those with political ambitions.

This is where religious bias begins to look like anti-LGBT attitudes and behavior. Even though individual people may not belong to a formal hate group or other special interest that has religious biases, they start to widely adopt hate rhetoric and attitudes. Meanwhile, followers continue to be deceived by the rhetoric in and propensity for social media that consistently carries the message.

Religious bias is so rooted in irrational thought and concepts that it is difficult for those fighting against religious bias to nullify it regardless of how much social media with positive messages they generate. Thus, the stage is set for the rise of fascists to power based on their promises to cleanse society of the people who the populace now blames for all their problems. Such biases spill over into many realms of society, as they have in recent years into immigration issues.

Religious bigots use social media warfare as much as possible, and they go well beyond self-validation and influencing to deception, confusion, and trolling. Religious bigotry rhetoric as well as efforts to expose and counter such rhetoric can be found in many social media posts. An informal survey of social media posts conducted on September 2, 2016, shows that these types of posts can be found in many places on the Internet. According to some sources, there was an increase in anti-Muslim posts in 2016. The following provides the essence of several posts:

- Anti-Muslim interest strike back at proposals for U.S. mosques.
- Cardinal Burke, anti-Muslim crusader?
- Islamic terrorism not just a statement of identity it is about MOTIVATION.
- Mom got intense in her anti Muslim reaction when she saw someone in a Hijab.
- Stop anti-Muslim fanatics from showing violence on social media!
- Who said tackling anti-Muslim hate was easy.
- You say you will keep America safe but your anti-Muslim rhetoric indicates otherwise.

5.9 Measuring the Social Media Presence of Special Interest Topics

Social media monitoring is a process by which analysts can determine how popular a topic is on social media sites or websites. A BackTweets search, indicating how many tweets related to a search term are archived on Twitter (backtweets.com), was conducted on October 13, 2016 along with a Yahoo search on the terms used to describe special interests in this chapter.

The term racism had the highest number of achieved tweets at 7,470,000; religious bias had the fewest archived tweets at 14,200. Environmental protection had

Table 5.4   Frequency of Term Usage for Special Interest/Groups

Topical Area	BackTweets Results: Archived Tweets	Yahoo Search Results (million)
Abortion	1,590,000	14.8
Environmental protection	76,800	52.8
Gay rights	3,740,000	14.4
Gun rights	3,360,000	15.2
Hate crime	763,000	13.3
Healthcare	1,850,000	23.4
LGBT rights	326,000	14.6
Racism	7,470,000	13.6
Religious bias	14,200	4.4

the highest number of Yahoo search results at 52.8 million, and religious bias had the fewest at 4.4 million search results. Full results of the searchers are shown in Table 5.4.

5.10 Conclusions

Many special interest groups use social media responsibly and constructively. On the other hand, there are special interest groups that flock to social media warfare to self-validate and to criticize anyone who disagrees with them. The following important conclusions can be drawn from the material presented in this chapter:

■ There are many very large and powerful groups actively involved in social media warfare; they expend considerable effort on self-validation, recruitment and indoctrination, influence, and relationship building.
■ Many smaller organizations rely on volunteers for the labor needed to keep them afloat; although social media warfare tactics help the small groups self-validate and recruit and indoctrinate, they have few resources to do much more.
■ Many organizations serving special health interests use social media warfare tactics, but they do not get involved in prolonged skirmishes regarding their position or their work.
■ People that commit hate crimes like to talk about the crimes on their social media accounts; and upon apprehension of hate crime perpetrators, law enforcement agencies routinely look at their social media pages and posts.

- Mainstream social media application providers work with law enforcement to fight hate and have policies that generally disallow hate speech.
- There is a strong relationship between hate and gun ownership in the United States, which manifests itself in acts of violence by domestic terrorists.
- Some anti-abortion extremists believe that violence and bloodshed are justified to support their different beliefs on abortion and have turned to murder, bombings, assault, vandalism, kidnapping, and arson.
- Social media warfare tactics are used by all sides of the environmental protection debate. Business and industry self-validate and work to influence policy makers; pro-environment forces work to recruit and indoctrinate citizens into the cause; eco-terrorists use reinforcement, recruitment, indoctrination, and deception tactics.
- Churches, religious leaders, conservative politicians, homophobic people, and anti-human rights organizations worked for decades in concert to battle expanded LGBT rights; and in social media posts, all their ground troops have done so in unison, with a consistent message and consistent animosity toward LGBT citizens.

5.11 Agenda for Action

Special interest groups vary in nature from hate groups to healthcare research, from religious organizations to shared-interest communities. Any type of special interest group can benefit from some social media warfare tactics and become a victim of tactics being used against it. Action steps for special interest groups should include, but not be limited to, the following areas:

- Each type of special interest group should observe and analyze which social media warfare tactics will work best for them and which tactics can do them the most harm.
- Human rights special interest groups should continue to monitor and catalog social media posts that promote discrimination, bigotry, and hate against the constituency that they serve.
- Each type of special interest organization should develop guidelines for their staff, volunteers, and supporters to follow when making social media posts and responding to other social media posts.
- Staff, volunteers, and supporters of special interest organizations should actively report social media post violations and hateful rhetoric or threats to the social media application provider.
- Law enforcement agencies should continue to monitor the social media warfare activities of hate groups and those groups that promote bigotry or violence.

5.12 Key Terms

Eco-terrorists are individuals or groups who oppose environmental policies or actions of governments and private companies, and who use a variety of methods to hinder or halt projects or operations.

Sovereign citizens are anti-government extremists who believe that even though they physically reside in this country, they are separate or "sovereign" from the United States. Thus, they believe that they don't have to answer to any government authority, including the courts, taxing entities, motor vehicle departments, or law enforcement.

Special interest terrorism is an act of violence or destruction by extremist special interest groups seeking to address specific issues and to influence segments of society, including the general public, to change attitudes about issues considered important to their causes.

5.13 Seminar Discussion Topics

Discussion topics for graduate- or professional-level seminars

■ What experience have seminar participants had in situations where social media warfare tactics were used to spread hate or threaten people? How were those incidents handled?

■ What experience have seminar participants had with special interest organizations that used social media warfare tactics of any type and for any reason?

■ How would seminar participants deal with hate group postings under different circumstances? Professional? Personal? Family?

5.14 Seminar Group Project

Divide participants into multiple groups with each group taking 10–15 minutes to develop a list of social media warfare tactics to counter hate rhetoric or racially, religious, or gender preference bias in social media posts. Upon completion, have groups exchange their lists of tactics, with groups taking 10–15 minutes to develop a short list of guiding principles for special interest group staff, volunteers, or supporters to deal with hate rhetoric or racially, religious, or gender preference bias in social media posts. Meet as a group and discuss the guiding principles selected by the groups to counter hate rhetoric or racially, religious, or gender preference bias in social media posts.

References

1. Federal Bureau of Investigation. 2014. Hate crime statistics. Accessed September 3, 2016. https://ucr.fbi.gov/about-us/cjis/ucr/hate-crime/2014/topic-pages/incidentsandoffenses_final.
2. Southern Poverty Law Center. Hate groups. Accessed September 3, 2016. https://www.splcenter.org/hate-map.
3. Federal Bureau of Investigation. What we investigate. Accessed September 3, 2016. https://www.fbi.gov/investigate/civil-rights/hate-crimes.
4. Mekouar, Dora. 2015. This is who America's gun owners are. *Voice of America* (blog). Accessed September 3, 2016. http://blogs.voanews.com/all-about-america/2015/07/01/this-is-who-americas-gun-owners-are/.
5. U.S. Department of Justice, Offices of the U.S. Attorneys. 2014. Domestic terrorism. Accessed September 4, 2016. https://www.justice.gov/usao/priority-areas/national-security/domestic-terrorism.
6. Jarboe, James F. 2002. Testimony before the House Resources Committee, Subcommittee on Forests and Forest Health. Accessed September 4, 2016. https://archives.fbi.gov/archives/news/testimony/the-threat-of-eco-terrorism.
7. Federal Bureau of Investigation. What are known violent extremist groups? Accessed September 4, 2016. https://cve.fbi.gov/whatare/?state=domestic.
8. Mueller, Robert S., III. 2005. Testimony before the Senate Committee on Intelligence of the U.S. Senate. Accessed September 4, 2016. https://archives.fbi.gov/archives/news/testimony/global-threats-to-the-u.s.-and-the-fbis-response-1.

Chapter 6

Social Media Warfare in the Political Electoral Process

The political electoral process is tumultuous in many countries around the world; it is sometimes characterized by violence and is most often laden with *ideological conflict* and divisiveness. The 2016 presidential election in the United States along with congressional, senatorial, and state-level races were no except to this long pattern of ideological conflict and divisiveness. Although social media warfare tactics have played a part in previous elections, especially during the Barack Obama campaigns of 2008 and 2012, social media warfare tactics took the main stage during the 2016 campaigns and elections. In will take several election cycles before it can be determined if social media helps or hurts candidates for public office. This chapter examines the role of social media warfare tactics and their use in the political electoral process in 2016 in the United States.

6.1 Media Convergence Comes of Age

Media convergence, or the melding of different media types into a multi-faceted stream of information and entertainment, has been a trend for over two decades. Video, text, photos, sound, and graphics were at one time all delivered from separate platforms and applications. Social media applications have led the way in enabling users to blend all these media types into a customizable stream that blends desirable media elements into a personalized content stream.

As events in the 2016 election progressed, so did the blending of media types. A post on a social media site could include news from broadcast television, print media, and graphic images from multiple sources. Users could post and share content from other media sources. Digital news applications could also blend such content as well as social media posts. News articles hosted on digital platforms began using social media posts as content, just as social media posts were blending in content from other media sources.

Sometimes, social media posts were about news or content from other sources. News sources started including social media posts as part of their stories and would often include several posts from different users as part of the news content. Old media relations formulas for dealing with print media or broadcast media are becoming obsolete. Media relations professionals are confronted with new ways to control media content and a more complex set of relationships to achieve media coverage for their clients. It has certainly made things more interesting and, after the elections of 2016 in the United States, the use of media platforms and how to penetrate news content with a desired perspective is forever changed.

It sounds simple, but all media and all news coverage seekers now face having to understand multiple channels into public exposure. This trend will also impact how social media warfare strategies will be deployed in the future as well as the success of any and all media campaigns.

6.2 Social Media Warfare Tactics of Candidates for Elected Office

Candidates for elected office used the entire range of social media warfare tactics discussed in previous chapters. However, the electoral process has its own set of unique targets and candidates often used social media warfare tactics carelessly and without thought. Candidates were not all equal in their ability to use social media warfare tactics and many committed gaffes; and when they didn't, their campaign staff often blundered for them.

The recklessness and lack of savvy on the part of candidates resulted in the use of social media warfare tactics as a mixed-up mess rather than in a clearly thought-out manner, and candidates often used defensive tactics to try to mount an offense and vice versa. Clearly, many of the candidates were downright amateurish in their use of social media. For the purpose of analyzing social media warfare tactics used in the 2016 campaigns, a separation of defensive and offensive tactics is unnecessary because although the candidates used various tactics, most of the time they just did not know what they were doing. Basically, political candidates themselves are horrible communicators, while some just did stupid things others were crass and crude. For some reason, a good portion of the population of the United States find the crass and crude appealing. A tailored list of

Table 6.1   Social Media Warfare Tactics in Political Campaigns

Blended threats: Combined activities to accomplish offensive or defensive objectives.
Confusion: Creating and perpetuating uncertainty among voters and contributors.
Deception: Making promises that will not or cannot be kept and the use of invalid or incorrect information.
Divisiveness: Instigating hatred and suspicion among categories of voters.
Exposure: Release of damaging information about opponents.
Influence: Convincing contributors, supporters, and voters on the validity and legitimacy of a position or action of a candidate.
Nullify opponents: Efforts to discredit opponents.
Persuasion of non-aligned entities: Trying to convince undecided contributors and voters of the validity and legitimacy of a position or action of a candidate.
Recruitment and indoctrination: Drawing people into supporting a candidate and teaching related doctrine rhetoric.
Reinforcing alliance partners: Showing support to organizations that endorse a candidate.
Relationship building: Establishing cooperative efforts with like-minded organizations, contributors, and voters.
Trolling: Posting opposing or critical messages to existing social media posts.

social media warfare tactics of the 2016 political electoral process is presented in Table 6.1.

One of the challenges in analyzing social media warfare posts by candidates during the 2016 election is determining what some of the candidates were really doing when they used social media. Fact checkers found a vast number of factual errors made by candidates when speaking or using social media during campaigns. Given the large number of factual errors, it is somewhat difficult to determine if the candidates were just ignorant about what they were saying, or they were deliberately trying to cause confusion by creating and perpetuating uncertainty among voters and contributors, or they were willing to say and do anything to deceive or cause divisiveness. The tactic of divisiveness is a natural part of election campaigns that helps to create groups of voters dedicated to one candidate or the other. This will require considerably more detailed research and analysis than allowed here.

6.3 Blunders in Social Media Warfare

There are three major types of blunders that fire up the social media world. Factual errors made by candidates, poor behavior on the part of a candidate including making racist or fascist statements, and the amateurish use of social media by a candidate.

Before social media was so popular and widely available, the factual errors that candidates made when speaking could take days or even weeks to come back to them, and in some cases they never came back to them in any form. Now, factual errors made anywhere by a candidate, in speech, print, or broadcast media, quickly come back to bite them. When candidates attempt to impress their constituency by espousing a particular position based on supposed factual information and that information is refuted by multiple sources, the social media world is set aflame, automatically. Opponents and the news media take joy in exposing errors made by candidates. It helps to discredit the candidate among undecided voters even if it does not penetrate the minds of a candidate's devoted supporters.

Poor behavior on the part of a candidate, including making racists, fascist, or sexist statements, will send shock waves through social media. Many candidates in 2016 rejected politically correct or well-mannered speech because their constituency supposedly had grown tired of having to be nice to people and wanted to reject modern liberal values. In 2016, candidates often abandoned correctness and fired off ridiculously anti-social statements during interviews, speeches, or in their social media posts. In some cases, it was the next day and in other cases the next hour that the social media world started commenting on the stupidity of a candidate or at least their crudeness and lack of sensitivity to the diverse population of the United States.

During the last several years, as more and more people started using social media, it became obvious that many users are not very conscious of how social media works. There were at least two major blunders made on social media in 2016. A few stories were floating around about an ISIS fighter who posted a selfie to his social media account. The selfie was taken in front of a building used by ISIS as some type of headquarters. The story had a short life, but supposedly, the building that the dumbest terrorist in the world took his selfie in front of was bombed within 24 hours. So much for the social media prowess of the modern terrorist.

Tied for blunder of the year with the terrorist selfie, was a selfie posted by Speaker of the House Paul Ryan with his large group of interns gathered on the steps of the U.S. Capitol building. Ryan stood tall and smiled for the camera to which he was showing off his interns, his more than predominately white interns. Perhaps Ryan did not read the latest projections from the U.S. Census Bureau about race and ethnicity in the United States. Or perhaps he just does not care about race and ethnicity in the United States. For the record, the U.S. Census Bureau projects that

- The non-Hispanic white population in the United States will peak in 2024 at 199.6 million, up from 197.8 million in 2012. Unlike other races or ethnic groups, however, the non-Hispanic white population is projected to slowly decrease, falling by nearly 20.6 million from 2024 to 2060.
- Meanwhile, the Hispanic population will more than double, from 53.3 million in 2012 to 128.8 million in 2060. Consequently, by the end of this period, nearly one in three U.S. residents will be Hispanic, up from about one in six.
- The black population is expected to increase from 41.2 million to 61.8 million over the same period. Its share of the total population will rise slightly, from 13.1% in 2012 to 14.7% in 2060.
- The Asian population is projected to more than double, from 15.9 million in 2012 to 34.4 million in 2060, with its share of the nation's total population climbing from 5.1% to 8.2 % in the same period [1].

The message in these projections for the white conservative Christian who would like to keep the nation racially pure, is that it is all over and they will not be a majority much longer. The message in these projections for political candidates is that they will not be able to keep their head in the sand about diversity in the country, at least not for very long.

Meanwhile, social media experienced a mild tsunami over Ryan's white interns post. The media in general was not particularly kind to Ryan, with the major news outlet stories frequently shared on social media. The wording that prompted such sharing included phrases such as "A crate of Wonder Bread isn't as white as that Republican intern selfie Paul Ryan took" [2]. Many Democrats responded by posting photos of their diverse intern groups.

6.4 Most 2016 Presidential Candidates Not Effective in the Use of Social Media Warfare

Candidates in the presidential primaries and the subsequent campaign for president of the United States were extensively followed in social media. Candidates also used social media warfare tactics in a variety of uncoordinated and random ways. Candidate messages on social media were as disjointed as the messages they relayed in debates and interviews. Most candidates could not hold together a prolonged discussion on how their positions compared with those of other candidates, instead they spent time bashing each other and bashing each other's political parties. This practice ended up being far less than productive for most of the candidates. It was all more reminiscent of a barroom brawl or a playground melee than it was a run for the presidency.

Donald Trump was the clear leader in the volume of social media posts and in the number of Twitter followers. To illustrate the disparity between Trump and the many other candidates, a count of followers and tweets was taken over Labor Day weekend 2016 (the first weekend in September). Trump had 11.4 million followers and had posted approximately 33,000 tweets. This put Trump ahead of all other candidates, and he was given a score of 100 for the number of followers and number of tweets, as can be seen in Table 6.2.

The rest of the candidates with active accounts on Labor Day weekend were then ranked in terms of the percentage of followers and percentage of tweets compared to Trump. For example, Hillary Clinton had 76.23% of the followers that Trump had and she had made only 24.24% of the number of tweets that came from Trump's account. On the other end of the continuum, Chris Christie had only 1.27% of the followers that Trump had and Christie had made only 9.09% of the number of tweets that came from Trump's account.

On Facebook, Clinton had 5.8 million Likes on her official page and Trump had 10.6 million Likes for his official Facebook page over the Labor Day weekend. Trump had a button that said "SHOP NOW" on his Facebook page, which linked to the website address https://shop.donaldjtrump.com/ and invited people

Table 6.2 Candidate Comparative Ranking on Twitter, Labor Day Weekend 2016

Candidate	Followers	Tweets
Trump	100	100
Clinton	76.32%	24.24%
Sanders	21.93%	45.45%
Carson	17.54%	9.09%
Rubio	14.04%	18.18%
Cruz	13.16%	51.52%
Paul	7.89%	30.30%
Bush	6.36%	12.12%
Fiorina	6.14%	12.12%
Huckabee	4.39%	18.18%
Kasich	3.77%	27.27%
Santorum	2.37%	18.18%
Christie	1.27%	9.09%

to "CHECK OUT THE NEW GEAR" and purchase a variety of political paraphernalia. Clinton had a button that said "Sign Up" that allowed visitors to enter their e-mail address and zip code and then provided an opportunity to make a financial contribution.

On Instagram, Clinton had 2 million followers and Trump had 2.4 million followers during the same time frame. A Yahoo search showed that Clinton had 13 million search results and Trump had 13.9 million search results. These comparisons are shown in Table 6.3.

There was only a moderate change in followers and Likes for the two presidential candidates after early September. Facebook Likes for Trump increased by 400,000, for Mrs. Clinton they increased about 800,000. These are certainly significant counts, but although for Trump that was less than a 4% increase and for Clinton it was a 14% increase, Clinton had about 60% of the Facebook Likes that Trump had achieved. Increases in other counts were similarly modest. More details on the changes in social media statistics are shown in Table 6.4.

The social media presence of both Trump and Clinton continued to grow in late October 2016, just before the election and at just about equal rates. One observer commented that the number of Facebook pages with each of the candidate's name in the title was increasing. This may have caused some confusion for fans as they were looking to Like the page of their favorite candidate (Table 6.5).

Table 6.3   Candidate Comparative Facebook Likes, Instagram Followers, and Yahoo Search Results, Labor Day Weekend 2016

Media	Trump	Clinton
Facebook Likes	10.6 million	5.8 million
Instagram Followers	2 million	2.4 million
Yahoo Search Results	13 million	13.9 million

Table 6.4   Candidate Social Media Status Update October 1, 2016

Media	Trump	Clinton
Facebook Likes	11 million	6.6 million
Instagram Followers	2.5 million	2.3 million
Yahoo Search Results	14.3 million	13.6 million
Twitter Followers	12 million	9.3 million
Tweets	33.4 thousand	8.6 thousand

Table 6.5 Candidate Social Media Status Update Late October 2016

Media	Trump	Clinton
Facebook Likes	11.5 million	7.2 million
Instagram Followers	2.7 million	2.5 million
Yahoo Search Results	16.2 million	15.3 million
Twitter Followers	12.6 million	9.8 million
Tweets	33.6 thousand	9.1 thousand

6.5 Campaign Staff Can Be a Liability in Social Media Warfare

Although social media can be relatively easy to become involved in, it brings with it long-term overhead costs for a campaign and one of the costs is associated with keeping control over social media usage. The 2016 campaign clearly showed that not all staff should be allowed to use social media tools without controlling how the tools are used and who gets to use the tools on behalf of an organization. Social media can help campaigns achieve numerous goals:

- Disseminate information about the candidate and campaign in a timely fashion
- Increase the impact of important messages to supporters, contributors, and voters
- Leverage networks of people to spread the message of the candidate and the campaign
- Tailor different messages to communicate with diverse audiences
- Personalize messages from candidates for particular audiences
- Keep the public engaged with the candidate and the campaign

Many campaign staff members, when paid, are hired on short notice and many others are volunteers. A limited number of campaign staff should be charged with managing social media for the campaign, and those who are selected to work on social media should be trained in ethics, protocols, and standards. It is clear that just because you take campaign staff out of their cultural environment does not mean you have taken their cultural environment out of them. In addition, campaign staff and volunteers that are not charged with social media responsibilities should be queried about their personal social media use to determine if they are or were involved in activities that may eventually be an embarrassment to the candidate or the campaign (e.g., if they have posted *hate messages*).

The 2016 campaigns and elections provide many lessons for future candidates and campaigns. One of those lessons is the necessity of properly managing social media usage to ensure that how social media warfare tactics are used is of actual benefit to the campaign and does not cause more harm than benefit. This can be accomplished by establishing *social media policies* to cover the content, subject matter, and tone that everyone in the campaign must adhere to including, and especially, the candidate.

Campaigns can hire social media consultants when resources are available. If there is a shortage of financial resources, campaign staff can still find guidance from several sources. The U.S. military services serve as an example of how to manage social media use and set polices for its use in a campaign. The service branches put a great deal of effort into social media and have a strong *social media presence*. *The United States Army Social Media Handbook* provides considerable guidance to all levels of the Army on how to best use social media to meet desired validation, relationship building, and communication to all the Army's constituents.

Campaign managers can prepare to use social media tools by addressing what types of controls need to be in place to properly manage social media use:

- Designating who in the campaign organization will establish policies and procedures necessary for governing the use of the social media tools
- Designating who in the campaign organization will be responsible for managing the use of the social media tools
- Designating who in the campaign organization will be able to post to social media accounts and how that can be controlled
- Designating who in the campaign organization will be responsible for the day-to-day monitoring of accounts including postings or comments
- Designating who in the campaign organization will be responsible for training employees on the appropriate use of the social media tools
- Determining how campaign managers should evaluate the results gained from using a social media application and how that will be accomplished

As a logical first step, a person or persons in the campaign organization should be designated responsibility over the use and control of the use of social media. But before campaign staff members get too far into the realm of social media, campaign managers should develop policies regarding the use of social media applications that are officially used by and represent the campaign. Social media staff and content producers need to understand the audience they are trying to reach, apply communication literacy skills, and follow *plain language* practices in written communications.

Because of the virtual unlimited exposure that the Internet provides, it is also reasonable to be concerned about how campaign staff, paid or volunteer, use social media or any Internet website, functionality, or social application. In addition, we have come to realize that people tend to do really stupid things on the Internet.

in many instances, using the Internet seems to make people very careless. People often start out using the Internet with the best of intentions, not knowing or thinking about potential negative consequences. Setting guidelines for personal social media use for campaign staff, is a good first step in addressing the issues. However, it should also be recognized that the candidate should demonstrate, through their own use of social media, including content and tone, how they expect campaign staff to manage their personal use of social media.

There are a few proprietary websites that provide helpful information. One very popular website is Netiquette (www.networketiquette.com), which provides the rules of good behavior online. Another helpful website is Education World (www.educationworld.com), which provides the ten commandments of computer ethics. Both may be helpful in providing ideas for training materials. Both sites are protected by copyright and permission is needed for reuse of material in most circumstances.

A campaign's social media policy should apply to a broad range of social media applications including, but not limited to

- Media sharing such as YouTube, Flickr, iTunes
- Blogging/microblogging such as WordPress, Blogger, Twitter
- Social networking applications such as Facebook, MySpace, LinkedIn, Ning
- Document sharing repositories such as Scribd, SlideShare, Socrata
- Social bookmarking sites such as Delicious, Digg, Reddit

Composing social media content takes skill and experience that not all campaign staff have at high enough levels to be effective. A review of social media content clearly shows that political campaigns have yet to master content creation. Some of the worst social media writers are the candidates themselves. A campaign relies on several delivery mechanisms to communicate, including social media applications that provide short bursts of information as well as websites that provide more in-depth material.

One of the most important writing practices is the use of plain language, and that can be more of a challenge than it seems. There is a plain language movement powered by groups of writers that provides guidance on plain language composition. The website is www.plainlanguage.gov.

Campaign writers should recognize that web content is not clear unless supporters and voters can find what they need, understand what they find, and use what they find to meet their needs. Plain language writers recommend that web content is composed in an inverted pyramid style, beginning with the shortest and clearest statement you can make about your topic, and putting the most important information at the top and the background information at the bottom. Topics should be split up into logical sections separated by informative headings and unnecessary information should be omitted [3].

6.6 Candidate Supporters Use of Social Media

Gaining supporters and voters is the goal of any electoral campaign. Supporters can use social media warfare tactics to help grow supporter bases by recruiting and indoctrinating friends, relatives, coworkers, or neighbors into supporting a candidate.

Most supporters use Facebook, and all campaigns are compelled to have some sort of Facebook presence. Facebook, as are other social media tools, is intended to be part of a larger integrated campaign communications strategy. Careful consideration should always be given to the nature of Facebook posts and activities. Posts that are likely to draw widespread or media attention or address a controversial topic should be cleared through media control processes of campaign management. Campaign social media warfare managers should establish best practices for using the Facebook page, among them

- Keeping content short and simple with posts of 250 characters or less to allow the post to be viewed in its entirety in a news feed and include a link to the campaign website
- Keeping length of comments 1000 characters or less
- Setting a schedule and determining frequency of posts
- Cross-promoting the Facebook page on other campaign social media channels and vice versa
- Posting links to the Facebook page on the campaign website
- Facebook can be used to engage supporters in two-way interaction and communication but that process must be managed and staffed
- Asking supporters to do something within a post or content such as Share, Like, or Comment [4]

Evaluation is an integral component managing all social media activities, and social media warfare staff should review Facebook Insights for page-specific metrics. Staff should also monitor increases in traffic to the campaign website, as well as mentions outside of Facebook, on blogs, websites, or articles.

Supporters should have as much guidance in their use of social media warfare tactics as possible. There should be a stated social media philosophy published by the campaign and posted on the campaign's website and social media pages. At a minimum, guidance should state that the campaign does not discriminate against any views, but does monitor social media content on all official social media sites and reserves the right to remove, without warning, any comments that contain abusive, vulgar, offensive, threatening, or harassing language, personal attacks of any kind, unsupported accusations, defamatory language, or offensive terms that target specific individuals or groups. In addition, a declaration should be made that campaign staff will remove spam and comments that are clearly off topic or contain gratuitous links to websites that are not relevant to discussions; and that campaign staff will ban from campaign social media platforms, users who repeatedly violate the comment or posting policies.

Supporters should be encouraged to use social media warfare tactics to aid the campaign but guidance will help to keep supporters focused and prevent any serious blunders in posting. One of the proprietary websites listed earlier provides very helpful information that can be used to guide supporters' use of social media. Netiquette is a very popular website that provides the rules of good behavior online.

Supporters should be discouraged from posting personal attacks against individuals and abusive, profane, or vulgar language, including offensive language targeting specific ethnic or racial groups. In addition, supporters should also be encouraged to avoid sexual content, overly graphic, disturbing, obscene, or offensive material in their supporting posts.

Supporters should also be repeatedly cautioned about posting *personally identifiable information* (PII), which is information that can be used to distinguish or trace an individual's identity, either alone or when combined with other personal or identifying information that is linked or linkable to a specific individual. PII may include, but is not limited to, an individual's name, social security number, physical address, e-mail address, Internet protocol (IP) address, phone number, or birth date [5]. Supporters should also be warned that non-PII can become PII whenever additional information is made publicly available or when combined with other available information. This could be used to identify an individual and determine their location. This information potentially poses a security threat to the supporter posting the information as well as a threat to the reputation of the campaign.

6.7 Monitoring Social Media Activity and Effectiveness

A monitoring and measurement process can help campaigns track the results of social media warfare efforts. There are two major categories of measurement: hard and soft data. By using these two types of measurements, campaign managers will see what is or is not working within the campaign social media strategy. The data can also help to reveal trends, new influencers in a campaign community, and different online channels and places to connect with supporters. These are some examples of hard and soft data:

- Hard data: Number of newsletter subscribers; number of followers on Twitter or fans on Facebook; staff time saved by using social media; cost savings from using social media; donations; increased rank in Google and Yahoo! search engine results; increased coverage in newspapers, TV news, and online
- Soft data: Engagement and interaction with supporters; reputation; loyalty; satisfaction; sentiment either positive or negative; feedback from supporters

There are several free online tools that can help campaign staff identify data quickly and easily. Examples include Facebook Insights, YouTube Insight, Insights dashboard, Klout, and Social Mention. Tools will continue to evolve, so campaigns staff should evaluate which social media applications the campaign will use and review the tools that can be used to measure activity. Once that is done, an evaluation process can be initiated and data can be generated at a reasonable frequency or after special events [6].

Campaign staff, volunteers, and supporters can also be mobilized to discover and report mentions of the campaign or candidate in social media posts made by other campaigns or the public. A reporting system can be established that allows monitors to send links to posts or a specific account to which the post can be shared. This provides campaign staff with insights into what people are posting about the campaign and reveals sources of false or misleading information.

6.8 Citizen Sources of Information

Voting rights in the United States have represented an ongoing battle since the founding of the country and, in some states, they are still hotly contested as conservatives attempt to stymie the voting rights of minorities and the poor in order to reduce the votes that liberal candidates get in elections. Originally, under the U.S. Constitution, only white male citizens over the age of 21 were eligible to vote. This racist and sexist injustice was fought against by voting rights advocates, and voting rights have been extended several times over the course of the country's history. Currently, any citizen over the age of 18 cannot be denied the right to vote, regardless of race, religion, sex, disability, or sexual orientation. In every state except North Dakota, citizens must register to vote, and laws regarding the registration process vary by state as do the obstacles to citizens actually casting a vote. Under the Fourteenth and Fifteenth Amendments to the U.S. Constitution, passed during the Reconstruction period after the Civil War, all male citizens, regardless of their race, received equal treatment under the law. This also meant that they could not be deprived of their voting rights without due process. The Fifteenth Amendment is specifically dedicated to protecting the right of all citizens to vote, regardless of their race. However, this was not the end of the voting rights struggle for African Americans because of widespread discrimination in some states, which resorted to the use of poll taxes, grandfather clauses, and literacy tests to discriminate. African Americans were not assured full voting rights until President Lyndon B. Johnson signed the Voting Rights Act in 1965. Women were denied the right to vote until 1920, when the Nineteenth Amendment was passed. Prior to that, women were only able to vote in select states [7].

Private citizens and campaign staff can find a great deal of information about politicians, elections, lobbying, and contributions at the Center for Responsive Politics, which is a research organization that tracks money in U.S. politics and its effect on elections and public policy (www.opensecrets.org). The mission of the organization is "to produce and disseminate peerless data and analysis on money in politics to inform and engage Americans, champion transparency, and expose disproportionate or undue influence on public policy" [8].

The U.S. Federal Election Commission (FEC) was created in 1975 to administer and enforce the Federal Election Campaign Act (FECA), which is the statute that governs the financing of federal elections (www.fec.gov). The duties of the FEC, which is an independent regulatory agency, are to disclose campaign finance information, to enforce the provisions of the law such as the limits and prohibitions on contributions, and to oversee the public funding of presidential elections.

The FEC is made up of six members, who are appointed by the president and confirmed by the Senate. Each member serves a 6-year term, and two seats are subject to appointment every 2 years. By law, no more than three commissioners can be members of the same political party, and at least four votes are required for any official commission action. This structure was created to encourage nonpartisan decisions. The chairmanship of the FEC rotates among the members each year, with no member serving as chairman more than once during his or her term [9].

Data available from the FEC include data tables for congressional candidate committees, national party committees, political action committees, independent expenditures, and electioneering communications are available for each semi-annual period in non-election years and available quarterly in election years. Presidential data tables are available semi-annually beginning in the year preceding presidential elections and quarterly in presidential election years.

The U.S. Election Assistance Commission (EAC) (www.eac.gov) was established by the Help America Vote Act of 2002 (HAVA). The EAC is an independent, bipartisan commission charged with developing guidance to meet HAVA requirements, adopting voluntary voting system guidelines, and serving as a national clearinghouse of information on election administration. EAC also accredits testing laboratories and certifies voting systems, and audits the use of HAVA funds. Other responsibilities include maintaining the national mail voter registration form developed in accordance with the National Voter Registration Act of 1993.

HAVA established the Standards Board and the Board of Advisors to advise EAC. The law also established the Technical Guidelines Development Committee to assist EAC in the development of voluntary voting system guidelines. The four EAC commissioners are appointed by the U.S. president and confirmed by the Senate. The EAC is required to submit an annual report to Congress as well as testify periodically about HAVA progress and related issues. The commission also holds public meetings and hearings to inform the public about its progress and activities. The EAC also provides frequently asked questions (FAQs) for voters (in seven languages) with information on registering to vote through casting a ballot on Election Day. The FAQs answer 14 common questions from citizens about voting in federal elections [10].

6.9 Conclusions

The 2016 presidential elections in the United States along with the congressional, senatorial, and state-level races were no exception to the long pattern of ideological conflict and divisiveness. Although social media warfare tactics have played a part in previous elections, and especially during the Barack Obama campaigns of 2008 and 2012, social media warfare tactics took the main stage during the 2016 campaigns and elections. The following are important conclusions drawn from the material presented in this chapter:

- Social media applications have enabled users to blend multiple media types into a customizable stream, which combines their desired media elements into a personalized content stream.
- Social media posts are often about news or content from other sources. Then, news sources started including social media posts as a part of news stories, often including several posts from different users as part of the news content.
- The entire range of social media warfare tactics discussed in previous chapters were deployed in an electoral process that has its own set of unique targets. Candidates many times used social media warfare tactics carelessly and without thought.
- There are three major types of blunders that fire up the social media world. Factual errors made by candidates; poor behavior on the part of a candidates, including making racist or fascist statements; and the amateurish use of social media by a candidate.
- Campaign staff cannot be allowed to use social media tools without controlling how the tools are used and who gets to use the tools on behalf of an organization.
- Composing social media content takes skill and experience and not all campaign staff have high enough skill levels to be effective writers.
- Supporters should be cautioned about posting personally identifiable information (PII), which is information that can be used to distinguish or trace an individual's identity, either alone or when combined with other personal or identifying information that is linked or linkable to a specific individual.
- A monitoring and measurement process can help campaigns track the results of social media warfare efforts.
- Voting rights in the United States have represented an ongoing battle since the founding of the country and, in some states, they are still hotly contested as conservatives attempt to stymie the voting rights of minorities and the poor in order to reduce the votes that liberal candidates get in elections.

6.10 Agenda for Action

Although social media warfare tactics have played a part in previous elections, and especially during the Barack Obama campaigns of 2008 and 2012, social media warfare tactics took the main stage during the 2016 campaigns and elections. Still, many candidates have been less than stellar when it comes to using social media warfare tactics. Action steps for political parties, campaigns, and candidates include, but are not limited to the following areas:

- Political parties would do well to add social media warfare tactics training to campaign education programs including fighting against negative offensive tactics and social media etiquette.
- Candidates for national offices should gain better control over their social media warfare activities, screen staff for previous social media activity, and train staff on the proper use of social media.
- Candidates for state and local offices should develop more effective social media warfare tactics and utilize many of the web resources that are available to train staff.
- All candidates for all offices should clearly indicate to supporters that they expect them to use proper social media etiquette when making posts in support of the candidate.
- Further research should be conducted by several related academic disciplines on the impact of social media warfare on the electoral process.

6.11 Key Terms

Hate messages are social media posts that use obnoxious language to ridicule or discriminate against minority or ethnic groups.

Ideological conflict is conflict perpetuated by radicalized groups against mainstream society and minority groups.

Media convergence is the melding of different media types into multi-faceted streams of information and entertainment including video, text, photos, sound, and graphics, which were at one time delivered from separate platforms and applications.

Netiquette is a group of principles and concepts that encourage the socially proper use of social media and other Internet applications.

Personally identifiable information (PII) is information that can be used to distinguish or trace an individual's identity, either alone or when combined with other personal or identifying information that is linked or linkable to a specific individual.

Plain language is straightforward writing that enables readers of all types and levels of education to better understand written content in any media through which it is delivered.

Social media policies specify who in an organization is responsible for social media operations and specify when, why, where, and how social media can be used on behalf of an organization; they also provide guidance on the inappropriate use of social media by corporate media staff and employees.

Social media presence is an organization's use of social media accounts and applications to communicate to individuals or groups as well as the mention, comments, discussions, and display of any material on any social media application that relates to or depicts an organization.

6.12 Seminar Discussion Topics

Discussion topics for graduate- or professional-level seminars:

■ What experience have seminar participants had with political campaigns where social media warfare strategies or tactics were deployed?
■ What would seminar participants do differently in their use of social media warfare tactics than what the candidates in the 2016 election campaigns did?
■ How would seminar participants control social media warfare tactics use for a political campaign?

6.13 Seminar Group Project

Divide participants into multiple groups with each group taking 10–15 minutes to develop a list of social media warfare blunders they observed during the 2016 elections in the United States. Upon completion, have groups exchange their lists of social media warfare blunders, with groups taking 10–15 minutes to develop measures to effectively prevent social media warfare blunders. Meet as a group and discuss the blunders selected by the groups and the measures to prevent blunders that were identified by the groups.

References

1. U.S. Census Bureau. U.S. Census Bureau projections show a slower growing, older, more diverse nation a half century from now. December 12, 2012. Accessed September 9, 2016. https://www.census.gov/newsroom/releases/archives/population/cb12-243.html
2. Brennan, Christopher. J, 2016. Paul Ryan blasted for picture of Congressional interns with few minorities. *New York Daily News*. Accessed September 9, 2016. http://www.nydailynews.com/news/politics/paul-ryan-blasted-lack-minorities-intern-photo-article-1.2715707.

3. Write Web Content. Accessed September 11, 2016. http://www.plainlanguage.gov/index.cfm.
4. Centers for Disease Control and Prevention. Social media at CDC: Facebook guidelines and best practices. Accessed September 11, 2016. http://www.cdc.gov/social-media/tools/guidelines/facebook-guidelines.html.
5. U.S. Department of the Treasury. Site policies and notices. Accessed September 11, 2016. from https://www.treasury.gov/SitePolicies/Pages/privacy.aspx.
6. U.S. Department of Agriculture. Social media monitoring and measurement. Accessed September 11, 2016. http://www.fns.usda.gov/sites/default/files/SNAP_ComChan_SocialMediaMeasurement.pdf.
7. The White House. Elections and voting. Accessed September 11, 2016. https://www.whitehouse.gov/1600/elections-and-voting.
8. Center for Responsive Politics. Our vision and mission: inform, empower and advocate. Accessed September 11, 2016. http://www.opensecrets.org/about/.
9. U.S. Federal Election Commission. About the FEC. Accessed September 11, 2016. http://www.fec.gov/about.shtml.
10. U.S. Election Assistance Commission (EAC). About EAC. Accessed September 11, 2016. http://www.eac.gov/about_the_eac/.

Chapter 7

Social Media Warfare for Support of Social Causes

Social causes come and go, some just fade away, while others result in the establishment of well-structured special interest groups and organizations that share a special interest. This chapter examines the use of social media warfare tactics to support social causes, not including the well-established special interests that were covered in Chapter 5: "Special Interest Groups' Use of Social Media as a Weapon." The social causes examined in this case study are connected to the Black Lives Matter movement, which started in 2014 when, at approximately noon on Saturday, August 9, 2014, Officer Darren Wilson of the Ferguson, Missouri Police Department shot and killed Michael Brown, an unarmed 18-year-old African American [1]. Since the killing of Michael Brown, there have been several other incidents where police have shot and killed African Americans. The Black Lives Matter movement responded reactively in all these cases, and social media warfare tactics were a key factor in the reactions to and protests associated with the incidents. This chapter covers social media warfare in support of social causes.

7.1 Ferguson, Missouri, Michael Brown, and a Social Media Warfare Tsunami

The City of Ferguson is a municipality of northern Saint Louis County, Missouri. It is one of 89 municipalities in Saint Louis County. According to the 2010 U.S. Census, Ferguson has approximately 21,000 residents. The overall population of Ferguson has remained relatively constant in recent decades, but a significant increase in African American residents has considerably shifted demographics. In 1990, Ferguson was predominantly white with 74% of the population identifying as white, and 25% as black. By 2000, African Americans made up 52% of the city's population. Ten years later, in 2010, 67% of Ferguson's population was black and 29% was white. Approximately 25% of the city's population lives below the federal poverty level [2].

In terms of social causes, never before was there such use of social media warfare tactics in the United States as began on August 9, 2014, when Officer Darren Wilson shot and killed Michael Brown. The shooting and subsequent protests gave rise to the Black Lives Matters movement, which was, and continues to be, fueled through social media. As events over the days unfolded, a massive volume of social media posts was generated, as were hundreds of hours of footage taken by major television news networks and the newly social media–empowered *citizen journalists*.

Over the next two weeks, there were often nightly protests and arrests. Police used teargas on protesters as well as news reporters. The police detained two reporters one from the *Huffington Post* and another from the *Washington Post*. The FBI then opened an investigation into the incident. When police decided not to release the name of the officer who shot and killed Michael Brown because of alleged threats on social media, there were more protests at the Saint Louis County Police Department headquarters.

The Missouri State Highway Patrol took control of security in Ferguson and was overseen by Captain Ron Johnson, an African American who grew up in the area. Largely organized through social media, protests and vigils appeared around the country to honor the memory of Michael Brown. Shortly after, the name of the officer that shot and killed Michael Brown was released: Darren Wilson.

Missouri's governor called the National Guard to Ferguson after protesters allegedly shot at police and threw things at them while others looted local businesses. The National Guard helped support the protection of Ferguson city offices and police headquarters and left much of the surrounding community vulnerable to the arson, looting, and extensive damage that occurred over the period of a few days.

A grand jury began investigating whether Ferguson police officer Darren Wilson should be criminally charged for the death of Michael Brown. This seemed to help calm things for a while, as did a visit from U.S. Attorney General Eric Holder for briefings on the investigation into possible civil rights violations related to the shooting of Michael Brown. As things continued to calm down, the National Guard began to withdraw.

During the period of unrest, protesters and others accused the City of Ferguson and its police department of racial bias and *economic exploitation* based on a policing and court system that was geared toward drawing revenue into the city as opposed to serving real *public safety issues*. City and court officials along with the police department continuously denied wrongdoing.

Also during this period, there was a rather severe polarization between white and black people of the community, surrounding areas, and throughout the State of Missouri. Police officials were bitter and angry toward anyone who questioned their integrity and who didn't support their use of force. Online fund-raising efforts for Officer Darren Wilson surpassed similar efforts for Michael Brown.

The local broadcast media curtailed its coverage of the conflict and the accusations of *predatory policing method* against the City of Ferguson and surrounding communities. The national media, however, continued to cover the situation in detail. Social media continued to be awash in discussions, accusations, hate messages, and pleas for peace.

Protests continued and police arrested clergy and activist-academic Cornel West as the Ferguson October movement culminated with Moral Monday protests. Activists along with hundreds of protesters marched from a church to the police station in a very organized demonstration. The community anxiously awaited a decision by a grand jury on whether Darren Wilson would be indicted or not; few people believed that the white criminal justice establishment of the Saint Louis area would seek justice for Michael Brown. When the governor stated that he would call up the National Guard to prevent any violence resulting from the grand jury decision, many people considered it to be the writing on the wall that Darren Wilson would not be indicted.

Racism in the surrounding communities and the State of Missouri was beginning to reach a fever pitch. It was as if the racists and white supremacists were rising like locusts or cicadas to make noise and spread hatred. Social media posts were scathingly racist. Even casual conversations were riddled with racist sentiment and comments. People who had never even been to Ferguson were condemning black protesters and Michael Brown. Meanwhile, Darren Wilson had widespread support among white people, especially bigots and white supremacist, which Missouri had in ample supply.

On November 24, 2014, a Saint Louis county grand jury declined to indict Officer Darren Wilson for firing six shots in the confrontation that killed Michael Brown. Protesters soon filled the streets near the Ferguson police station. A police car and some stores were torched and other stores were looted and objects were thrown at police. Gunfire was allegedly heard and there were later reports of automatic weapons being fired. It started snowing a couple of days later and protests subsided. Meanwhile, local authorities continued to deny that they were guilty of *discriminatory policing practices*. Protests arose across the country fueled by and organized through social media, which law enforcement agencies were monitoring.

On March 4, 2015, U.S. Department of Justice Civil Rights Division released its report on its investigation into the Ferguson Police Department. The report confirmed what members of the community and the protesters claimed the Ferguson Police Department and the Ferguson courts were doing, especially to African Americans. A key summary paragraph from the report [3] appears in Table 7.1.

Table 7.1 Summary Statements from Investigation of the Ferguson Police Department, U.S. Department of Justice Civil Rights Division, March 4, 2015

Ferguson's law enforcement practices are shaped by the city's focus on revenue rather than by public safety needs. This emphasis on revenue has compromised the institutional character of Ferguson's police department, contributing to a pattern of unconstitutional policing, and has also shaped its municipal court, leading to procedures that raise due process concerns and inflict unnecessary harm on members of the Ferguson community. Further, Ferguson's police and municipal court practices both reflect and exacerbate existing racial bias, including racial stereotypes. Ferguson's own data establish clear racial disparities that adversely impact African Americans. The evidence shows that discriminatory intent is part of the reason for these disparities. Over time, Ferguson's police and municipal court practices have sown deep mistrust between parts of the community and the police department, undermining law enforcement legitimacy among African Americans in particular.

The report also concluded that Ferguson court practices impose unnecessary harm overwhelmingly on African Americans and are run in ways counter to public safety. Most strikingly, it was revealed that the court issues municipal arrest warrants not based on public safety needs, but rather as a routine response to missed court appearances and required payment of fines. In 2013 alone, the court issued over 9000 warrants on cases stemming in large part from minor violations such as parking infractions, traffic tickets, or housing code violations. Jail time would be considered far too harsh a penalty for the great majority of these code violations, yet Ferguson's municipal court routinely issued warrants for people to be arrested and incarcerated for failing to pay related fines and fees on time. Under state law, failure to appear in municipal court for a traffic charge involving a moving violation can result in license suspension. Ferguson had made this penalty even more onerous by only allowing the suspension to be lifted after payment of a fine is made in full. Many pending cases still included such charges that were imposed before a court recently eliminated them, making it as difficult as before for people to resolve these cases [3].

On Thursday, March 17, 2016, the Justice Department and City of Ferguson resolved a lawsuit against the city with the Agreement to Reform the Ferguson Police Department and Municipal Court to Ensure Constitutional Policing [4]. Under the agreement, Ferguson is to implement reforms to bring about *constitutional and effective policing*. These are the areas covered by the agreement:

- Community policing and engagement: Creating a *community engagement strategy* that requires meaningful engagement between Ferguson Police Department (FPD) officers and all segments of the Ferguson community.

■ Bias-free police and court practices: Requiring implicit bias-awareness training of all court staff and FPD personnel and ensuring that Ferguson does not discriminate on the basis of race or other characteristics.

■ Stops, searches, and arrests: Ensuring that FPD's stop, search, citation, and arrest practices adhere to the Fourth Amendment of the Constitution and do not discriminate on the basis of race or any other protected characteristic; and prohibiting Ferguson from developing or implementing any law enforcement action in order to generate revenue.

■ First Amendment: Protecting all individuals' First Amendment rights, including their right to record public police activity, lawfully complain about police activity free from retaliation, and engage in lawful protest.

■ Use of force: Reorienting FPD's use-of-force policies toward de-escalation and avoiding force except where necessary; retraining all officers; and investigating all uses of force thoroughly, objectively, and in a timely manner.

■ Officer supervision: Requiring close and effective supervision of officers; requiring FPD officers and other personnel wear and use body-worn and in-car cameras; and requiring supervisors to review camera footage as part of misconduct and force investigations.

■ Accountability: Requiring Ferguson and FPD to fully and fairly investigate all allegations of officer misconduct and take corrective and disciplinary action.

■ Civilian oversight: Establishing a civilian review board to review, generate findings, and recommend disciplinary action for investigations of complaints involving excessive force, abuse of authority, the use of discriminatory slurs, and other misconduct; review FPD policies and training plans; serve on officer hiring and promotion panels; and review crime, racial profiling, and complaint data.

■ Officer assistance and support: Ensuring that officers are provided access to support services, including physical and mental health services, and requiring Ferguson to develop protocols to ensure that officers are provided relief support during public demonstrations and periods of civil unrest.

■ Recruitment: Requiring Ferguson to develop a recruitment plan that will assist FPD in attracting and retaining a highly qualified officer workforce.

■ Mental health crisis intervention: Requiring that Ferguson and FPD implement and train officers in specialized responses to incidents involving individuals in mental health crisis.

■ Data collection, reporting, and transparency: Requiring FPD to collect the data on its operations needed for it to continue to learn and improve upon its police and court practices.

■ School resource officers (SROs): Ensuring that Ferguson SROs have the skills to work lawfully, productively, and fairly with youth; requiring SROs to divert students toward alternatives; and minimizing the use of force in schools.

- Municipal court reform: Enacting reforms to ensure that municipal code enforcement is driven by public safety, not a desire to raise revenue; implementing an amnesty program for all open cases and associated warrants initiated prior to January 1, 2014; eliminating unnecessary fees and altering the court's fine and warrant practices to ensure due process; increasing transparency of court operations; eliminating the use of secured money bonds; ensuring that no person will be jailed for being poor; and ensuring the independence of the court from the city prosecutor and the impartiality of the municipal judge.

An independent monitor was to be selected by the Justice Department and the City of Ferguson to assess implementation of the consent decree, provide technical assistance to Ferguson, and report on Ferguson's implementation of reforms through periodic public reports. The consent decree required two consecutive years of compliance by Ferguson before the agreement could be terminated.

The settlement agreement helped to vindicate the citizens of Ferguson and partially satisfy members of the Black Lives Matter movement. But by that point the movement had gained momentum as demonstrated by activities that took place between the time the Saint Louis County grand jury declined to indict Darren Wilson and the U.S. Justice Department released its report on policing in Ferguson. Both the citizens of Ferguson and the supporters of the Black Lives Matter movement clearly demonstrated the power of social media warfare tactics to motivate and mobilize people to support a social cause.

It should be noted that, upon further investigation, it was found that numerous municipalities in Saint Louis Country relied on the same policing and court practices as Ferguson to increase their revenues. The Missouri legislature took steps to impose dollar limits on what municipalities can generate through such practices. However, this is still a hotly contested issue in Missouri and municipalities are trying to fight back and protect their revenue streams regardless of how harmful and discriminatory their practices are toward minorities and the poor.

7.2 Eric Garner and Other Cases

People being killed due to a *policing style* is not new, but the use of social media warfare tactics to expose such incidents is new. An analysis of the killing of Amadou Diallo by New York City police officers in February 1999 concluded that that event was neither an act of racist violence nor an accident; instead, it was the result of a worst-case scenario of a dangerous and reckless style of policing [5]. In addition to the Michael Brown case discussed previously, there have been several other cases of police killing African American and other citizens. Since the death of Michael Brown, many of these cases have involved citizen journalists and have had an incredible social media response.

In August, 2011, a federal jury convicted five officers from the New Orleans Police Department (NOPD) on 25 counts in connection with a shooting involving police that took place on the Danziger Bridge in the days after Hurricane Katrina and the extensive cover-up of those shootings. The incident resulted in the death of two civilians and the wounding of four others. Four officers were convicted in connection with the shooting of multiple victims, two of whom died. The four officers and a supervisor were also convicted of helping to obstruct justice during the subsequent investigations. The evidence at trial established that officers opened fire on an unarmed family on the east side of the bridge. According to testimony, the second shooting occurred minutes later on the west side of the bridge, where officers shot at a 40-year-old man with severe mental disabilities. Witnesses testified that Ronald Madison was shot in the back as he ran away. Furthermore, an officer stomped and kicked Madison while wounded, but not yet dead. Madison later died at the scene [6].

On December 2, 2014, a grand jury in Staten Island decided not to bring criminal charges against police officers involved in the death of Eric Garner in July of 2014. The incident was captured on video by citizen journalists. The day after the announcement, the U.S. Justice Department stated it would proceed with a federal civil rights investigation into Garner's death [7]. There were numerous protests across the United States that required very little organization and leadership, many of which arose as a result of social media warfare recruitment and indoctrination tactics, which emerged organically as supporters of the Black Lives Matter movement and other organizations worked in unison to respond to the grand jury announcement. Social media was on fire and protests were again organized across the country while law enforcement monitored social media to try and keep ahead of the protesters.

About a week after the video of Garner exploded onto social media, other citizen journalists filmed a New York City Police Department (NYPD) officer using a banned chokehold during a Harlem subway station arrest and NYPD officers dragging a Brooklyn grandmother from her apartment in only her underwear. Another video showed an officer in Brooklyn pulling a gun on a man pinned to the ground; the man was suspected of smoking marijuana [8].

The Russian punk art collective Pussy Riot hit social media with a video tackling police brutality in the United States. It was the group's first English-language video, which took its title, "I Can't Breathe," from the last words of Eric Garner, 43, whose choking death at the hands of an officer sparked nationwide protests in the United States. The music video was released on February 18, 2015 [9].

In April 2015, a white South Carolina police officer was charged with the murder of a black male, Walter Scott, after a citizen-journalist video showed the officer shooting Scott eight times in the back as he ran away. As Scott lay on the ground, the video shows the officer putting him in handcuffs. Users of social media sites, including Twitter, had a huge reaction to the video, with people mostly commenting that without the video, no action would have been taken against the police officer [10].

In July of 2016, police were involved in the fatal shootings of Alton Sterling in Baton Rouge, Louisiana and Philando Castile in Falcon Heights, Minnesota [11]. At the time of this writing, these cases were not completely resolved. In both cases, citizen journalists captured part of the incidents on video, and social media activists launched protests and disseminated information as quickly as possible.

The list of cases seems endless but the examples presented in this chapter show that citizen journalists, social media warfare activists, and on-the-scene witnesses are responsible for collecting evidence and disseminating it widely through social media. This trend is probably far from over and the police are striking back in any way they can to minimize the impact that social media warfare has on removing secrecy from police activity and bringing greater transparency to police activity.

7.3 Police in the United States Feel under Siege

Although policing is a difficult and dangerous job anywhere in the world, it is more so in some places than others. The United States is no exception and police officers face dangerous situations everyday they are on the job. In 2012, there were 48 felonious deaths of police officers in 26 states, the U.S. Virgin Islands, and Puerto Rico. The number of officers killed as a result of criminal acts in 2012 decreased by 24 when compared with the 72 officers who died in 2011. Five- and 10-year comparisons show an increase of seven felonious deaths compared with the 2008 figure (41 officers) and a decrease of four deaths compared with 2003 data (52 officers) [12].

In 2013, there were 27 felonious deaths of police officers in 16 states. The number of officers killed as a result of criminal acts in 2013 decreased by 22 when compared with the 49 officers killed in 2012. Five- and 10-year comparisons show a decrease of 21 felonious deaths compared with the 2009 figure (48 officers) and a decrease of 30 deaths compared with 2004 data (57 officers) [13].

Preliminary statistics for 2014 showed that 51 law enforcement officers were feloniously killed in the line of duty in 2014. This is an increase of almost 89% when compared with the 27 officers killed in 2013. (Note that from 1980 to 2014 an average of 64 law enforcement officers were feloniously killed per year. The 2013 total, 27, was the lowest during this 35-year period.) By region, 17 officers died as a result of criminal acts that occurred in the Southern United States, 14 officers in the Western United States, 8 officers in the Midwest region of the country, 8 in the Northeast, and 4 in Puerto Rico [14]. In 2016, the number of police officers shot and killed in the United States was 44% higher than in 2015 (18 police officers). By July 2016, 26 police officers had been killed including the five killed in the Dallas sniper attack, according to data from the National Law Enforcement Officers Memorial Fund.

Forty-nine law enforcement officers were killed accidentally while performing their duties in 2013. The majority (23 officers) were killed in automobile accidents.

The number of accidental line-of-duty deaths increased by one from the 2012 total (48 officers) [13]. In 2014, an additional 44 officers were accidentally killed in the line of duty. This total represents five officers fewer than the 49 officers who were accidentally killed in 2013 [14]. In addition to these deaths, thousands of police officers are injured every year in the line of duty in the United States.

As a result of deaths and injuries, police officers and police associations often react to any circumstance where they feel they are not being fully supported by their departments or the governments for which they work. Police associations often react negatively to calls for *civilian oversight boards* that review police conduct because they feel these boards will not be fully on their side. In fact, civilian oversight boards are not supposed to take anyone's side, they are supposed to conduct fair and impartial reviews of alleged police misconduct.

Some police officers and police associations have also reacted negatively to transparency efforts, such as requiring officers to wear body cameras that record their actions during encounters with the public or with criminal elements. In other situations, police officers have allegedly tried to stop citizen journalists from filming their activities when making an arrest or interacting with the public. In the Ferguson case, police officers also detained journalists and encroached on freedom of the press, and some officers had complaints about the in-depth coverage that broadcast journalists were providing of the incidents and protesters, and they blamed the media for the magnitude of the Ferguson events.

Police officers and police departments have used social media warfare tactics for self-validation, to influence the public and policy makers, and to entrap sexual predators online. These activities are covered more in-depth in Chapter 13: "Law Enforcement Response to Social Media Warfare."

7.4 Social Media Warfare to Support Social Causes around the World

Many governments continue to use direct and overt means to repress civil society within their countries. Social media warfare tactics are employed by groups ranging from those seeking improved human rights to those working to overthrow a government. This has put incredible pressure on governments to control social media application access.

Social protest against immigration is becoming widespread in Europe as the influx of refugees from the Middle East continues to disrupt the status quo. Social media is used by those protesting immigration as well as terrorists who have perpetrated horrible attacks against civilians. The famed Arab Spring uprisings in Egypt and Tunisia were in part fueled by social media, or at least the governments of those countries feared as much and they attempted to cripple the use of social media by people they considered dissidents.

Chapter 2, "Civilian Government Use of Social Media to Attack, Defend, or Control," provides details on the efforts of many countries to quash freedoms of the press and freedoms of dissent and on how the governments work to control access to social media warfare weapons that can be used against them. When control of the Internet and social media is mentioned, many people instantly think of China, Iran, or North Korea. But there are many countries that have laws and can exercise extreme measures when trying to control social media. Some of the worse offending countries are considered friendly toward or allies of the United States. Countries that attempt to control Internet and social media use are listed in Table 7.2.

When journalists were detained by the police during the unrest in Ferguson, Missouri, it raised alarm among journalist and those who support freedom of the press and free speech. The Ferguson police may not have even considered that detaining and arresting journalists is one of the ways that oppressive regimes control free speech and thus try to control dissent in their countries. What the

Table 7.2   Countries Known to Control Speech and Internet Content

Afghanistan	Jordan	Saudi Arabia
Algeria	Kazakhstan	Serbia
Angola	Kenya	Seychelles
Austria	Korea	Singapore
Azerbaijan	Democratic People's	Somalia
Bahrain	Republic Korea	South Africa
Bangladesh	Republic of Kuwait	South Sudan
Belarus	Kyrgyz Republic	Sri Lanka
Brazil	Laos	Sudan
Brunei	Lebanon	Suriname
Burma	Libya	Swaziland
Burundi	Madagascar	Syria
Cambodia	Malaysia	Tajikistan
China	Mauritius	Tanzania
Congo, Democratic	Mexico	Thailand
Republic	Montenegro	Turkey
Congo, Republic of	Mozambique	Turkmenistan
Cuba	Nauru	Uganda
Djibouti	Nicaragua	Ukraine
Ecuador	Niger	Ukraine-Crimea
Egypt	Nigeria	United Arab
Equatorial Guinea	Oman	Emirates
Eritrea	Pakistan	Uzbekistan
Ethiopia	Peru	Venezuela
Gambia	Qatar	Vietnam
Indonesia	Romania	Yemen
Iran	Russia	Zambia
Iraq	Rwanda	Zimbabwe

Ferguson police did when they detained journalists is what oppressive regimes do frequently, and that is how they keep news of dissent and civil disobedience under control. Police states often detain, arrest, harass, beat, jail, and execute journalists.

7.5 Conclusions

Since the killing of Michael Brown on August 9, 2014, there have been several other incidents where police have shot and killed citizens. The Black Lives Matter movement acted reactively in all of those cases that involved African Americans, and social media warfare tactics were a key factor in the reactions to and protests against all of the incidents. Important conclusions can be drawn from the material presented in this chapter:

■ Social media warfare tactics have been effective in social causes for recruiting and indoctrination as well as influencing and coordinating protest activities.
■ Citizen journalists who records or film police actions or actions by other agents of the state have become an integral part of supporting social media warfare against perceived oppression and wrongdoing on the part of authorities.
■ Social media warfare tactics that expose wrongdoing have enabled people across the country and around the world to react and mobilize against incidents that concern them.
■ Many people believe that without citizen journalists filming police actions justice would not be served for many victims of police violence.
■ Many police officers and police associations oppose efforts to increase transparency and hold officers more accountable for their actions.
■ Many police officers and police associations oppose citizen journalists filming or otherwise recording their activities.

7.6 Agenda for Action

The support of social causes by individual citizens and action groups helps bring constructive change to nations and communities. Social media warfare tactics enable individual citizens and action groups to recruit, influence, and communicate. Unless social media suddenly disappears, it will play a bigger and more important role in individual citizen and action group pursuit of their agendas and their ability to coalesce into special interest groups that can more strongly influence voters and policy makers. Action steps should include, but not be limited to

■ Establishing and supporting research efforts that examine the role of social media warfare tactics in social causes and social change.
■ Developing methods to more comprehensively monitor and measure the impact of social media warfare tactics in situations of civil disobedience.

- Protecting citizen journalists' rights to record police action or actions of any government representative or entity and share that recording with fellow activists and the public.
- Continuing to advocate for the rights of social activists and citizen journalists around the world to exercise free speech and freedom of press.
- Taking steps to assure that law enforcement monitoring of social media complies with all applicable laws and does not violate individual privacy.

7.7 Key Terms

Bias-free police and court practices are criminal justice practices that do not discriminate against any type of minority and treats all citizens equally.

Citizen journalist is an individual who uses technology such as smartphones to record police or government representative actions and disseminate that evidence to the community at large and to interested activists.

Civilian oversight boards are independent boards not comprised of police officials or officers that review and examine complaints of police misconduct.

Community engagement strategy is a policing strategy that brings citizens and civic groups into a partnership with policing practices and public safety concerns.

Constitutional and effective policing is the use of policing practices that simultaneously protect the constitutional rights of citizens while effectively addressing public safety concerns.

Discriminatory policing practices are practices that target specific segments of the population including minorities of any type.

Economic exploitation in this context is the excessive fining and penalizing of citizens for minor offenses in order to raise revenue for a governmental entity.

Policing style is the manner and procedural conduct by which policing is managed in a community.

Predatory policing methods are policing methods that are not designed to protect life or property but are geared toward raising revenue for a governmental entity.

Public safety issues encompass actions or conditions that impede the everyday functioning of a community and the protection of life and property.

7.8 Seminar Discussion Topics

Discussion topics for graduate- or professional-level seminars:

- What experience have seminar participants had working for or supporting a social cause where social media warfare tactics were deployed?
- What do seminar participants think the best social media warfare tactics are to support or be active in a social cause?

■ How would seminar participants try to neutralize social media warfare tactics used to support or be active in a social cause?

7.9 Seminar Group Project

Divide participants into multiple groups with each group taking 10–15 minutes to develop a list of social media warfare tactics that could be used to support a social cause. Upon completion, have groups exchange their lists of social media warfare tactics, with groups taking 10–15 minutes to develop measures to effectively counter the social media warfare tactics used to support a social cause. Meet as a group and discuss the tactics selected by the groups and the countermeasures for the tactics developed by the groups.

References

1. U.S. Department of Justice. 2015. Memorandum: Department of Justice report regarding the criminal investigation into the shooting death of Michael Brown by Ferguson, Missouri police officer Darren Wilson. Accessed September 12, 2016. https://www.justice.gov/sites/default/files/opa/press-releases/attachments/2015/03/04/doj_report_on_shooting_of_michael_brown_1.pdf.
2. *United States of America v the City of Ferguson.* 2016. Accessed September 12, 2016. https://www.justice.gov/opa/file/823486/download.
3. U.S. Department of Justice Civil Rights Division. 2015. Investigation of the Ferguson Police Department. Accessed September 12, 2016. https://www.justice.gov/sites/default/files/opa/press-releases/attachments/2015/03/04/ferguson_police_department_report.pdf.
4. U. S. Department of Justice Office of Public Affairs. 2016. Justice Department and City of Ferguson, Missouri, resolve lawsuit with agreement to reform Ferguson Police Department and Municipal Court to ensure constitutional policing. Accessed September 12, 2016. https://www.justice.gov/opa/pr/justice-department-and-city-ferguson-missouri-resolve-lawsuit-agreement-reform-ferguson.
5. Lynch, Timothy. 2000. We own the night: Amadou Diallo's deadly encounter with New York City's Street Crimes Unit. Accessed September 13, 2016. https://www.ncjrs.gov/App/Publications/abstract.aspx?ID=182886.
6. U.S. Department of Justice. 2011. New Orleans police officers convicted of civil rights violations in Danziger Bridge case: Officers convicted of killing two victims and for extensive cover-up of crimes. Accessed September 13, 2016. https://www.justice.gov/opa/pr/new-orleans-police-officers-convicted-civil-rights-violations-danziger-bridge-case.
7. U.S. Department of Justice. 3, 2014. Statement by Attorney General Holder on federal investigation into death of Eric Garner. *Justice News.* Accessed September 13, 2016. https://www.justice.gov/opa/speech/statement-attorney-general-holder-federal-investigation-death-eric-garner.

8. U.S. Congressman Hakeem Jeffries Web page. 2014. Eric Garner protest march moved amid new calls for independent investigation. April 19, 2014. Accessed September 13, 2016. http://jeffries.house.gov/media-center/in-the-news/eric-garner-protest-march-moved-amid-new-calls-for-independent.
9. Radio Free Europe. Radio Liberty. 2015. Pussy Riot protests police abuse in video tribute to Eric Garner. Accessed September 13, 2016. http://www.rferl.org/content/pussy-riot-video-takes-on-us-police-abuse/26856769.html.
10. Voice of America. 2015. White South Carolina police officer charged in black man's death. Accessed September 13, 2016. http://www.voanews.com/a/white-south-carolina-police-officer-black-man-shooting-death/2710866.html.
11. The White House. 2016. President Obama on the fatal shootings of Alton Sterling and Philando Castile. Accessed September 13, 2016. https://www.whitehouse.gov/blog/2016/07/07/president-obama-fatal-shootings-alton-sterling-and-philando-castile.
12. FBI National Press Office. 2013. FBI releases 2012 statistics on law enforcement officers killed and assaulted. Accessed September 13, 2016. https://archives.fbi.gov/archives/news/pressrel/press-releases/fbi-releases-2012-statistics-on-law-enforcement-officers-killed-and-assaulted.
13. FBI National Press Office. 2014. FBI releases 2013 statistics on law enforcement officers killed and assaulted. Accessed September 13, 2016. https://www.fbi.gov/news/pressrel/press-releases/fbi-releases-2013-statistics-on-law-enforcement-officers-killed-and-assaulted.
14. FBI National Press Office. 2015. FBI releases 2014 preliminary statistics for law enforcement officers killed in the line of duty. Accessed September 13, 2016. https://www.fbi.gov/news/pressrel/press-releases/fbi-releases-2014-preliminary-statistics-for-law-enforcement-officers-killed-in-the-line-of-duty.

Chapter 8

Mercenaries and Activists of Social Media Warfare

There has long been a place for mercenaries in warfare and social media warfare is no different than other types of warfare when it comes to the use of mercenaries. *Social media warfare mercenaries* and activists are a blend of techies, writers, and activists who can be employed or otherwise motivated to support or oppose a cause or an organization. This chapter examines the types of social media warfare mercenaries, how to hire them, and how to use their talents in social media warfare.

8.1 Types of Social Media Warfare Mercenaries

Mercenaries are a necessity for mounting any substantial social media warfare campaign. There are thousands of them available and most call themselves social media consultants, managers, or writers. When working in social media on behalf of their clients, they take on many different roles. They can be surrogates, supporters, friends, fans, imposters, antagonists, protagonists, advocates, or adversaries. Basically, social media warfare mercenaries can take on any role they need to in order to participate in social media events, conversations, and interactions. The difference between an effective social media warfare mercenary and a less effective one is how skillfully they play their role in social media—that is, how effectively they can pass themselves off as regular social media users.

There are many social media warfare roles, including the strategists who look at the big picture over a long term, the planners who design a specific campaign, and the operatives who execute plans. The social media warfare mercenary can be employed by any type of organization or individual that needs to be involved in social media. This includes governments, military organizations, corporations, special interest groups, political campaigns, celebrities, and law enforcement agencies. A mercenary can take on any role in social media warfare interactions, but it is important that they are convincing in that role. A teenage girl, for example, may find it difficult to play the role of a grandfather.

When needed, social media warfare mercenaries come with or create a personality: screen name or handle, a photo, a social or professional profile, an educational background, a job, hobbies, and family. This means that it can be very difficult to tell if a person visible in social media posts or content is real or contrived. The posts, comments, and Likes seen on different social media platforms may in fact not be done by regular users but by a social media warfare mercenary.

Social media warfare mercenary services can be engaged through agencies or consulting firms just as advertising services are contracted or firms are placed on a retainer. Freelance services can be contracted for activities such as writing or editing. Freelancers can be hired on an individual basis or they can be contracted through an Internet clearinghouse.

8.2 Examples of Work Performed by Social Media Warfare Mercenaries

The author uses and recommends the Internet clearinghouse for media services of all types: Fiverr (www.fiverr.com). A wide variety of services are available on Fiverr, including general social media services such as management, marketing, design, search engine optimization, product promotion, and content marketing. Basically, the buyer needs to know what to look for and how to read the *Gig Page*, where sellers describe their Gig and the Gig's terms, and where buyers can place an order. *Gigs* are services offered on Fiverr [1].

There are other websites that provide opportunities to hire social media freelancers that social media warfare managers can check on for contracted services. These sites are constantly evolving and need to be checked on for currently available services. There are also dozens of consulting and service firms that provide social media warfare services on a contractual basis, including

- Customer experience management
- Dedicated reputation management and protection and social media management services
- Ecommerce integration with social media services
- Event coverage services in social media
- Follower and fan growth services
- Managing social media channels
- Marketing lead generation services

- Posts to Facebook, Twitter, and Google+
- Social media advertising management
- Social media campaign management and services
- Social media community management and growth services
- Social media management teams
- Social media monitoring
- Social media posting and social media presence reporting services
- Social media strategy development
- User-generated content management services
- Vanity URL and domain names for engagement and marketing
- Writing and scheduling social media posts

8.3 Social Media Warfare Rangers and Activists

Rangers are generally rather secretive people with special talents and abilities that distinguish them and set them apart. They often work and live on the fringes of society and remain secluded but in touch with the world around them. Rangers ultimately work for a cause although their methods are not always in line with social norms and conventions.

Anonymous is a loosely knit group of hacktivists that hack or break into computer systems. They are motivated by social justice causes. They are social media warfare rangers and have been credited with hacking actions against the Church of Scientology, the United States, Israel, Tunisia, as well as the systems of other countries. They have also taken on the Ku Klux Klan (KKK), the Islamic State of Iraq and Syria (ISIS), child pornography sites, and the Westboro Baptist Church. Corporate hacks allegedly have included PayPal, MasterCard, Visa, and Sony. Anonymous has supported WikiLeaks and the Occupy movement [2,3]. The activities of Anonymous have been celebrated and appreciated by people who believe in the value of social justice and the fight against evil no matter where it lurks because that fight is in the public interest. Guy Fawkes masks are also popular among these social justice seekers.

Another group of social media warfare rangers are the people who support and provide journalistic services to the WikiLeaks organization. WikiLeaks is a global media organization and library founded by publisher Julian Assange in 2006. It has published more than 10 million documents of classified or otherwise restricted official materials related to war, spying, and corruption. WikiLeaks has a relationship and secure communication links with over 100 important media organizations around the world. WikiLeaks has won numerous journalism awards [4].

Many hacking collectives have come and gone over the last 40 years; some developed reputations for pursuing social justice, including Goatse Security, Chaos Computer Club, and the Hacking Team. There have also been many Internet activists who have used social media to support and promote their work on environmental protection, human rights, and transparency in government. Internet activists are basically volunteers who come together based on shared beliefs and the desire to work for change.

There are also several non-profit organizations that fight for Internet freedom that are involved in educational efforts as well as lobbying and Internet activism. The Free Press, for example "fights to save the free and open internet, curb runaway media consolidation, protect press freedom, and ensure diverse voices are represented in our media" (www.freepress.net) [5]. "The Declaration of Internet Freedom" (www.internetdeclaration.org) is supported by the Free Press. The intent of the declaration is to keep the Internet free and open. "The Declaration of Internet Freedom" is also supported by numerous activist organizations that support freedom and human rights, including the Alliance for Community Media, the American Civil Liberties Union, Amnesty International, the Center for Democracy and Technology, the Center for Digital Democracy, the Electronic Frontier Foundation, and the Media Mobilizing Project [6].

8.4 Rangers and Activists Use of Social Media Warfare Tactics

Although rangers and activists use the wide variety of social media warfare tactics that other digital warriors use, they have a unique approach and perspective to how they deploy these tactics. Exposure or the release of damaging information about corrupt corporations, governments, and individuals is one of a ranger's most important tactics. While activists rely heavily on influence as a tactic—working to convince potential contributors, supporters, and policy makers of the validity and legitimacy of fighting corrupt corporations, governments, and individuals—they also heavily rely on recruitment and indoctrination tactics to recruit people into supporting the fight against corrupt corporations, governments, and individuals. The variety of tactics and their tailored use by rangers and activists are shown in Table 8.1.

Most rangers and activists strongly believe in their work and use that belief to justify their use of tactics that seek social justice and expose corruption. Rangers are fearless and take considerable risks in support of their missions. Activists are persistent in their efforts and are willing to take on corporations, governments, and very powerful individuals. Social activists, unlike eco-terrorists and hate mongers, do not intend harm. They participate in social discourse and debate, lobby elected officials, and use the court system to effect change.

Both rangers and activists have a wide base of grassroots support and use that support to raise funds for their efforts. They are heroes to many people and foes to corrupt governments, corporations, and the powerful individuals they challenge. As discussed in earlier chapters, there are many countries that try to suppress activists and quash the freedom of press and freedom of speech, which rangers and activists almost universally fight against. Social media warfare has become an essential weapon for both rangers and activists.

Table 8.1   Ranger and Activist Use of Social Media Warfare Tactics

Blended threats: Joint social media warfare activities between activist groups using a variety of tactics
Divisiveness: Working to prevent corrupt corporations and governments from working in conjunction with each other to oppress or exploit people
Exposure: Release of damaging information about corrupt corporations, governments, and individuals
Influence: Convincing potential contributors, supporters, and policy makers of the validity and legitimacy of corrupt corporations, governments, and individuals.
Nullify opponents: Efforts to discredit opponents
Persuasion of non-aligned entities: Efforts to convince undecided contributors, supporters, and policy makers of the validity and legitimacy corrupt corporations, governments, and individuals
Recruitment and indoctrination: Drawing people into supporting the fight against corrupt corporations, governments, and individuals
Reinforcing alliance partners: Showing support for organizations that fight against corruption, oppression, and so on
Relationship building: Establishing cooperative efforts with like-minded organizations that fight against corruption, oppression, and so on
Trolling: Posting opposing or critical messages to existing social media posts, done by oppressive and corrupt governments, corporations, and individuals

8.5 Conclusions

Rangers and activists fight against incredible odds. In some countries, they end up dead or incarcerated for their work and the fight for freedom. Mercenaries generally fight for anyone who pays them whether they believe in what they are doing is good or evil. Important conclusions can be drawn from the material presented in this chapter:

■ Mercenaries in social media warfare are readily available for hire and can bring a wide variety of skills and tactics to the theater of war.
■ Rangers continue to fight for their beliefs and will risk their lives and freedom in support of their efforts.
■ Activists are generally very dedicated to the causes they support and many put in countless hours of work for no pay in pursuit of social justice and fairness.

- Most rangers and activists strongly believe in their work and use that belief to justify their use of tactics to seek social justice and expose corruption.
- "The Declaration of Internet Freedom" is supported by numerous activist organizations that support freedom and human rights and oppose government oppression and corruption.
- Social media warfare mercenary services can be engaged through agencies or consulting firms in the same way that advertising services are contracted or firms are put on a retainer.

8.6 Agenda for Action

Social media warfare mercenaries, rangers, and activist have found that the Internet and social media applications provide them with a new set of weapons to either fight for hire or fight for a cause. The fight for freedom, overcoming oppression, and achieving social justice on the Internet is just beginning. Corrupt governments, corporations, and individuals will not fall easily, but activists will not be going away any time soon, if ever. Action steps should include, but not be limited to, the following areas:

- Rangers and activists should be leery of governments cooperating with each other in order to halt their efforts. Much of that cooperation is pursued in the fight against terrorism.
- Social media warfare mercenaries should use caution when accepting work from oppressive governments or corrupt corporations because they themselves may become victims in the fight against evil.
- Individuals or organizations that hire social media warfare mercenaries should carefully check the background of people they hire to prevent problems, such as infiltration into their organizations.
- Those individuals or organizations that hire social media warfare mercenaries should not provide excessive amounts of information about the missions or goals of the organization in order to prevent problems such as exposure of potentially damaging information.
- Activists should carefully examine the performance and fund-raising records of the organizations they support to ensure that those organizations are not corrupt or misappropriating funds.

8.7 Key Terms

Custom offers are exclusive proposals that a seller can create in response to specific requirements of a buyer on Fiverr.
Gigs® are services offered on Fiverr.

Gig Extras are additional services offered on top of the seller's Gig for an additional price defined by the seller on Fiverr.

Gig Page a Gig Page on Fiverr is where the seller describes their Gig and the Gig's terms, and the buyer can purchase the Gig.

Rangers are rather secretive groups of people with special talents; they often work and live on the fringes of society and remain secluded but in touch with the world around them.

Social media warfare mercenaries are individuals or groups that perform social media tasks as agents or imposters on behalf of organizations that desire to have a social media presence or disrupt the social media activities of other people or organizations.

8.8 Seminar Discussion Topics

Discussion topics for graduate- or professional-level seminars:

- What experience have seminar participants had employing mercenary organizations or individuals in social media warfare?
- What experience have seminar participants had with Internet activist organizations or individuals in social media warfare?
- What experience have seminar participants had with rangers or ranger organizations in social media warfare?

8.9 Seminar Group Project

Divide participants into multiple groups with each group taking 10–15 minutes to develop a list of social media warfare tactics that rangers employ in their activities. Upon completion, have groups exchange their lists of social media warfare tactics with groups taking 10–15 minutes to develop defensive measures to effectively counter the tactics used by rangers. Meet as a group and discuss the offensive tactics selected by the groups and the defensive measures to counter the tactics that were developed by the groups.

References

1. Fiverr. Fiverr's terms of service. Accessed September 15, 2016. https://www.fiverr.com/terms_of_service.
2. Wikipedia. Anonymous (group). Accessed September 16, 2016. https://en.wikipedia.org/wiki/Anonymous_(group).

3. Raza, Ali. 2016. 8 most awesome hacks conducted by Anonymous hackers. *HackRead*, Accessed September 16, 2016. https://www.hackread.com/8-most-awesome-hacks-conducted-by-anonymous-hackers/

4. WikiLeaks. 2015. What is WikiLeaks? Accessed September 16, 2016. https://wikileaks.org/What-is-Wikileaks.html.

5. Free Press. What we do. Accessed September 16, 2016. http://www.freepress.net/about.

6. Free Press. The declaration of Internet freedom. Accessed September 16, 2016. http://www.internetdeclaration.org/.

Chapter 9

Social Media as a Weapon to Recruit and Inspire Violent Extremists

Almost all organizations must recruit to keep their ranks filled, and the process of using social media to accomplish that is discussed in several chapters of this book. The conflict in Syria and Iraq is currently attracting *Western-based extremists* who want to engage in violence. This chapter focuses on the terrorist Islamic State of Iraq and the Levant (ISIL), also referred to as the Islamic State of Iraq and Syria (ISIS), and its noted efforts to recruit and inspire new members. Efforts to stop ISIL from successful recruitment and *radicalization* of devotees are also discussed, including the development of counter narratives.

9.1 ISIL's Recruitment Efforts Using Social Media Warfare

The conflict in Syria and Iraq is currently the most attractive overseas theater for Western-based extremists who want to engage in violence. The FBI estimates upward of 150 Americans have traveled or attempted to travel to Syria to join extremist groups. Although this number is small in comparison to the number of European travelers, it is important to consider the influence that groups like ISIL have on individuals located in the United States who might be inspired to commit acts of violence.

The FBI has long been concerned about the possibility of homegrown extremists becoming radicalized by information available on the Internet and through social media warfare. ISIL is known for using widespread social media campaigns to propagate its extremist ideas. Propaganda includes various English-language publications circulated via social media, videos of ISIL-held hostages, and videos glorifying ISIL.

Online supporters of ISIL use various social media platforms to call for retaliation against the United States and other countries. ISIL has advocated for lone-wolf attacks and used social media warfare tactics to inspire such actions. Several incidents that occurred in the United States and Europe indicate the call to arms has been effective among ISIL supporters and sympathizers. The FBI has long contended that individuals inspired by foreign terrorist groups could quietly arm themselves with the expertise and tools to carry out attacks in the United States, and this has proved to be a realistic concern [1].

Several sources indicate that there are as many as 90,000 pro-ISIS tweets daily and others suggest that there may be as many as 200,000 such tweets per day. Accounts belonging to other foreign terrorist organizations, such as Jabhat al-Nusra, Al-Qaeda's branch in Syria, have had over 200,000 followers. Official Twitter accounts belonging to Jabhat al-Nusra operated much like those belonging to ISIS, tweeting similar extremist content. YouTube videos depicting violent acts against Westerners have been used to incite others to take up arms and wage jihad.

ISIS's use of social media is believed to resonate with vulnerable populations, particularly Muslim converts and susceptible alienated youth. However, radicalization of U.S. citizens and residents is not limited to any single social or demographic profile. Instead, U.S. citizens and residents who have been radicalized to support and fight for Islamic extremists have come from all walks of life [2].

ISIL aggressively promotes its hateful message, attracting like-minded extremists, including Westerners, and persistently uses the Internet to communicate. ISIL blends traditional media platforms, glossy photos, in-depth articles, and social media campaigns that can go viral in a matter of seconds. No matter the format, the message of radicalization now spreads faster than it did just a few years ago. Unlike other groups, ISIL has constructed a narrative that touches on all facets of life, from career opportunities to family life to a sense of community. The message is not just tailored to those who are overtly expressing symptoms of radicalization, rather it is seen by many people who click through the Internet every day, receive social media push notifications, and participate in social networks. Ultimately, many of these individuals are seeking a sense of belonging. Children and young adults have been drawn deeper into the ISIL narrative. These individuals are often comfortable with virtual communication platforms, especially social media networks [3].

Terrorists are using a variety of social media warfare tactics to build their ranks and influence people and organizations to align with terrorists and provide support. These tactics are listed in Table 9.1.

Table 9.1   Social Media Warfare Tactics Used by Terrorists

Deception: False promises and invalid information in order to gain supporters and fighters
Confusion: Creating and perpetuating uncertainty among populace and organizations regarding the validity of counter and alternative narratives used by anti-terrorist forces
Divisiveness: Instigating hatred and suspicion among populace and anti-terrorist forces
Exposure: Unauthorized release of damaging information about anti-terrorist forces
Trolling: Post opposing messages to existing posts supporting counter and alternative narratives used by anti-terrorist forces
Relationship building: Establishing cooperative efforts with like-minded people or terrorist organizations
Nullify opponents: Efforts to discredit anti-terrorist forces and their counter and alternative narratives.
Blended threats: Combined activities to accomplish offensive objectives
Recruitment and indoctrination: Drawing individuals to terrorism and to supporting the terrorist position using the same negative narrative

9.2 Apprehension and Arrest of Terrorist Supporters in the United States

There are numerous cases of law enforcement officers apprehending and arresting terrorist supporters in the United States. Since 2014, the U.S. Department of Justice and the Federal Bureau of Investigation (FB) have arrested approximately 65 individuals in ISIL-related matters. Many of these arrests helped to prevent violence and attacks in the United States. In addition, the U.S. Treasury and the State Department imposed sanctions on more than 30 ISIL-linked senior leaders, financiers, foreign terrorist facilitators, and organizations in an attempt to isolate ISIL from international financial systems [4]. The following is a summary of material found through a September 15, 2016, Web search of FBI and U.S. District Attorney publications regarding those cases.

▪ On December 22, 2015, Jalil Ibn Ameer Aziz, 19 years old, a U.S. citizen and resident of Harrisburg, Pennsylvania, was charged in an indictment with conspiring and attempting to provide material support to ISIL. He was later charged in a superseding indictment with solicitation to commit a crime of violence and transmitting a communication containing a threat to injure. According to the indictment, from July 2014 to December 17, 2015, Aziz knowingly conspired to provide, provided, and attempted to provide material support, including personnel and services, to ISIL. The superseding indictment alleges that during the same period, Aziz solicited, commanded, induced, and endeavored to persuade others to kill and attempt to kill officers and employees of the United States. The superseding indictment further alleges that he knowingly tweeted the names, addresses, photographs, and military branches of approximately 100 U.S. service members to followers and viewers of his Twitter account. The communication also contained threats to injure the service members, stating "kill them in their own lands, behead them in their own homes, stab them to death as they walk their street thinking that they are safe." Aziz used at least 57 different Twitter accounts to advocate violence against the United States and its citizens, to disseminate ISIL propaganda, and to espouse pro-ISIL views. Aziz allegedly used his Twitter accounts and other electronic communication services to assist persons seeking to travel to and fight for ISIL [5].

■ In June 2016, Ardit Ferizi, aka Th3Dir3ctorY, a citizen of Kosovo, pleaded guilty before a U.S. district judge to providing material support to ISIL and accessing a protected computer without authorization and obtaining information. Ferizi admitted to stealing the personally identifiable information of over 1000 U.S. service members and federal government employees, and providing it to ISIL with the understanding that they would incite terrorist attacks against those individuals. The case against Ferizi was the first of its kind involving terrorism and cyber threats [6].

■ In July 2016, Haris Qamar, 25 years old, was arrested on charges of attempting to provide material support and resources to ISIL. According to the affidavit in support of the criminal complaint, on May 26, Qamar and FBI confidential witness (CW) discussed ISIL's need of photos of possible targets in and around Washington, D.C., for use in a video that ISIL was purportedly making to encourage lone-wolf attacks in the Washington, D.C., area. Qamar allegedly offered CW ideas of where to take these photographs, including the Pentagon and numerous landmarks in Arlington and Washington, D.C., which could be targeted for terrorist attacks. A conversation was audio and video recorded when CW picked up Qamar in a vehicle and they drove to area landmarks on the list Qamar had developed. Qamar allegedly said "bye bye DC, stupid ass kufar, kill'em all." Qamar and CW met again on June 10 and drove to a location in Arlington to take additional photos for the ISIL video. The FBI first learned of Qamar as he operated over 60 variations of the Twitter handle "newerajihadi," which Qamar used to express his support of ISIL and share videos and photos of extreme violence, including beheadings and mass shootings. For example, after terrorists murdered employees of the *Charlie Hebdo* magazine in Paris in January

2015, Qamar tweeted his prayer for another similar attack with even more casualties [7].

■ In July 2016, Mohamed Bailor Jalloh, 26 years old, a former member of the U.S. Army National Guard, was arrested for attempting to provide material support to ISIL. According to the complaint, Jalloh is alleged to have attempted to provide services by assisting in the procurement of weapons to be used in what he believed was going to be an attack on U.S. soil committed in the name of ISIL, and that he attempted to provide material support to ISIL by providing money to assist in the facilitation of individuals seeking to join ISIL. Jalloh told the confidential human source (CHS) that he was a former member of the Virginia Army National Guard, but that he had decided to quit after listening to online lectures by Anwar al-Aulaqi, a deceased leader of Al-Qaeda in the Arabian Peninsula. He stated that he recently had taken a six-month trip to Africa, where he had met with ISIL members in Nigeria and first began communicating online with the ISIL member who later brokered his introduction to the CHS. During their meeting, Jalloh also told the CHS that he often thought about conducting an attack and that he knew how to shoot guns. Jalloh praised the gunman who killed five U.S. military members in a terrorist attack in Chattanooga, Tennessee, in July 2015, and stated that he had been thinking about conducting an attack similar to the November 2009 attack at Fort Hood, Texas [8].

■ Erick Jamal Hendricks, 35 years old, tried to recruit people to train together and conduct terrorist attacks in the United States on behalf of ISIL, according to a criminal complaint. In June 2015, an individual (CW-1) was arrested in the Northern District of Ohio after attempting to purchase an AK-47 assault rifle and ammunition from an undercover law enforcement officer. CW-1 had pledged allegiance to ISIL in social media and made statements expressing interest in conducting attacks in the United States. Hendricks had contacted CW-1 over social media to recruit him in the spring of 2015. Hendricks allegedly told CW-1 that he needed people and wanted to meet in person; that there were several brothers located in Texas and Mexico; that he was attempting to get brothers to meet face to face; and that he wanted to get brothers to train together. CW-1 said that Hendricks tested his religious knowledge and commitment, inquiring about his willingness to commit jihad, to die as a martyr and his desire to enter jannah (paradise). CW-1 understood these statements to mean that Hendricks was recruiting people to train together for the purpose of conducting a terrorist attack in the United States and to see if CW-1 was suitable for recruitment, according to the allegations. Hendricks also allegedly communicated over social media with several other people, including an undercover FBI employee (UCE-1). According to the complaint, on April 16, 2015, Hendricks instructed UCE-1 to download the document "GPS for the Ghuraba in the United States" which included a section entitled "Final Advice" and advocated that brothers and sisters should not allow themselves to go to jail, to "Boobie trap your homes, to lay in wait for them and to never leave your home without your AK-47 or M16" [9].

■ In August 2016, Nicholas Young, 36 years old, who was employed as a police officer with the Washington D.C. Metro Transit Police Department, was arrested on charges of attempting to provide material support to a designated foreign terrorist organization. Law enforcement first interviewed Young in September 2010 in connection with his acquaintance, Zachary Chesser, who one month later pleaded guilty to providing material support to terrorists. Over the next several years, Young had numerous interactions with undercover law enforcement officers and a cooperating witness regarding Young's knowledge of or interest in terrorist-related activity, many of which were recorded. Several meetings Young had with an undercover law enforcement officer in 2011 included another of Young's acquaintances, Amine El Khalifi, who later pleaded guilty to charges relating to attempting a suicide bombing at the U.S. Capitol building in 2012. Young told FBI agents that he traveled to Libya twice in 2011 and he had been with rebels attempting to overthrow the Muammar Qaddafi regime. Baggage searches revealed that Young traveled with body armor, a Kevlar helmet, and several other military-style items [10].

Numerous other cases involved efforts by people to travel to Syria and join or provide material support to ISIL. There are also several cases of individuals attempting to recruit fighters for ISIL or raise funds for their efforts. The following headlines come from a September 17, 2016 Web search of the FBI website:

■ Federal Jury Convicts Three Minnesota Men for Conspiring to Join ISIL and Commit Murder in Syria
■ Rochester Man Charged with Attempting to Provide Material Support to ISIL
■ Tenth Minnesota Man Charged with Conspiracy to Provide Material Support to ISIL
■ New York Man Pleads Guilty to Attempting to Provide Material Support to ISIL
■ Maryland Man Charged with Attempting to Provide Material Support to ISIL
■ Bronx Man Charged in Manhattan Federal Court with Attempting to Provide Material Support to ISIL
■ San Joaquin County Man Sentenced to 12 Years in Prison for Attempting to Join ISIL
■ Former New Jersey Resident Charged with Conspiracy and Attempt to Provide Material Support to ISIL

- Maryland Man Indicted for Conspiring to Provide and for Providing Material Support to ISIL
- Former New Jersey Resident Admits Conspiring to Provide Material Support to ISIL
- U.S. Citizen Arrested for Attempting to Provide Material Support to ISIL and Other Federal Offenses
- Two California Men Arrested on Charges of Conspiring to Provide Material Support to ISIL
- Georgia Man Pleads Guilty to Attempting to Provide Material Support to ISIL
- Orange County Man Who Admitted He Attempted to Provide Material Support to a Terrorist Organization by Joining ISIL Sentenced to 15 Years in Federal Prison
- Manassas Man Sentenced to 11 Years for Providing Material Support to ISIL
- Hudson County, New Jersey Man Sentenced to 15 Years in Prison for Conspiring to Provide Material Support to ISIL
- New Jersey Man Charged with Conspiracy to Provide Material Support to ISIL and Witness Tampering
- Ohio Man Pleads Guilty to Attempting to Provide Material Support to ISIL and Possessing Firearms as a Felon
- Fifth Defendant Charged with Attempt and Conspiracy to Provide Material Support to ISIL
- Bolingbrook Man Pleads Guilty to Attempting to Provide Material Support to ISIL
- Wife of Dead ISIL Leader Charged in Death of Kayla Jean Mueller
- New Jersey Man Charged with Conspiracy to Provide Material Support to ISIL
- Lackawanna Man Indicted on Charges of Attempting to Provide Support to ISIL
- Texas Resident Charged with Conspiracy to Provide Material Support to ISIL
- U.S. Army National Guard Soldier and His Cousin Indicted for Conspiring to Support Terrorism (ISIL)
- U.S. Air Force Veteran Charged with Attempting to Provide Material Support to ISIL
- California Resident Pleads Guilty to Providing Material Support to ISIL and Making False Statements
- Three Brooklyn Residents Charged with Attempt and Conspiracy to Provide Material Support to ISIL
- Fourth Brooklyn Resident Charged with Attempt and Conspiracy to Provide Material Support to ISIL

■ Madison Man Charged with Attempting to Provide Material Support to ISIL
■ New York Man Pleads Guilty to Conspiracy to Provide Material Support to ISIL in Connection with Planned New Year's Eve Attack

9.3 International Response to Terrorist Use of Social Media Warfare

The FBI and the U.S. Department of Homeland Security (DHS) work in cooperation with INTERPOL to share information on terrorist operations. INTERPOL has an agenda to fight against terrorism that includes examination of social media use by terrorist organizations. INTERPOL's Counter-Terrorism Fusion Centre is a global hub for intelligence on transnational terrorist networks shared by member countries worldwide. A dedicated project on foreign terrorist fighters was established in July 2013. Major projects focus on terrorist use of social media and the Internet and hostage-taking for ransom [11].

The DHS, FBI, the Department of State, and other agencies are not only challenging justifications for violence, but affirming American ideals of inclusiveness and opportunity as well. These efforts include countering violent extremist narratives that feed on disenchantment and a sense of exclusion with positive affirmations of national unity. The basic philosophy behind this is that a complex issue such as violent extremist radicalization and recruitment requires a nuanced path to guide a whole-of-government approach [12]. Governments around the world are putting more and more pressure on social media providers to be proactive in keeping terrorist propaganda and content off social media platforms. The question at the core of this issue is: What is freedom of expression and free speech versus the incitement to terrorism? Many governments around the world have a rather narrow concept of what comprises free speech, as is pointed out by the U.S. Department of State in its annual report on human rights around the world.

The United Nations Security Council (UNSC) has applauded the extraordinary efforts by states to stem the flow of foreign terrorist fighters to and from conflict zones, while also urging more work on the issue because of growing recruitment by extremist groups, from more than 100 countries. The 15-member UNSC expressed grave concern over the increase of foreign fighters joining the Islamic State in Iraq and the Levant/al-Sham (ISIL/ISIS or Da'esh), Al-Qaeda, and other groups. The UNSC has reiterated concern about the dangers posed by foreign fighters, both in zones of combat and their country of origin. It has asked for member states to improve prevention, interdiction, and enforcement efforts through intensified national activities and international cooperation, particularly information-sharing, undertaking priority actions with assistance from others where needed, as expeditiously as possible.

According to the UNSC, laws that criminalize recruiting, organizing, transporting, or equipping foreign terrorist fighters were particularly needed in many states. In addition, the UNSC noted with concern that only 51 member states were reportedly using advance passenger information to address the scourge of terrorism, and it urged all to support evidence-based traveler risk assessment and screen procedures without resorting to profiling based on stereotypes founded on grounds of discrimination prohibited by international law.

In addition, the UNSC noted that terrorist recruitment efforts that targeted youths, increasingly young women as well as men, have created the need for member states to more effectively identify and work with relevant local community leaders to address radicalization, and that much more work must be done to prevent terrorists from exploiting social media warfare technology to incite support for violence.

The UNSC has also called for strengthened international, regional, and public-private cooperation for all those purposes, with due respect for human rights and fundamental freedoms. It has also urged greater cooperation with INTERPOL, calling on nations to increase exchange of information and use of the agency's foreign terrorist fighter database.

In addition to security and legal and intelligence measures, UNSC members have stressed the need to provide a *counter narrative to radicalization*, addressing root causes and working with communities in that regard [13]. This means addressing conditions conducive to terrorism or the various social, economic, political, and other factors that contribute to circumstances in which individuals might become terrorists, including community-oriented approaches to terrorism or counterterrorism objectives, or policies and measures that are pursued through locally driven, cooperative initiatives, tailored to local contexts to increase effectiveness. Such practices include a *community-targeted approach* to terrorism and counterterrorism policies and practices that, driven by the security priorities of a state, target communities for intelligence-gathering and enforcement activities to detect suspected terrorists and thwart their activities, especially active plans for attacks.

UNSC members have recommended that special investigation techniques be used to gather information, such as electronic or other forms of surveillance and undercover operations, in a way that does not alert the targeted persons and for the purpose of detecting and investigating terrorism and organized-crime-related offenses [14]. These activities include the monitoring and interception of social media content. There are numerous terrorist organizations that are internationally recognized as a threat to global security [15]:

- Abdallah Azzam Brigades (AAB)
- Abu Nidal Organization (ANO)
- Abu Sayyaf Group (ASG)
- Al-Aqsa Martyrs Brigade (AAMB)

- al-Mulathamun Battalion
- al-Nusrah Front
- Al-Qaeda (AQ)
- Al-Qaeda in the Arabian Peninsula (AQAP)
- Al-Qaeda in the Islamic Maghreb (AQIM)
- Al-Shabaab
- Ansar al-Dine (AAD)
- Ansar al-Islam (AAI)
- Ansar al-Sharia in Benghazi
- Ansar al-Sharia in Darnah
- Ansar al-Sharia in Tunisia
- Ansaru
- Army of Islam (AOI)
- Asbat al-Ansar (AAA)
- Aum Shinrikyo (AUM)
- Basque Fatherland and Liberty (ETA)
- Boko Haram
- Communist Party of the Philippines/New People's Army (CPP/NPA)
- Continuity Irish Republican Army (CIRA)
- Gama'a al-Islamiyya (Islamic Group) (IG)
- Hamas
- Haqqani Network (HQN)
- Harakat ul-Jihad-i-Islami (HUJI)
- Harakat ul-Jihad-i-Islami/Bangladesh (HUJI-B)
- Harakat ul-Mujahidin (HUM)
- Hezbollah
- Indian Mujahedeen (IM)
- ISIL Sinai Province (formally Ansar Bayt al-Maqdis)
- ISIL-Khorasan (ISIL-K)
- Islamic Jihad Union (IJU)
- Islamic Movement of Uzbekistan (IMU)
- Islamic State of Iraq and the Levant (formerly Al-Qaeda in Iraq)
- Islamic State of Iraq and the Levant's Branch in Libya (ISIL-Libya)
- Jaish-e-Mohammed (JEM)
- Jaysh Rijal al-Tariq al Naqshabandi (JRTN)
- Jemaah Anshorut Tauhid (JAT)
- Jemaah Islamiya (JI)
- Jundallah
- Kahane Chai (Kach)
- Kata'ib Hezbollah (KH)
- Kurdistan Workers Party (PKK) (Kongra-Gel)
- Lashkar-e-Jhangvi (LJ)
- Lashkar-e-Tayyiba (LeT)

- Liberation Tigers of Tamil Eelam (LTTE)
- Mujahidin Shura Council in the Environs of Jerusalem (MSC)
- National Liberation Army (ELN)
- Palestine Liberation Front (PLF)
- Palestinian Islamic Jihad (PIJ)
- PFLP-General Command (PFLP-GC)
- Popular Front for the Liberation of Palestine (PFLF)
- Real Irish Republican Army (Real IRA)
- Revolutionary Armed Forces of Colombia (FARC)
- Revolutionary People's Liberation Party/Front (DHKP/C)
- Revolutionary Struggle (RS)
- Shining Path (SL)
- Tehrik-e-Taliban Pakistan (TTP)

9.4 Using Social Media Warfare Tactics to Fight Terrorist Groups

Countering the violent extremism that is driving terrorist threats is a *multi-generational challenge*. Lasting victories over terrorism and the violent extremist ideologies that underpin it are not found on the battlefield, but rather in mindsets, and within communities, schools, and families. The U.S. Department of State and U.S. Agency for International Development (USAID) are actively involved in countering terrorist threats and building capacity and resilience to prevent future terrorist threats. The United States works with a committed consortium of international partners, including governments, the United Nations, regional organizations, civil society, and the private sector, to prevent the spread of violent extremist ideologies and networks worldwide. The U.S. Department of State and USAID along with international partners are supporting a wide range of programs and initiatives to counter violent extremism (CVE), including but not limited to

- Improving and sharing analysis of violent extremism
- Developing skills, expertise, and strategies to counter violent extremism
- Promoting the role of *civil society leaders*, especially youth and women, in countering and preventing violent extremism
- Strengthening community–police and community–security force relations as ingredients for countering and preventing the spread of violent extremism
- Building *community resilience* to recruitment and radicalization to violent extremism
- Promoting counter narratives, including through strategic communications
- Elevating the role of religious voices and promoting educational initiatives to build resilience against extremist recruitment

- Preventing radicalization of violence in prisons and rehabilitation/reintegration of violent extremists
- Engaging the private and charitable sectors to support community-led solutions globally to create opportunity and address violent extremism
- Strengthening multilateral initiatives to counter violent extremism

One very long-term effort using social media warfare tactics is the process of promoting counter narratives, including through strategic communications. This also involves the expansion of innovative public diplomacy efforts to support counter narratives and *counter messaging* to mitigate recruitment and radicalization to violent extremism in key countries through social media and other information technologies and platforms.

These efforts include support for *alternative narratives* and counter messaging that amplify the voices of victims and survivors of terrorism and former violent extremists and training them on ways to broadcast their message in a way that emphasizes the negative impact of violent extremism on families and communities. This can be accomplished by employing social media warfare tactics that use widely accessible technologies such as the Internet, smartphones, radio, television, and text messaging for maximum message dissemination to vulnerable communities.

These initiatives require support for online media training programs and tech camps. The media-tech camps provide training and knit together influential community and religious leaders to enhance their use of technology to more effectively counter ISIL's narrative and propaganda [16].

The U.S. Department of State Office of the Special Representative to Muslim Communities is helping to lead efforts to develop and implement counter narratives by building respectful and strong long-term relationships between the U.S. government and Muslim communities, especially the next generation of Muslims. This is being done in part by supporting indigenous organic and credible alternative narratives that counter violent extremism and by building online and offline global action networks of like-minded leaders. There are several steps in the process, starting with engaging people-to-people at the grassroots level and scouting out talented creative change makers who can positively impact their communities through social media as well as other media [17].

One step in countering violent extremist messaging and promoting alternative narratives, is the support of the interagency Global Engagement Center (GEC) that fosters efforts to help government and non-governmental partners to counter ISIL's messaging and promote alternative narratives. The establishment of the Sawab Center in Abu Dhabi, was the first-ever joint online messaging program to counter ISIL propaganda by directly exposing its criminal nature, challenging its doctrine of hate and intolerance, and highlighting coalition successes [18]. The GEC has plans to provide seed funding and other support to non-government organizations and media start-ups focused on countering violent extremist messaging [19].

A regional summit for countering violent extremism (CVE) in South and Central Asia was convened by the government of Kazakhstan in June of 2015 in Astana. The event brought together government officials, civil society, and private sector representatives from the region to explore select themes from the action agenda outlined by international actors at the White House summit to counter violent extremism held in February 2015. In addition to exchanging experiences and lessons learned, participants put forward concrete proposals for furthering efforts to prevent and counter violent extremism in the region.

The discussions also focused on the importance of developing *positive narratives* against violent extremism, not just counter narratives to argue point-for-point with extremists but to also *alternative master narratives* that can be powerful incentives for positive action. It was emphasized that the message, the medium, and the messenger are all integral to effective messaging. How, with whom, and when interventions are conducted are as much a part of the message as the content itself. For messaging to be effective and resonate with key audiences, it should be emotive and engaging, and locally driven. In this effort, the credibility of interlocutors is key and it is therefore important to insulate and protect *credible voices* to allow them to continue their work [20].

The GEC and many anti-terrorist organizations are using several social media warfare tactics to go head-to-head against terrorist use of social media warfare tactics with counter and alternative narratives. The tactics used along with a brief explanation for each are shown in Table 9.2.

9.5 How the 2016 Presidential Primaries in the United States Aided Terrorists

The GEC is working to counter terrorist and terrorism by engaging Muslim communities in leading efforts to develop and implement counter narratives and alternative narratives. The GEC and participating entities are working to build a respectful and strong long-term relationships between the ant-terrorism governments and Muslim communities. This is essential to engage the next generation of Muslims. As pointed out earlier, there are several steps to the process, starting with engaging people-to-people at the grassroots level and scouting out talented creative change makers who can positively impact their communities through social media. It is also emphasized that the message, the medium, and the messenger are all integral to effective messaging. To accomplish these goals requires positive interaction between anti-terrorism individuals and organizations and the vulnerable populations and regions of the world that could be swayed to support terrorism.

Table 9.2   Counter Narrative and Alternative Narrative Social Media Warfare Tactics

Exposure: Release of discrediting information about individual terrorist leaders or fighters or their organizations
Influence: Convincing citizens and policy makers to oppose terrorism and act against terrorists
Nullify opponents: Debasing the philosophy of terrorists with an alternative or counter narrative
Persuasion of non-aligned entities: Convincing potential terrorists or supporters to not be involved with or support terrorism
Recruitment and indoctrination: Drawing individuals away from terrorism and to supporting the fight against terrorism and adopting the same alternative positive narrative
Reinforcing alliance partners: Showing support for individuals and organizations that fight against terrorism
Relationship building: Establishing cooperative efforts with like-minded organizations that fight against terrorism
Trolling: Posting opposing or critical messages to existing social media posts made by terrorists or their supporters, using an alternative or counter narrative.

Instead of participation in the process that the GEC and aligned entities are supporting and working hard to build, many candidates in the 2016 U.S. presidential primaries and elections as well as campaigns for other offices did just the opposite. They helped to perpetuate hate and a reputation that most people in the United States hate and mistrust Muslims. Candidates swayed anti-Muslim populations into supporting them by feeding into their fear, hatred, and mistrust of Muslims. They did so in person, on television, and through social media.

Far too often when there were incidents in the United States involving Muslim perpetrators, the nation and the candidates immediately blamed Islam. This contrasts their reactions when a white supremacy supporter is involved in a terror attack or crimes; in these cases, they are quickly labeled mentally ill. Most people in the United States believe that if a Muslim perpetrates such crimes it is because of Islam not mental illnesses.

The anti-Muslim rhetoric supported by the candidates does sway the voting population because many people in the United States could be said to be bigots and are paranoid about Muslims. The anti-Muslim rhetoric of the 2016 U.S. election campaigns was accompanied by anti-immigration rhetoric that fed the desire of some Americans to keep the United States a white Christian-dominated society;

a society that they believe still exists even though it barely exists at this point and what is left of it will be short lived. The candidates have convinced people that immigrants are taking jobs away from them when the fact of that matter is that most jobs that immigrants have in the United States are jobs that citizens will not do or cannot perform.

The anti-Muslim rhetoric and hate generated by the 2016 campaigns created fear in many Muslim populations around the world. Vulnerable populations and regions of the world that might be swayed to support terrorism are becoming convinced that the United States is in fact a hateful nation that holds prejudiced views against Muslims. If the message of the candidates and their delusional supporters is the only message that Muslims around the world receive from the United States, then the divide between Muslims and non-Muslims will remain very wide for a very long time.

The candidates are clearly not aware of the need for a counter and alternative narrative within the culture of the United States, just as it is needed in other places in the world. The perpetuation of anti-Muslim rhetoric by the candidates can be just as damaging as the anti-Western, anti-Christian, and anti-American narratives of the terrorists. The hateful rhetoric and narrative in the United States pushes Muslims away just as much as the rhetoric and narrative of the terrorists pulls Muslims closer to them. It all says so much about the lack of social responsibility of the candidates for president of the United States in 2016.

9.6 Conclusions

Online supporters of ISIL use various social media platforms to call for retaliation against the United States and other countries. ISIL advocates lone-wolf attacks and uses social media warfare tactics to inspire such actions. The FBI has long been concerned about the possibility of homegrown extremists becoming radicalized by information available on the Internet and though social media warfare. Important conclusions can be drawn from the material presented in this chapter:

- Law enforcement agencies clearly warn that it is important to consider the influence groups like ISIL have on individuals located in the United States who might be inspired to commit acts of violence.
- ISIS's use of social media is believed to resonate with vulnerable populations, particularly Muslim converts and susceptible alienated youth. However, radicalization of U.S. citizens and residents is not limited to any single social or demographic profile.
- There have been numerous cases where law enforcement officers have apprehended and arrested terrorist supporters in the United States.
- INTERPOL's Counter-Terrorism Fusion Centre is a global hub for intelligence on transnational terrorist networks shared by member countries worldwide.

■ Governments around the world are putting more and more pressure on social media providers to be proactive in keeping terrorist propaganda and content off social media platforms. The question at the core of the issue is, what is freedom of expression and free speech versus the incitement to terrorism?

■ In addition to security and legal and intelligence measures, United Nations Security Council members have stressed the need to provide a counter narrative to radicalization, addressing root causes and working with communities in that regard.

■ Countering the violent extremism that is driving terrorist threats is a multi-generational challenge and victories over violent extremist ideologies that underpin it are not found on the battlefield, but rather in mindsets.

■ Narratives against violent extremism, not just counter narratives that argue point-for-point with extremists, can be powerful incentives for positive action, especially alternative master narratives, and the message, the medium, and the messenger are all integral to effective messaging.

■ Many candidates in the U.S. presidential primaries and elections helped to perpetuate hate and the idea that most of people in the United States hate and mistrust Muslims. Candidates swayed anti-Muslim populations into supporting them by feeding into their fear, hatred, and mistrust of Muslims.

■ The hateful rhetoric and narrative in the United States pushes Muslims away just as much as the rhetoric and narrative of the terrorists pulls Muslims closer to them.

9.7 Agenda for Action

Countering the violent extremism that is driving terrorist threats is a multi-generational challenge, and victories over the violent extremist ideologies that underpin it are not found on the battlefield, but rather in mindsets. Narratives against violent extremism, not just counter narratives that argue point-for-point with extremists, can be powerful incentives for positive action, especially alternative master narratives, and the message, the medium, and the messenger are all integral to effective messaging. Action steps should include, but not be limited to, the following areas:

■ Provide further training for law enforcement agencies to monitor and investigate violent extremist social media content so that they can identify and conduct surveillance of radicalized individuals.

■ Continue the dialogue between governments, law enforcement agencies, and social media service and application providers on how to stem the flow of violent extremist messaging on social media.

■ Provide more funding for NGOs and private start-ups to develop and deliver alternative master narratives delivered by credible voices.

- Train and educate candidates for public office on positive alternative messages regarding the Muslim population and Muslim countries.
- Develop counter messaging to mitigate the impact of hate speech in countries around the world.
- Develop alternative positive messages for U.S. citizens and residents to replace the hate speech and prejudicial attitudes that currently dominate the culture.

9.8 Key Terms

Alternative master narratives are designed to replace violent extremist narratives by offering an entire cultural, political, or social philosophy that eliminates the appeal of the extremist narrative.

Alternative narratives are those narratives that are designed to replace radical or extremist narratives; they are intended to provide viable alternatives to radicalization.

Civil society leaders are individuals who hold government, business, or religious positions that enable them to influence their societies, communities, and individuals.

Community resilience is the social beliefs and norms of a local population that enables the community to resist radicalization and neutralizes the impact of the radical narrative.

Community-targeted approach is a set of methods and techniques designed to engage individuals or groups in the communities where they live to diminish the possibility of radicalization and identify radicalized individuals or groups.

Counter messaging is the process of matching radical extremist messages on a head-to-head basis in order mitigate the recruitment and radicalization to violent extremism.

Counter narrative to radicalization is a narrative that neutralizes or invalidates the narrative designed to radicalize individuals or groups.

Credible voices are those voices of trusted community leaders, religious leaders, and intellectuals who can provide a positive influence on a society or community.

Multi-generational challenge describes a long-term approach of assimilating and socializing individuals and groups.

Positive narratives are designed to negate violent extremist messages and provide powerful incentives for positive action.

Radicalization is the process indoctrinating previously non-violent individuals or groups into anti-social violent ideologies and actions.

Western-based extremists are citizens or residents of Western countries who engage or who want to engage in violence against the governments or residents of the countries in which they reside.

9.9 Seminar Discussion Topics

Discussion topics for graduate- or professional-level seminars:

- What experience have seminar participants had in situations where social media warfare tactics were used to recruit and indoctrinate?
- What experience have seminar participants had in situations where social media warfare tactics were used to counter terrorist recruiting efforts?
- What experience have seminar participants had in developing counter and alternative narratives against terrorism?
- What do seminar participants believe comprises a master narrative that can help counter terrorism?

9.10 Seminar Group Project

Divide participants into multiple groups with each group taking 10–15 minutes to develop a list of social media warfare narratives that can be used to counter the terrorist narrative. Upon completion, have groups exchange their lists of social media warfare tactics, with groups taking 10–15 minutes to develop master narratives that can be developed using the narratives. Meet as a group and discuss the offensive tactics selected by the groups and the defensive measures to counter the tactics that were developed by the groups.

References

1. Steinbach, Michael. 2015. ISIL in America: Domestic terror and radicalization. Statement before the House Judiciary Committee, Subcommittee on Crime, Terrorism, Homeland Security, and Investigations. Accessed September 17, 2016. https://www.fbi.gov/news/testimony/isil-in-america-domestic-terror-and-radicalization.
2. U.S. House of Representatives, Subcommittee on National Security, Committee on Oversight and Government Reform. 2015. Radicalization: Social media and the rise of terrorism. Accessed September 17, 2016. http://oversight.house.gov/wp-content/uploads/2016/04/10-28-15-Radicalization-Social-Media-and-the-Rise-of-Terrrorism.pdf.
3. U.S. Federal Bureau of Investigation. Social media. (no date provided). Accessed September 17, 2016. https://www.fbi.gov/about/leadership-and-structure/national-security-branch/social-media.
4. The White House, Office of the Press Secretary. 2016. Maintaining momentum in the fight against ISIL. Accessed September 17, 2016. https://www.whitehouse.gov/the-press-office/2016/01/15/fact-sheet-maintaining-momentum-fight-against-isil.
5. U.S. Department of Justice Office of Public Affairs. 2016. Pennsylvania man charged with additional ISIL-related offenses, defendant originally charged with providing material support to ISIL. Accessed September 17, 2016. https://www.justice.gov/opa/pr/pennsylvania-man-charged-additional-isil-related-offenses.

6. U.S. Department of Justice Office of Public Affairs. 2016. ISIL-linked hacker pleads guilty to providing material support. Accessed September 17, 2016. https://www.justice.gov/opa/pr/isil-linked-hacker-pleads-guilty-providing-material-support

7. Department of Justice, U.S. Attorney's Office, Eastern District of Virginia. 2016. Virginia man charged with attempting to provide material support to ISIL. Accessed September 17, 2016. https://www.justice.gov/usao-edva/pr/virginia-man-charged-attempting-provide-material-support-isil.

8. Department of Justice, U.S. Attorney's Office, Eastern District of Virginia. 2016. Former Army National Guard member arrested for attempting to provide material support to ISIL. Accessed September 17, 2016, from https://www.justice.gov/usao-edva/pr/former-army-national-guard-member-arrested-attempting-provide-material-support-isil.

9. U.S. Department of Justice Office of Public Affairs. 2016. North Carolina man charged with conspiring to provide material support to ISIL. Accessed September 17, 2016. https://www.justice.gov/opa/pr/north-carolina-man-charged-conspiring-provide-material-support-isil.

10. Department of Justice, U.S. Attorney's Office, Eastern District of Virginia. 2016. Fairfax man arrested for attempting to support ISIL. Accessed September 17, 2016. https://www.justice.gov/usao-edva/pr/fairfax-man-arrested-attempting-support-isil.

11. INTERPOL. Counter-Terrorism Fusion Centre. Accessed September 17, 2016. http://www.interpol.int/Crime-areas/Terrorism/Counter-Terrorism-Fusion-Centre.

12. Office of the President of the United States. 2011. Strategic Implementation Plan for Empowering Local Partners to Prevent Violent Extremism in the United States. Accessed September 17, 2016. https://www.whitehouse.gov/sites/default/files/sip-final.pdf.

13. United Nations Security Council. 2015. Action against threat of foreign terrorist fighters must be ramped up, Security Council urges in high-level meeting. Accessed September 17, 2016. http://www.un.org/press/en/2015/sc11912.doc.htm.

14. Organization for Security and Cooperation in Europe. 2014. Preventing terrorism and countering violent extremism and radicalization that lead to terrorism: A community-policing approach. Accessed September 17, 2016. http://www.osce.org/atu/111438?download=true.

15. U.S. Department of State, Bureau of Counterterrorism. Foreign terrorist organizations. (no date provided). Accessed September 17, 2016. http://www.state.gov/j/ct/rls/other/des/123085.htm.

16. U.S. Department of State. 2015. U.S. Department of State and USAID supported initiatives to counter violent extremism. Accessed September 18, 2016. http://www.state.gov/r/pa/prs/ps/2015/02/237647.htm.

17. U.S. Department of State Office of the Special Representative to Muslim Communities. *Voices.* Accessed September 18, 2016. www.state.gov/documents/organization/155334.pdf.

18. U.S. Department of State, Bureau of Counterterrorism and Countering Violent Extremism. 2016. Country reports on terrorism 2015. Accessed September 18, 2016. http://www.state.gov/j/ct/rls/crt/2015/257522.htm.

19. U.S. Department of State. 2016. A new center for global engagement. Accessed September 18, 2016. http://www.state.gov/r/pa/prs/ps/2016/01/251066.htm.

20. Global Center on Cooperative Security. Preventing and countering violent extremism in South and Central Asia: Key outcomes. Accessed September 18, 2016. www.state.gov/documents/organization/245705.pdf.

Chapter 10

Social Media Warfare for Celebrities and Famous People

Thousands of celebrities and famous people around the world adopt social media warfare tactics for self-promotion or to support charitable causes of their choice. Most of the time, celebrities use social media to promote positive narratives and support causes that are in the public interest. Sometimes, however, celebrities communicate negative narratives and provide an undesirable role model for social behavior. This chapter examines the positive work and outcomes of celebrity use of social media warfare tactics as well as the impact that negative messaging by celebrities can have on society.

10.1 Ways Celebrities Use Social Media Warfare Tactics

Celebrities all have one thing in common: they must self-promote and participate in promotional campaigns that maintain an image and name recognition. Such celebrities include film and television stars, musicians and musical performers, athletes, authors, and famous people. Social media warfare tactics have become a mainstay of these promotional efforts. Celebrities contribute to numerous *positive message promotional activities*.

In addition to self-promotion, many celebrities and famous people participate in supporting charitable causes or positive messaging to support constructive personal and social behavior. In these efforts, celebrities and famous people lend their fame and recognition to promote efforts to build a positive society. In turn, they receive recognition for doing good deeds and this promotes their positive image.

Then, there are those celebrities and famous people who self-promote for profit, name recognition, or just plain, old narcissism, and they do so in a manner that disregards social decorum and positive messaging. Unfortunately, these boisterous socially irresponsible few often have large numbers of followers that consume and are motivated by negative messaging and anti-social behavior.

There have also been instances of scam artists and dishonest business people misappropriating the name or image of celebrities and famous people to promote products, sell unreliable or unproven products or nonexistent services. Such campaigns often come and go quickly and are difficult to prevent. Other campaigns may use celebrity name variations or imply that a deceased person had always been a fan and supporter of a product. The following sections examine the various uses and outcomes of social media warfare tactics by celebrities and famous people.

10.2 Non-Profit Promotional Activities of Celebrities and Famous People

In addition to self-promotion, many celebrities and famous people participate in supporting charitable causes or positive messaging to support constructive personal and social behavior. They lend their fame and recognition to promote efforts to build a positive society. In turn, they are recognized for doing good deeds and work and that helps promote their positive image.

One of the most outstanding examples of celebrity and positive messaging for a charitable organization is the National Celebrity Cabinet of the American Red Cross. The talented individuals on the Red Cross National Celebrity Cabinet donate their time, skills, passion, and energy to help the Red Cross highlight important initiatives and responses. Cabinet members include Amy Grant, Dr. Phil McGraw, Heidi Klum, Jane Seymour, Peyton Manning, and dozens more. All these celebrities have a strong social media presence, as does the American Red Cross [1].

Celebrities also do considerable work for U.S. diplomacy. The United States generally carries out its foreign policy through the work of the State Department and its government-appointed officers, but *citizen diplomacy* is also an important part of diplomacy, and when high-profile celebrities contribute to those efforts, they can have a far-reaching impact.

Celebrities are commissioned by the State Department to be special envoys for specific causes. An example of this is *sports diplomacy*, which takes advantage of a universal interest in sports to bridge the gap between the United States and other countries. These programs help the State Department appoint different sports celebrities to reach out to the world community. In 2007, Cal Ripken Jr., a baseball player, was named as the second Special Sports Envoy.

Celebrity diplomats come from other backgrounds than sports. American Music Abroad is another State Department program that brings American musicians of diverse styles to a worldwide audience. The State Department invites actors, artists, poets, and chefs, among others to serve as diplomats. U.S. embassies often host programs, performances, or workshops put on by these individuals. This serves to break down cultural barriers and build positive narratives with foreign countries. One area that has had a significant impact is *culinary diplomacy*.

Celebrities who are not officially appointed by the State Department can still act as diplomats if their work advances U.S. interests. George Clooney's efforts to bring awareness to the crisis in Darfur have stirred international support. The U.S. embassy in Rome inspired Lady Gaga to advance her advocacy of LGBT rights by performing at EuroPride Rome in 2011. These celebrities, along with many others, work in conjunction with the State Department's mission to advance freedom, democracy, and human rights.

Five-time World Skating Champion Michelle Kwan talked to students during a visit to the Dandelion School for Children of Migrants in Beijing, China. Kwan was appointed as an American Public Diplomacy Envoy and visited China to promote cross-cultural dialogue with youths. Celebrity diplomacy covers many areas, including culinary diplomacy, American music abroad, and American poetry [2].

Another major endeavor involving celebrities and their social media influence was the launch of the Let Girls Learn initiative. There are 62 million girls around the world who are not in school and millions more are fighting to stay there. In a show of support for girls' education and empowerment around the world, nearly 30 artists and athletes, as well as a host of global non-profits and businesses, joined with the U.S. federal government to launch Let Girls Learn. This effort aims to elevate a conversation about the need to support all girls in their pursuit of a quality education. Brought together by heinous acts of violence and intimidation against girls in different parts of the world, celebrities gathered in New York and Los Angeles to lend their voices to a common message: The right to education is universal and unambiguous. The U.S. Agency for International Development (USAID) is coordinating "Let Girls Learn." USAID has an impressive arsenal of content and social media outlets, including "extreme possibilities (the USAID storytelling hub), the USAID *Impact* blog, Medium, Exposure, Storify, Vimeo, YouTube, Facebook, Twitter, Instagram, Pinterest, and LinkedIn [3].

Numerous celebrities support efforts to inform the public about health issues. One example is Katie Couric's televised colon cancer awareness campaign that is supported by social media. There is a series of national health observances—special days, weeks, or months—dedicated to raising awareness about important health topics. The U.S. Department of Health and Human Services supports a website

Table 10.1   National Health Observances with Toolkit Support

Month	Observances
January	Cervical Health Awareness Month
February	American Heart Month Teen Dating Violence Awareness Month
March	Colorectal Cancer Awareness Month
April	Alcohol Awareness Month
May	National Physical Fitness and Sports Month Melanoma/Skin Cancer Detection and Prevention Month
June	National Safety Month June 27 National HIV Testing Day
August	National Immunization Awareness Month
September	National Childhood Obesity Awareness Month Fruits and Veggies—More Matters Month
October	National Breast Cancer Awareness Month
November	American Diabetes Month
World AIDS Day	World AIDS Day

and social media efforts that provide information on more than 200 national health observances with up-to-date information and outreach materials on national health observances (https://healthfinder.gov/NHO/). Healthfinder also provides toolkits for individuals or organizations that want to get involved in a specific observance. The toolkit includes a sample announcement, sample Tweets, e-cards, a Web badge, and resources that can be shared. Table 10.1 lists the observances held during each month of the year [4].

10.3 Positive Message Promotional Activities of Celebrities and Famous People

Celebrities all have one thing in common, they must self-promote and participate in promotional campaigns that maintain an image and name recognition. Film, television, music, and literary celebrities generally self-promote or participate in promotional campaigns when a new film, recording, or written work is going to be released and during the initial release period for the product.

It is standard practice at this point that any new release will have a space on producers' or celebrities' websites; a social media component that allows fans to

Table 10.2   Social Media Warfare Tactics for Celebrity Promotion

Influence: Convincing potential purchasers of the quality of a product or performance
Nullify opponents: Preemptively discrediting critics by creating an image of quality of a product or performance
Persuasion of non-aligned entities: Convincing non-potential purchasers of the quality of a product or performance to sway them into buying or not objecting to a product or performance
Recruitment and indoctrination: Drawing non-fans or non-followers to join the ranks of supporters and fans and getting them to espouse the same doctrine as existing fans
Reinforcing alliance partners: Showing support for individuals and organizations that have assisted with the product or performance

share on their preferred social media application; and a variety of supporting material, including behind the scenes photos, commentaries, and video clips. Social media warfare tactics are a mainstay of these promotional efforts. The primary tactics used during promotional efforts include influence, nullify opponents, persuasion, recruitment, and reinforcement of alliance partners. The tactics are shown in Table 10.2.

The interest of fans and followers has prompted the creation of advertising and promotion efforts that move beyond the standard, and social media is enabling producers to leverage a variety of alternative promotional opportunities. A relatively recent movie release, *The Martian*, was able to leverage support from NASA with interesting stories about the technology that appears in the movie. NASA is already working with or developing several of those technologies including habitat, plant farms, water recovery, oxygen generation, the Mars spacesuit, the rover, ion propulsion, solar panels, and more. This technology is discussed and showcased on a NASA website with full reference to the movie *The Martian*. The NASA website is fully equipped with a set of social media sharing icons [5].

Celebrities, especially those in film and television, have long been instruments of product promotion whether it was automobiles, clothes, or movie-themed fast-food toys. All of that is commonplace, but it has become easier to accomplish with social media cross-promotions. Celebrities have portrayed characters of all types including those with illnesses or diseases or those trying to treat and care for those with diseases. This has helped viewers expand their knowledge and concern about those diseases.

The U.S. Centers for Disease Control (CDC) has an Entertainment Education Program that provides expert consultation, education, and resources for writers and producers who develop scripts with health storylines and information. This is important because 88% of Americans learn about health issues from television. The CDC recognizes that prime time and daytime television programming are great outlets for health messages but is concerned about the accuracy of those messages. The CDC works in partnership with Hollywood, Health and Society (HH&S) at the University of Southern California's Norman Lear Center to share public health information with storyline creators [6]. The CDC provides a variety of resources to writers and producers:

- Tip sheets: Contain easy-to-use, credible information on pressing health issues; they include information such as who's at risk, typical symptoms, prevention messages, and case examples.
- HH&S staff hold meetings for show creators and network officials to inform them of the full range of services available, including consultations and visits from CDC experts.
- Expert panel discussions are also planned in coordination with organizations like the Writers Guild of America and the Robert Wood Johnson Foundation to examine the implications of dramatizing critical health issues.

There have been many CDC Entertainment Education Program outreach successes over the years. These are some of the public health issues covered in television programs:

- Traumatic brain injury and the Lifetime Movie Network
- HIV/AIDS and MTV during World AIDS Day
- HIV/AIDS and Tyler Perry Studio's comedy, *Meet the Browns*
- Asperger's syndrome and NBC-TV's *Parenthood*
- Cancer and the CW's *90210*
- CDC advised big-budget movies, such as the 2011 film *Contagion* and the 2010 Warner Brother's film *I Am Legend*

The Sentinel Awards for Health are presented annually by HH&S and CDC. The awards were established in 2000 to recognize television storylines that promote health topics and audience awareness. CDC evaluates nominees during the first round of selection based on their scientific accuracy and health message. In the second round, HH&S select finalists based on their entertainment value. Categories include prime time drama and comedy, daytime drama, and Spanish-language telenovela.

Over a 4-year period, 700 HH&S-assisted programs were aired. Fourteen finalists were chosen from almost 80 entries for the 2016 Sentinel Awards, showcasing a diverse range of topics including healthcare, sexual abuse, Ebola and climate change. Storylines are recognized in these categories: drama, comedy, serial drama, TV movie, climate change, reality, talk show, documentary, children's programming, and Spanish language [7]. HH&S has worked with many popular shows, including *All My Children*, *Body of Proof*, *Boston Legal*, *General Hospital*, *Grey's Anatomy*, *CSI*, *Elementary*, *60 Minutes*, and *Law and Order* [8].

10.4 Celebrities and Famous People who Generate Negative Messaging

There are some celebrities who self-promote for profit and name recognition and do so in a manner that disregards social decorum and positive messaging. In some cases, celebrities are widely known as negative role models and for creating negative messaging through anti-social and sometimes illegal activities. Unfortunately, these boisterous, socially irresponsible few often have large followings that consume and are motivated by negative messaging and anti-social behavior. There are more teens on Instagram than any other social media platform and many follow their favorite actors, singers, and athletes. With celebrities racking up millions of followers, it's unfortunate that some of them use their reach and power to promote the use of alcohol and drugs.

According to the National Institute on Drug Abuse for Teens (NIDA for Teens), Wiz Khalifa, Diplo, Rihanna, and Nicki Minaj have posted hundreds of pictures with or of drugs and alcohol. Miley Cyrus posted a photo of herself wearing a t-shirt stating "I'm In Love With The Coco" that by many accounts is a reference to an O.T. Genasis song about cocaine, "CoCo". More than 7% of Snoop Dogg's Instagram photos involve drugs or alcohol.

Beyond pictures of people doing drugs, many drug dealers are turning to Instagram to advertise their products, according to NIDA for Teens. They post piles of pills and baggies full of weed with the same artistic filters applied to any other pictures. Though Instagram's community rules prohibit sharing images that break the law, new drug-related hashtags and new user accounts have been known to pop up frequently [9].

Justin Bieber was arrested in January 2014 on drinking under the influence (DUI) charges. Based on his talent, success, and reach, he could have been a terrific role model for teens. Instead, he seems to have chosen a path to self-destruction. He was arrested while street racing in a Lamborghini. The star admitted to police in Florida that he had been drinking, smoking marijuana, and taking prescription drugs all at the same time. Mixing drugs and alcohol while street racing sends a very negative message especially when people could have been killed, including Bieber himself [10].

NIDA for Teens keeps up-to-date on drug use trends and social media and cultural trends that may impact drug abuse. At the end of 2012, NIDA for Teens noticed a huge spike in the number of searches on the NIDA for Teens website for information on Molly, a club drug made from MDMA (short for 3,4-methylene-dioxymethamphetamine), which is most commonly known as Ecstasy or Molly, the pure form of MDMA.

Molly is abused at clubs and concerts and is referred to in electronic music. Rap and hip hop are mentioning the drug more often. In 2012, several major artists released songs that referenced Molly:

- Kanye West in "Mercy": "Something about Mary, she gone off that Molly/ now the whole party is melted like Dalí."
- Trinidad James in "All Gold Everything:" "Popped a Molly and now I'm sweating, woo!"
- Rihanna in "Diamonds:" "Palms rise to the universe, as we moonshine and Molly, feel the warmth, we'll never die, we're like diamonds in the sky."

While many of these songs focus on the euphoria Molly can cause, they leave out the dangers it poses to the brain and body. Molly may be a hot topic in pop culture, but most teens steered clear of the drug. In 2012, NIDA's Teens Monitoring the Future survey found that only 7.2% of 12th graders had used Ecstasy in their lifetime, a 4.5% decrease from 2011 [11].

NIDA for Teens uses social media warfare methods to expose the negative side of drug use and to influence people by posting real-life stories about drug abuse and the impact of drug abuse. Many of these posts are designed to teach lessons about drug abuse:

- "Glee" Cast Members Speak Out about Drug Abuse
- "Amy" and "Kurt Cobain: Montage of Heck"—Up Close and Very Personal
- Amy Winehouse: Death by Misadventure
- Celebs and Drugs: A Cycle of Arrests and Rehab
- Demi Lovato's Road to Recovery
- Dopers' Downfall May Be Cycling's Salvation—Tour de France 2015: End of an Era
- Elton John Reflects on Drug Addiction
- Former "Jersey Shore" Star in Recovery from Painkiller Addiction
- How Does Pro Football Tackle Players' Drug Use?
- In Memoriam: Lost to Addiction and Mental Illness
- Lindsay Lohan on Why Recovery Can Be So Hard
- Macklemore Talks Drug Abuse, Addiction, and Recovery
- Philip Seymour Hoffman's Death and the Terrible Toll of Addiction
- Real Life: The Choices We Make
- Whitney Houston: Cocaine and Heart Disease
- Wired to Win? Drug Testing Comes to Sports

10.5 Misleading Endorsements Using Celebrity Names and Images

There have been instances of scam artists and dishonest business people misappropriating the name or image of celebrities and famous people to promote products and sell unreliable products or nonexistent services. Such campaigns often come and go quickly and are difficult to prevent. Other campaigns may use celebrity name variations or imply that a deceased person was a fan and supporter of a product.

It is reported that Babe Ruth was the first celebrity to make lots of money from product endorsements [12]. In fact, a search of Babe Ruth items on eBay shows him in numerous magazine ads for liquor, cigarettes, watches, beverages, baseball gloves, candies, and underwear. He died in 1948 and his image and name have been used in dozens of advertising campaigns since then, the legitimacy of all these campaigns has not been confirmed and his lifetime and after-death endorsement earnings are unknown.

The U.S. Federal Trade Commission (FTC) has received complaints and opened investigations into the false advertising of unproven products marketed by making false claims about their effectiveness. Some of these cases involved e-mail messages that appear to come from family members, friends, or other contacts. The e-mails had links to fake news sites that used celebrity names to promote products and make them appear legitimate [13].

Some advertising campaigns that have used celebrity endorsers have been found to be misleading. The Consumer Financial Protection Bureau (CFPB) conducted a focus group study on reverse mortgage advertisements that found many participants were left with misimpressions about the product. After viewing the ads, consumers were confused about reverse mortgages being loans, and they were left with the false impression that they are a government benefit or that they would ensure customers could stay in their homes for the rest of their lives. Many ads featured celebrity spokespeople discussing the benefits of reverse mortgages without mentioning the risks. Most consumers recalled TV ads that featured spokespeople portrayed as reliable and trustworthy. One consumer in one focus group said, "When it's a former Congressman endorsing it, it makes it sound like a good idea" [14].

A study in the July 2016 publication *Pediatrics* examined the use of music celebrities by the food industry to endorse sugary soft drinks and nutrient-poor foods through multi-million-dollar campaigns. The study, "Popular Music Celebrity Endorsements in Food and Non-Alcoholic Beverage Marketing," found 65 entertainers associated with the 2013 and 2014 Billboard Hot 100 chart that had one or more food and beverage endorsements between 2000 and 2014. The study also looked at the nutritional value of endorsed products and found 81% were unhealthy, according to the Nutrient Profile Index. No celebrities endorsed fruits, vegetables, or whole grains. Of the non-alcoholic beverage endorsements, 71% were for sugar-sweetened beverages, with only three endorsements for water or water-related products, such as a filter [15].

Endorsements are an important tool for advertisers and they can be persuasive to consumers. Several celebrity endorsers have run into unexpected difficulties as the products they were endorse became known for defects, associated with companies that are not in compliance with truth-in-advertising laws, or with companies found to be exploiting child labor in other countries.

The FTC publication "Concerning the Use of Endorsements and Testimonials in Advertising" provides guidelines designed to help advertisers of all types, including television, print, radio, blogs, word-of-mouth marketing, and social media, to make sure that they meet guideline standards. For example, advertisers are advised that using unrepresentative testimonials may be misleading if they are not accompanied by information describing what consumers can generally expect from use of the product or service. In addition, the Endorsement Guides let endorsers know "that they shouldn't talk about their experience with a product if they haven't tried it, or make claims about a product that would require proof they don't have." The Endorsement Guides also state that if there is a connection between the endorser and the marketer of a product that would affect how people evaluate the endorsement, it should be disclosed. The Endorsement Guides are not regulations, so there are no civil penalties associated with them. But if advertisers don't follow the guides, the FTC may decide to investigate whether the practices are unfair or deceptive under the FTC Act [16]. The following is a list of headlines from a September 19, 2016 Web search of FTC cases that dealt with deceptive advertising:

- Warner Brothers Settles FTC Charges It Failed to Adequately Disclose It Paid Online Influencers to Post Gameplay Videos (July 2016)
- Operators of Phony Doctor Certification Program and Misleading Health and Lifestyle Websites Settle FTC Charges (June 2016)
- FTC Approves Final Order Prohibiting Machinima, Inc. from Misrepresenting that Paid Endorsers in Influencer Campaigns are Independent Reviewers (March 2016)
- FTC Sues Marketers Who Used Gag Clauses, Monetary Threats, and Lawsuits to Stop Negative Consumer Reviews for Unproven Weight-Loss Products (September 2015)
- Xbox One Promoter Settles FTC Charges That It Deceived Consumers with Endorsement Videos Posted by Paid Influencers (September 2015)
- FTC Halts Deceptive Marketing of Bogus Weight-Loss Products (May 2015)
- FTC Approves Final Order Barring AmeriFreight from Deceptively Touting Online Consumer Reviews and Failing to Disclose Incentives It Provided to Reviewers (April 2015)
- FTC Stops Automobile Shipment Broker from Misrepresenting Online Reviews (February 2015)

- Sony Computer Entertainment America to Provide Consumer Refunds to Settle FTC Charges Over Misleading Ads for PlayStation Vita Gaming Console (November 2014)
- Public Relations Firm to Settle FTC Charges That It Advertised Clients' Gaming Apps through Misleading Online Endorsements (August 2010)

10.6 When Endorsement Deals Fall Apart

Athletes get great endorsement contracts that can generate millions of dollars over their lifetime. The latest addition to the endorsement arena is celebrity chefs. They author cookbooks, get television shows, open restaurants, and use social media to drive their empires. Then there are the spokespeople for various businesses, like Jared Fogle for Subway.

Some athletes exhibit bad behavior like physically abusing their spouse, gambling, dog fighting, cheating on their spouse repeatedly, or taking performance enhancing drugs. Some have even killed. There could be racist incidents in someone's past that comes back to haunt. A worst-case scenario may be getting caught trying to lure teenage girls into meetings using a social media account.

All these examples have happened and tens of millions of dollars in endorsement contracts have disappeared quickly. Sponsoring companies do not like scandal and they do not like their brands tarnished by a relationship with endorsers that generate bad press and social media warfare storms. Sponsors cut ties quickly, they run far, and they run fast.

10.7 Conclusion

When celebrities and famous people around the world use or support social media warfare tactics to support charitable organizations and causes, they can make major positive contributions to society. Most of the time celebrities use social media to promote positive narratives and support causes that are in the public interest. There are times, however, when celebrities communicate negative narratives and provide an undesirable role model for social behavior. Important conclusions can be drawn from the material presented in this chapter:

- Social media warfare tactics have become a mainstay of celebrity promotional efforts.
- Celebrities and famous people participate in supporting charitable causes or positive messaging to support constructive personal and social behavior.
- There have been instances of scam artists and dishonest business people misappropriating the name or image of celebrities to promote products and sell unreliable or unproven products or nonexistent services.

- One of the most outstanding examples of celebrity and positive messaging for a charitable organization is the National Celebrity Cabinet of the American Red Cross.
- Celebrities have done considerable work for U.S. diplomacy. Celebrities can be commissioned by the State Department to be special envoys for specific causes. One such example is sports diplomacy.
- The CDC works in partnership with Hollywood, Health & Society (HH&S) at the University of Southern California's Norman Lear Center to share public health information with storyline creators and provides a variety of resources to writers and producers.
- Some celebrities self-promote in a manner that disregards social decorum and positive messaging and are widely considered negative role models and promoters of negative messaging based on their anti-social and sometimes illegal activities.
- The National Institute on Drug Abuse for Teens uses social media warfare methods to expose the negative side of drug use and to influence people by posting real-life stories about drug abuse and the impact of drug abuse.
- Some advertising campaigns using celebrity endorsers were determined to be misleading by the Consumer Financial Protection Bureau (CFPB).
- Sponsoring companies do not like scandal and they do not like their brands tarnished by having a relationship with endorsers that generate bad press and social media warfare storms.

10.8 Agenda for Action

Most of the time, celebrities use social media to promote positive narratives and support causes that are in the public interest. Sometimes, however, celebrities communicate negative narratives and providing an undesirable role model for social behavior. Action steps should include, but not be limited to, the following areas:

- Establish and support research efforts addressing negative messaging by celebrities in social media.
- Support more efforts to generate alternative and counter messaging against negative messages generated by celebrities, including those of violence, drug abuse, and alcohol abuse.
- Celebrities should carefully examine the products they are endorsing or promoting regarding their negative impact on health and social behavior.
- Celebrities should publicly stand up against negative messaging in social media by other celebrities as well as the businesses that sponsor celebrity endorsements that promote negative social behavior.

10.9 Key Terms

Citizen diplomacy is what is performed by non-professional diplomats to promote specific cultural or political agendas on behalf of their country.

Culinary diplomacy is the process of using culinary celebrities and a culinary context and agenda to promote improved relations and cultural exchanges between nations.

Positive message promotional activities are those that promote positive social behavior and counter negative messaging.

Sports diplomacy is the process of using sport celebrities and a sport context and agenda to promote improved relations and cultural exchanges between nations.

10.10 Seminar Discussion Topics

Discussion topics for graduate- or professional-level seminars:

- What experience have seminar participants had in situations where celebrities or famous people have generated and promoted positive messaging using social media warfare strategies or tactics?
- What experience have seminar participants had in situations where celebrities or famous people have generated and promoted negative messaging using social media warfare strategies or tactics?
- What experience have seminar participants had in situations where celebrities or famous people have worked on global issues or diplomacy using social media warfare strategies or tactics?

10.11 Seminar Group Project

Divide participants into multiple groups with each group taking 10–15 minutes to develop a list of negative social media messages. Upon completion, have groups exchange their lists, with groups taking 10–15 minutes to develop defensive measures to effectively counter the negative social media messaging. Meet as a group and discuss the negative messaging identified by the groups and the tactics developed to counter the negative messaging.

References

1. American Red Cross. National Celebrity Cabinet members. Accessed September 20, 2016. http://www.redcross.org/supporters/celebrities/celebrity-cabinet-members.

2. The U.S. Department of State. How do celebrities become diplomats? Accessed September 20, 2016. http://diplomacy.state.gov/discoverdiplomacy/diplomacy101/people/202511.htm.
3. U.S. Agency for International Development (USAID). 2014. Broad coalition of celebrities, athletes, non-profits join with USAID to Let Girls Learn. Accessed September 21, 2016. https://www.usaid.gov/news-information/press-releases/june-20-2014-broad-coalition-celebrities-athletes-non-profits-join-usaid-let-girls-learn.
4. U.S. Department of Health and Human Services. National health observances. Accessed September 21, 2016. https://healthfinder.gov/NHO/default.aspx.
5. NASA. 2015. Nine real NASA technologies in 'The Martian'. Accessed September 21, 2016. https://www.nasa.gov/feature/nine-real-nasa-technologies-in-the-martian.
6. U.S. Centers for Disease Control. 2015. Entertainment education. Accessed September 21, 2016. http://www.cdc.gov/healthcommunication/ToolsTemplates/EntertainmentEd/index.html.
7. Hollywood, Health and Society. 2016 Sentinel Awards. Accessed September 21, 2016. https://hollywoodhealthandsociety.org/events/2016-sentinel-awards.
8. Hollywood, Health and Society. Shows we've worked with. Accessed September 21, 2016. https://hollywoodhealthandsociety.org/about-us/shows-weve-worked.
9. National Institute on Drug Abuse for Teens. 2015. InstaBuzzed: Celebrities, drugs, and social media. *Drugs and Health* (blog). Accessed September 20, 2016. https://teens.drugabuse.gov/blog/post/instabuzzed-celebrities-drugs-and-social-media.
10. National Institute on Drug Abuse for Teens. 2014. Justin Bieber: A warning to all teens. *Drugs and Health* (blog). Accessed September 20, 2016 from https://teens.drugabuse.gov/blog/post/justin-bieber-warning-all-teens.
11. National Institute on Drug Abuse for Teens. 2013. Rap music and Molly. *Drugs and Health* (blog). Accessed September 20, 2016. https://teens.drugabuse.gov/blog/post/rap-music-and-molly.
12. Nodjimbadem, Katie. 2016. Babe Ruth hit a home run with celebrity product endorsements. *Smithsonian.com*. Accessed September 20, 2016. http://www.smithsonianmag.com/smithsonian-institution/how-babe-ruth-hit-home-run-celebrity-product-endorsements-180960038/.
13. U.S. Federal Trade Commission. 2016. FTC charges marketers used massive spam campaign to pitch bogus weight-loss products. Accessed September 21, 2016. https://www.ftc.gov/news-events/press-releases/2016/06/ftc-charges-marketers-used-massive-spam-campaign-pitch-bogus.
14. U.S. Consumer Financial Protection Bureau. 2015. CFPB study finds reverse mortgage advertisements can create false impressions. Accessed September 21, 2016. http://www.consumerfinance.gov/about-us/newsroom/cfpb-study-finds-reverse-mortgage-advertisements-can-create-false-impressions/.
15. American Academy of Pediatrics. 2016. Music celebrities popular among teens are used to promote unhealthy foods. Press Release. Accessed September 21, 2016. https://www.aap.org/en-us/about-the-aap/aap-press-room/pages/Music-Celebrities-Popular-Among-Teens-Are-Used-to-Promote-Unhealthy-Foods.aspx.
16. U.S. Federal Trade Commission. Advertisement endorsements. Accessed September 21, 2016. https://www.ftc.gov/news-events/media-resources/truth-advertising/advertisement-endorsements.

Chapter 11

Child Victims in Social Media Warfare

There are many ways individuals or groups can become victims of social media warfare. The Islamic State of Iraq and the Levant (ISIL) example discussed in other chapters is certainly an extreme example of what can be done to people using social media warfare. Far removed from that conflict is an ongoing onslaught of attacks against children. These can take the form of cyberbullying, slander and exposure campaigns, revenge actions, sexual harassment, exploitation, sextortion, and child pornography. This chapter examines some of the ways children are harmed by other individuals who used these adverse social media warfare tactics against them.

11.1 Cyberbullying: The New Social Media Menace to Children

Bullying is unwanted, aggressive behavior generally found among school-aged children that involves a real or perceived power imbalance. The behavior is repeated, or has the potential to be repeated, over time. Both kids who are bullied and who bully others may have serious, lasting problems. Approximately 20% of schoolchildren report they are bullied each year.

To be considered bullying, the behavior must be aggressive and include an imbalance of power and repetition. Kids who bully use power such as physical strength, access to embarrassing information, or popularity to control or harm others. Power imbalances can change over time and in different situations, even if they involve the same people. Repetitive bullying behaviors happen more than once or have the potential to happen more than once. Bullying includes actions such as making threats, spreading rumors, attacking someone physically or verbally, and excluding someone from a group on purpose.

There are several types of bullying. Verbal bullying is saying or writing mean things and includes teasing, name-calling, inappropriate sexual comments, taunting, or threatening to cause harm. Social bullying, sometimes referred to as relational bullying, involves hurting someone's reputation or relationships. Social bullying can include leaving someone out on purpose, telling other children not to be friends with someone, spreading rumors about someone, and embarrassing someone in public. Physical bullying involves hurting a person's body or possessions and can include hitting/kicking/pinching, spitting, tripping/pushing, taking or breaking someone's things, or making mean or rude hand gestures [1].

Cyberbullying is bullying that takes place using electronic technology. Electronic technology includes devices and equipment such as cell phones, computers, and tablets as well as communication tools including social media sites, text messages, chat, and websites. Examples of cyberbullying include mean text messages or e-mails, rumors sent by e-mail or posted on social networking sites, and embarrassing pictures, videos, websites, or fake profiles.

The 2013–2014 School Crime Supplement (National Center for Education Statistics and Bureau of Justice Statistics) indicates that 7% of students in Grades 6–12 experienced cyberbullying. *The 2013 Youth Risk Behavior Surveillance Survey* finds that 15% of high school students (Grades 9–12) were electronically bullied in the past year.

Kids who are being cyberbullied are often bullied in person as well. Additionally, kids who are cyberbullied have a harder time getting away from the behavior. Cyberbullying can happen 24 hours a day, 7 days a week, and reach a kid even when he or she is alone. It can happen anytime of the day or night. Cyberbullying messages and images can be posted anonymously and distributed quickly to a very wide audience. It can be difficult and sometimes impossible to trace the source. Deleting inappropriate or harassing messages, texts, and pictures is extremely difficult after they have been posted or sent.

Sextortion is a type of online sexual exploitation in which individuals coerce victims into providing sexually explicit images or videos of themselves, often in compliance with offenders' threats to post the images publicly or send the images to victims' friends and family. The Federal Bureau of Investigation (FBI) has seen a significant increase in sextortion activity against children who use the Internet, typically ages 10–17, but any age child can become a victim of sextortion.

Social media can be used for positive activities, like connecting kids with friends and family, helping students with school, and for entertainment. But these tools can also be used to hurt other people. Whether done in person or through technology, the effects of bullying are similar. Some of the effects of cyberbullying are shown in Table 11.1 [2].

Table 11.1   Effects of Cyberbullying

It has been observed that kids who are cyberbullied are more likely to
- Use alcohol and drugs
- Skip school
- Experience in-person bullying
- Be unwilling to attend school
- Receive poor grades
- Have lower self-esteem
- Have more health problems

11.2 Guidance on Responding to Cyberbullying against Children

The U.S. Department of Health and Human Services (HHS) provides guidance for parents and children on how to prevent cyberbullying. The HHS urges parents to talk with their children about cyberbullying and other online issues on a regular basis and to stay informed about the websites children visit and their other online activities.

Installing *parental control software* or monitoring programs are one option for monitoring a child's online behavior, but parents cannot rely solely on these tools. Parents should

- Have a sense of what their children do online and in texts.
- Learn about the sites they like.
- Try out the devices they use.
- Ask for their passwords, but tell them it will only use them in case of emergency.
- Ask a friend to, or follow kids on social media sites or ask another trusted adult to do so.
- Encourage children to immediately report if they, or someone they know, is being cyberbullied. Explain that their computers and cell phones will not be taken away if they confide in parents about a problem they are having.
- Establish rules about appropriate use of computers, cell phones, and other technology.
- Provide guidance to children about what they post or say online.
- Tell them not to share anything that could hurt or embarrass themselves or others.
- Teach children how to keep their passwords safe and not share them with friends [3].

It is important that parents document and report instances of cyberbullying. Parents should immediately take the following steps:

- Do not respond to and do not forward cyberbullying messages.
- Keep evidence of cyberbullying. Record the dates, times, and descriptions of instances when cyberbullying has occurred.
- Save and print screenshots, e-mails, and text messages. Use this evidence to report cyberbullying to web and cell phone service providers.
- Block the person who is cyberbullying.

Cyberbullying often violates the terms of service established by social media sites and Internet service providers. Parents should review the terms of service and conditions or rights and responsibilities sections of the social media applications or websites their children use. The terms of service generally describe content or activities that are or are not appropriate and how to block users and change settings to control who can contact a child or family.

Cyberbullying activities considered to be a crime and that should be reported to law enforcement include threats of violence, child pornography or sending sexually explicit messages or photos, taking a photo or video of someone in a place where he or she would expect privacy, and stalking and hate crimes.

Cyberbullying can also create a disruptive environment at school and is often related to in-person bullying. The school can use the information to help inform prevention and response strategies. In many states, schools are required to address cyberbullying in their anti-bullying policy. Some state laws also cover off-campus behavior that creates a hostile school environment [4].

11.3 Threat of Online Predators to Children

Every year, thousands of children become victims of crime whether through kidnappings, violent attacks, sexual abuse, or online predators that uses social media warfare tactics to confuse and deceive them. The mission of the FBI's Violent Crimes Against Children program (VCAC) is threefold:

- To decrease the vulnerability of children to sexual exploitation
- To develop a nationwide capacity to provide a rapid, effective, and measured investigative response to crimes against children
- To enhance the capabilities of state and local law enforcement investigators through programs, investigative assistance, and task force operations

The VCAC program provides a rapid, proactive, and comprehensive capacity to counter all threats of abuse and exploitation of children when those crimes fall under FBI jurisdiction. The FBI employs multi-disciplinary and multi-agency teams to investigate and prosecute crimes that cross legal, geographical, and jurisdictional boundaries. This facilitates the identification and rescue of child victims and reduces the vulnerability of children to in-person and online sexual exploitation and abuse and reduces the negative impact of domestic and international parental rights disputes. Investigative priorities include

- Child abductions including non-ransom child abductions and domestic parental kidnapping
- Child sexual exploitation enterprises that operate domestic child prostitution and the online networks and enterprises that make them possible
- Contact offenses against children including domestic travel with intent to engage in illegal sexual activity with children
- Child sex tourism (international travel to engage in sexual activity with children)
- Production of *child pornography*
- Mass distribution of child pornography; possession of child pornography
- International parental kidnapping
- Other crimes against children within the FBI's jurisdiction are investigated in accordance with available resources

These efforts solidified during investigations into the disappearance of a juvenile in May 1993, when FBI special agents from the Baltimore field office and detectives from the Prince George's County Maryland Police Department identified two suspects who had sexually exploited numerous juveniles over a 25-year period. The investigation into these activities determined that adults were routinely using computers to transmit sexually explicit images to minors and, in some instances, to lure minors into engaging in illicit sexual activity.

Further investigation and discussions with experts, both within the FBI and in the private sector, revealed that the use of computer telecommunications was rapidly becoming one of the most prevalent techniques by which some sex offenders shared pornographic images of minors and identified and recruited children into sexually illicit relationships. In 1995, based on information developed during this investigation, the Innocent Images National Initiative, which was initially part of the FBI Cyber Division, was created to address the illicit activities conducted by users of commercial and private online services and the Internet.

In 2000, the Crimes Against Children program was established by the FBI and it was under this umbrella program that other programs such as the Innocence Lost National Initiative and Child Abduction Rapid Deployment teams were implemented to provide additional resources and response tools to combat the ever-present problems of child prostitution, child abduction, and child sex tourism.

In October 2012, the Crimes Against Children program and the Innocent Images National Initiative merged to form the VCAC program in the Criminal Investigative Division. The program continues the efforts of previous programs by providing centralized coordination and analysis of case information that is national and international in scope. This requires close cooperation not only among FBI field offices and legal attachés but also with state, local, and international governments.

Many *child sexual exploitation* investigations are conducted undercover by FBI field offices by Child Exploitation Task Forces (CETFs), which combine the resources of the FBI with those of other federal, state, and local law enforcement agencies. Many of these investigations are worked in coordination with Internet Crimes Against Children (ICAC) Task Forces.

Unfortunately chat rooms and other social networking and online media forums offer the advantage of immediate communication around the world, providing pedophiles with an anonymous means of identifying and recruiting child victims into sexually illicit relationships. Thus, the ICAC program expanded its scope to include investigations involving all areas of the Internet and online services:

- Internet websites that post child pornography
- Internet newsgroups
- Internet relay chat (IRC) channels
- Online groups and organizations (eGroups)
- Peer-to-peer (P2P) file-sharing programs
- Bulletin board systems (BBSs) and other online forums
- Social networking venues

FBI agents and task force officers are real social media warfare operatives that go online using fictitious screen names and engage in real-time chat or e-mail conversations with subjects in order to obtain evidence of criminal activity. Investigation of specific online locations can be initiated based on a citizen complaint, a complaint by an online service provider, a referral from a law enforcement agency, or uncovering the name of an online location that suggests there may be illicit activity.

The ICAC program has been highly successful and has proved to be a logical, efficient, and effective method to identify and investigate individuals who are using the Internet to sexually exploit children. To date, there have been five VCAC program subjects placed on the FBI's ten most wanted fugitives list:

1. Eric Franklin Rosser (placed on list 2000; captured in 2001)
2. Michael Scott Bliss (placed on list 2002; captured in 2002)
3. Richard Steve Goldberg (placed on list 2002; captured in 2007)
4. Jon Savarino Schillaci (placed on list 2007; captured in 2008)
5. Eric Justin Toth (placed on list 2012; captured in 2013)

The Violent Crimes Against Children International Task Force (VCACITF) is an expert cadre of international law enforcement officers working together to provide a global response to crimes against children through strategic partnerships, the aggressive engagement of relevant law enforcement, and the extensive use of liaison, operational support, and coordination. One of the primary missions of the VCACITF is to combat child sex tourism.

Child sex tourism (CST) is defined as travel abroad to engage in the commercial sexual exploitation of a child under the age of 18. Some CST offenders, usually novices to the commercial sex trade, plan their travel through U.S.-based tour companies or tour operators, whereas other offenders plan their travel independently. Information on procuring children in foreign destinations is readily available in pedophile newsgroups and forums on the Internet.

In certain countries where there is a thriving commercial sex industry, such information can be obtained through taxi drivers, hotel concierges, and newspaper advertisements. Studies show Southeast Asian countries particularly Cambodia, the Philippines, and Thailand are the most common destinations for child sex tourism. Latin American countries such as Costa Rica, Mexico, and Brazil are also emerging destinations for CST. An estimated 25% of child sex tourists in the previously mentioned Southeast Asian countries are U.S. citizens, and an estimated 80% of CST offenders in Latin American countries are U.S. citizens.

The FBI's Criminal Investigative Division of which the VCAC program is a part, in conjunction with the International Operations Division, carries out joint operations overseas with governments in some of the top CST destinations. These operations target child sex tourists who do not plan their illegal activities from the United States but rather seek to procure children once they arrive at their destination.

The purpose of the operations is to coordinate with foreign law enforcement to gather evidence against American offenders that is admissible in U.S. courts, with the goal of extraditing those offenders back to the United States for prosecution. The VCAC program coordinates all efforts with FBI legal attachés in these countries to provide training, equipment, and logistical support to these joint operations [5].

11.4 Social Media Warfare to Rescue Missing and Exploited Children

The National Center for Missing and Exploited Children (NCMEC) operates a CyberTipline (www.cybertipline.com) that allows parents and children to report child pornography and other incidents of sexual exploitation of children by submitting an online form. The NCMEC also maintains a 24-hour hotline at 1-800-THE-LOST and a website at www.missingkids.com.

Complaints received by the NCMEC that indicate a violation of federal law are referred to the FBI for appropriate action. An FBI analyst reviews the information received by the CyberTipline. Analysts conduct research and analyses to identify individuals suspected of any of the following crimes:

- Possession, manufacture, and/or distribution of child pornography
- Online enticement of children for sexual acts
- Child sexual tourism and/or other sexual exploitation of children

Once a potential suspect is identified, FBI analysts compile an investigative packet that includes the applicable CyberTipline reports, subpoena results, public records search results, the illegal images associated with the suspect, and a myriad of other information that is forwarded to the appropriate FBI field office for investigation.

In 2008, the FBI, working with the NCMEC, began operation "Rescue Me," an aggressive program that uses image analysis to determine the identity of child victims depicted in child sexual exploitation material found on the Internet or from other sources. Focusing on items seen in the backgrounds of child pornography images and videos, analysts attempt to answer four basic questions to identify and subsequently rescue victimized children:

- What useful clues are there in the background? (e.g., What is visible on the walls? Are there distinct clothes or commercial labels visible?)
- Can a time frame for when the pictures/videos were taken be determined?
- What is the physical location of the children in the photos/videos (e.g., country, state, hotel room, etc.)?
- Who are the children in the photos/videos?

In February 2004, the FBI established the Endangered Child Alert program (ECAP) as a new proactive approach to identify unknown individuals involved in the sexual abuse of children and the production of child pornography. A collaborative effort between the FBI and the NCMEC, ECAP seeks national and international exposure of unknown adults (referred to as John/Jane Does) whose faces and/or distinguishing characteristics are visible in child pornography images. These faces and or distinguishing marks (i.e., scars, moles, tattoos, etc.) are displayed on the "seeking information" section of the FBI website as well as various other media outlets in hopes that someone from the public can identify them. As a result of the ECAP, the faces of many Jane/John Does have been broadcast on cooperating television shows.

The FBI's VCAC program provides a quick and effective response to all incidents of crimes against children. The first few hours after a child is abducted are critical, and that is why established Child Abduction Rapid Deployment (CARD) teams were established in October 2005. CARD teams are comprised of experienced personnel with a proven track record in violent crimes against children investigations, especially cases where a child has been abducted by someone other than a family member. The teams work closely with FBI Behavioral Analysis Unit representatives, National Center for the Analysis of Violent Crime coordinators, and Child Exploitation Task Force members.

CARD teams are capable of quickly establishing an on site command post to centralize investigative efforts and operations. Other assets they bring to the table include a new mapping tool to identify and locate registered sex offenders in the area, national and international lead coverage, and the Child Abduction Response

Plan to guide investigative efforts. CARD teams are primarily involved in non-family child abductions, ransom child abductions, and mysterious disappearances of children. They work with state and local law enforcement to protect and save the lives of innocent children.

Family child abductions, a parent kidnapping his or her own child and fleeing for parts unknown, often overseas, happen often. Under the 1982 Missing Children's Act, the circumstances surrounding the disappearance must indicate that the child was removed from the control of his or her legal custodian without the custodian's consent, or the circumstances of the case must strongly indicate that the child is likely to have been abused or sexually exploited. Two federal criminal investigative options and one non-criminal or civil method may be pursued when a child is abducted by a parent and taken over state lines or outside the United States:

■ The International Parental Kidnapping Crime Act (IPKCA) of 1993: A criminal arrest warrant can be issued for a parent who takes a juvenile under 16 outside of the United States without the other custodial parent's permission.

■ Unlawful flight to avoid prosecution (UFAP) Parental Kidnapping: When criminal charges are filed by a state that requests help, a criminal arrest warrant can be issued for an abducting parent who flees across state lines or internationally. In nations that have signed The Hague Convention on the Civil Aspects of International Child Abduction, there is a civil process that facilitates the return of abducted children under 16 years of age to their home countries.

Criminal processes enable the arrest of the abducting parent but do not specifically order the return of the child, although the child is usually returned when the parent is apprehended. The civil process, on the other hand, facilitates the return of the child but does not seek the arrest or return of the abductor. Thus, a criminal process would not be pursued if circumstances indicate it will jeopardize an active Hague Convention civil process.

It is important to understand that the FBI has no investigative jurisdiction outside the United States except on the high seas and other locations specifically identified by U.S. Congress. The FBI works through existing partnerships with international authorities through the U.S. Department of State, the Legal Attaché program, and INTERPOL. The Department of State receives approximately 1200 new Hague and non-Hague cases annually.

The FBI authority in parental kidnapping cases stems from the Fugitive Felon Act as part of Title 18, U.S. Code, Section 1073–UFAP. For the FBI to assist with a UFAP arrest warrant, the following criteria must be met:

■ There must be probable cause to believe the abducting parent has fled interstate or internationally to avoid prosecution or confinement.

- State authorities must have an outstanding warrant for the abductor's arrest charging him/her with a felony under the laws of the state from which the fugitive flees.
- State authorities must agree to extradite and prosecute that fugitive from anywhere in the United States if the subject is apprehended by the FBI.
- The local prosecuting attorney or police agency should make a written request for FBI assistance.
- The U.S. Attorney must authorize the filing of a complaint, and the federal arrest process must be outstanding before the investigation is instituted.

In 1932, Congress gave the FBI jurisdiction under the Lindbergh Law to immediately investigate any reported mysterious disappearance or kidnapping involving a child of tender age usually 12 years old or younger. Child abductions by strangers are often complex and high-profile cases and time is of the essence. FBI CARD teams are deployed soon after an abduction is reported to a local FBI field office, to FBI headquarters, or to the NCMEC, or in other cases when the FBI determines an investigation is warranted.

In June 2003, the FBI, in conjunction with the Department of Justice Child Exploitation and Obscenity Section and the NCMEC, launched the Innocence Lost National Initiative. This combined effort was aimed at addressing the growing problem of domestic sex trafficking of children in the United States. To date, more than 4800 children have been rescued. Investigations have successfully led to the conviction of more than 2000 pimps, madams, and their associates who exploit children through prostitution. These convictions have resulted in lengthy sentences, including multiple life sentences and the seizure of real property, vehicles, and monetary assets [5]. Presented here is a list of major cases:

- 2015: 149 sexually exploited children recovered in Operation Cross Country IX
- 2014: 168 trafficking victims recovered in Operation Cross Country VIII
- 2013: 105 sexually exploited children recovered in Operation Cross Country VII
- 2012: Nearly 80 juveniles recovered in Operation Cross Country VI
- 2010: 69 children rescued during Operation Cross Country V
- 2009: More than 50 children rescued during Operation Cross Country IV
- 2009: 48 children recovered in Operation Cross Country III
- 2008: 47 children rescued in Operation Cross Country II
- 2008: 389 arrested in Operation Cross Country
- 2005: National crackdown identified 30 child victims

There are several federal government statutes relating to crimes against children:

- Section 1073. Unlawful Flight to Avoid Prosecution (UFAP) or Giving Testimony
- Section 1201. Kidnapping

- Section 1204. International Parental Kidnapping
- Section 1462. Importation or Transportation of Obscene Matters
- Section 1465. Transportation of Obscene Matters for Sale or Distribution
- Section 1466. Engaging in the Business of Selling or Transferring Obscene Matter
- Section 1467(a). Criminal Forfeiture
- Section 1470. Transfer of Obscene Material to Minors
- Section 1591. Sex Trafficking of Children or by Force, Fraud, or Coercion
- Section 2241. Aggravated Sexual Abuse
- Section 2243. Sexual Abuse of a Minor or Ward
- Section 2251. Sexual Exploitation of Children
- Section 2251A(a)(b). Selling or Buying of Children
- Section 2252. Certain Activities Relating to Material Involving the Sexual Exploitation of Minors
- Section 2252A. Certain Activities Relating to Material Constituting or Containing Child Pornography
- Section 2253(a). Criminal Forfeiture
- Section 2254. Civil Forfeiture
- Section 2257. Record Keeping Requirements
- Section 2260(a)(b). Production of Sexually Explicit Depictions of a Minor for Importation into the United States
- Section 2421. Transportation Generally
- Section 2422. Coercion and Enticement
- Section 2423(a)(b). Transportation of Minors
- Section 2425. Use of Interstate Facilities to Transmit Information About a Minor [5]

11.5 Child Pornography Is at Home on the Internet

Distribution of child pornography and adult obscenity has expanded exponentially with advances in computer technology and increased availability and popular use of the Internet. This globalization of criminal activity is a significant challenge to the U.S. Department of Justice capacity to investigate and prosecute these crimes. Child pornography is relatively easy to identify. Obscenity is less easy to identify and the legal definition of obscenity was established by the U.S. Supreme Court in *Miller v California*, 413 U.S. 15 (1973). Under this ruling, the following three conditions must be met before material is considered obscene and subject to prosecution:

- The average person, applying contemporary community standards, would find that the material appeals to the prurient interest.

■ The work depicts or describes, in a patently offensive way, sexual conduct specifically defined by the applicable state law.
■ The work, taken as a whole, lacks serious literary, artistic, political, or scientific value.

Increasingly, obscenity is transmitted via the Internet and this has caused confusion as to which community standards should be applied in determining whether material is obscene. The Executive Office for U.S. Attorneys (EOUSA), and the FBI as a matter of policy, pursues major producers and traffickers of obscene materials.

The National Obscenity Enforcement Unit was established in 1987. The unit was later renamed the Child Exploitation and Obscenity Section (CEOS) to reflect its work on child sexual exploitation crimes. CEOS attorneys assist the U.S. Attorney's Offices (USAOs) in investigations, trials, and appeals of child pornography cases. These cases include the prosecution of individuals who possess, manufacture, or distribute child pornography; who sell, buy, or transport children interstate or internationally to engage in sexually explicit conduct; who travel interstate or internationally to sexually abuse children; who abuse children on federal lands; and who transport obscene material in interstate or foreign commerce.

Occasionally, due to their expertise, CEOS attorneys may prosecute cases themselves. In addition to assisting prosecutors, the CEOS has several other responsibilities relating to child pornography and child exploitation issues. These include advising USAOs on child victim witness issues; developing proposals for policies, legislation, government practices, and regulations; and training federal, state, local, and international prosecutors, investigators, and judges [6].

The CEOS and its High Technology Investigative Unit (HTIU), created in 2002, are experts in prosecuting child exploitation cases, and in investigating high-technology child exploitation crimes. CEOS attorneys and HTIU computer forensic specialists investigate and prosecute defendants who violate federal child exploitation laws and also assist the 94 USAOs in investigations, trials, and appeals related to these offenses [7].

The NCMEC maintains the CyberTipline, an online reporting system for Internet service providers (ISPs) and the public to report online child pornography. It receives over 90,000 child pornography (possession, manufacture, and distribution) tips per year. From 2005 to 2009, U.S. attorneys prosecuted 8352 child pornography cases, and in most instances, the offenders used digital technologies and the Internet to produce, view, store, advertise, or distribute child pornography.

Prior to the mid-1990s, Internet access and the availability of digital home recording devices (still, video, and web cameras) were very limited, thereby confining the production and distribution of child pornography material to relatively few individuals. Now the ease with which a person can move from viewing child pornography to producing and distributing child pornography is illustrated in numerous cases. In addition, advances in computer memory storage, the speed of downloading and uploading, and advances in file-sharing technologies make it very easy to quickly transfer or receive large volumes of child sex abuse images. Numerous technologies are used by offenders including peer-to-peer (P2P) networks, Internet relay chat (IRC), newsgroups, bulletin boards, photo-sharing sites, and social networking sites, among others. Experts posit, and common sense suggests, that the easy accessibility to this material online draws new offenders to the crime [8].

Children tend to be trusting online and will befriend people of any age or sex that they may not know. Offenders take advantage of this naïveté and target children who openly engage others online or have a strong social networking presence. In most instances, they openly post pictures or videos of themselves. Offenders can gain information from the online presence of potential victims by reviewing posts and friends lists and pose as an acquaintance, another teen from the same or a different school, or a stranger with similar interests. Friends lists may serve as a source to identify additional victims once the sextortion process starts. Once a child becomes a victim of sextortion, the victimization may last for years. Victims have reported having to meet demands for sexually explicit images and videos multiple times per day. The FBI has identified cases in which children committed suicide, attempted suicide, or engaged in other acts of self-harm due to their sextortion victimization. In one instance, the victim purposely engaged in activity that resulted in hospitalization to get a break from the offender's demands. As soon as the victim was released from hospital, the victimization continued.

People involved in child pornography are from all over the United States and the world and come from a wide variety of backgrounds. The following list represents a small sample of cases found during a September 22, 2016, search of the FBI and U.S. Attorney's websites:

- Alabama man indicted for producing child pornography involving multiple victims
- Alaskan physician convicted of Internet child pornography crimes
- Albuquerque man pleads guilty to federal child pornography charges
- Appalachian man pleads guilty to receiving child pornography
- Birmingham man sentenced to 30 years in prison for child exploitation and child pornography
- British man sentenced to 85 years in prison for trafficking child pornography
- Bronx man arrested for possessing and distributing child pornography
- California man sentenced to over 16 years in prison for producing child pornography
- Chesapeake man sentenced to 11 years in child pornography case
- Cleveland sex offender faces child pornography charges
- Columbia man indicted for producing child pornography
- Delaware man indicted for child pornography offenses and planning to meet 14-year-old for sex

- Former acting HHS cybersecurity director sentenced to 25 years in prison for engaging in child pornography enterprise
- Former airman sentenced for child pornography crimes
- Former Belleville resident pleads guilty to receipt of child pornography and possession of prepubescent child pornography
- Former church staff member sentenced to 50 years in prison for child sexual exploitation and possessing child pornography
- Former pharmacy technician indicted for attempting to entice a minor online and child pornography offenses
- Former U.S. Army Corps of Engineers employee sentenced to 30 years in prison for transportation and possession of child pornography
- Former U.S. Army reservist sentenced for production of child pornography
- Former U.S. Coast Guard officer sentenced for child pornography
- Former U.S. congressional staffer pleads guilty to receiving child pornography
- Former U.S. Navy lt. commander and Catholic priest pleads guilty to child pornography charges
- Illinois man sentenced to 11 years in prison for attempting to entice a minor
- Indiana gospel singer found guilty of sexual exploitation of a minor and distribution of child pornography
- Indiana man sentenced to 35 years in prison for producing child pornography
- Joplin man sentenced for child porn
- Kenyan child pornography producer sentenced to life in prison for participation in Dreamboard website
- Kern county man pleads guilty to receipt and distribution of child pornography in "sextortion" case
- Lawrence man sentenced for distributing child pornography
- Louisiana man sentenced to 20 years in prison for engaging in child exploitation enterprise and production of child pornography
- Maryland man sentenced to 10 years for transporting child pornography into United States
- Memphis man sentenced for distributing child pornography
- Miami resident guilty of receiving child pornography
- Milwaukee man sentenced to 10 years in prison for receiving child pornography
- Minnesota national guardsman pleads guilty to producing child pornography while deployed to Afghanistan
- Monona man sentenced for possessing child pornography
- Newport man sentenced for child pornography possession
- Ogdensburg man charged with producing child pornography
- Omaha man sentenced to 5 years for child pornography
- Painesville man indicted on child pornography charges
- Reading man charged with possession of child pornography
- Recidivist child sex offender sentenced to life in prison for child pornography-related offenses

- Retired master deputy sheriff sentenced to 20 years in prison for child pornography charges
- Rochester man guilty of possessing child pornography
- Sedalia sex offender pleads guilty to child pornography
- Shelton attorney charged with child pornography offenses
- Texas man sentenced to 300 months in prison for sexual abuse of orphans while working in Malawi
- Two individuals sentenced to federal prison for participation in long-running online child pornography ring
- Virginia man pleads guilty to production of child pornography
- Virginia music volunteer sentenced to 300 months in prison for production of child pornography

11.6 Conclusions

This chapter examined some of the ways children have been harmed by individuals who that used adverse social media warfare tactics against them. It also reviewed what law enforcement agencies do to prevent harm to children from Internet attacks and how law enforcement responds when harm has been done. Important conclusions can be drawn from the material presented in this chapter:

- Bullying is unwanted, aggressive behavior generally found among school-aged children that involves a real or perceived power imbalance. Approximately 20% of schoolchildren report they are bullied each year and there is a trend toward cyberbullying.
- Parents are the first line of defense against cyberbullying and the Department of Health and Human Services provides guidance for parents and children on how to prevent cyberbullying. This includes urging parents to talk with their children about cyberbullying and other online issues on a regular basis and to stay informed about the websites children visit and their other online activities.
- Every year, thousands of children become victims of crime whether through kidnappings, violent attacks, sexual abuse, or online predators who use social media warfare tactics to confuse and deceive them.
- Chat rooms and other social networking and online media forums offer the advantage of immediate communication around the world, providing pedophiles with an anonymous means of identifying and recruiting child victims into sexually illicit relationships.
- FBI agents and task force officers are real social media warfare operatives who that go online into predicated locations using fictitious screen names and engaging in real-time chat or e-mail conversations with subjects in order to obtain evidence of criminal activity against children.

- Prior to the mid-1990s, Internet access and the availability of digital home-recording devices (still, video, and web cameras) were very limited, thereby confining the production and distribution of child pornography material to relatively few individuals and within small circles.
- Distribution of child pornography and adult obscenity expanded exponentially with advances in computer technology and increased availability and popular use of the Internet.

11.7 Agenda for Action

Every year, thousands of children become victims of crime whether through kidnappings, violent attacks, sexual abuse, or online predators that uses social media warfare tactics to confuse and deceive them. Distribution of child pornography and adult obscenity expanded exponentially with advances in computer technology and increased availability and popular use of the Internet. Action steps should include, but not be limited to, the following areas:

- Support and expand research efforts addressing the threats that children face in all forms of social media warfare.
- Training is a critical step in enabling law enforcement officers to deal with the threats and abuses that children face on the Internet and in social media, and that training should be expanded at all levels law enforcement academies, universities, and advanced professional training.
- Support and expand efforts to teach children, at a young age, how to identify and deal with threats they encounter on the Internet and through social media, including taking legislative action at the state level to fund such efforts.
- Support and expand efforts to train educators how to teach children to identify and deal with threats they encounter on the Internet and through social media.
- Support and expand efforts to train scout and club leaders how to teach children to identify and deal with threats they encounter on the Internet and through social media and encourage such learning through awards and recognition.

11.8 Key Terms

Child pornography is sexually explicit or themed images or recordings involving minors less than 18 years of age.

Child sexual exploitation is the recruitment or involvement of minors less than 18 years of age in any sexual capacity.

Cyberbullying is bullying that takes place using electronic technology including devices and equipment such as cell phones, computers, and tablets as well as communication tools including social media sites, text messages, chat, and websites.

Family child abductions are abductions of a child by a family member who does not have legal custody of the child.

Parental control filtering software is design to allow parents to electronically control how their children can use the Internet and social media and to monitor and generate reports on a child's computer usage.

11.9 Seminar Discussion Topics

Discussion topics for graduate- or professional-level seminars:

- What experience have seminar participants had in situations where social media warfare strategies or tactics were used against children?
- What experience have seminar participants had in situations where they tried to protect children from social media warfare strategies or tactics being used against children?
- What experience have seminar participants had in situations where law enforcement was involved in protecting children from cyber predators?

11.10 Seminar Group Project

Divide participants into multiple groups with each group taking 10–15 minutes to develop a list of defensive social media warfare tactics to protect children online. Upon completion, have groups exchange their lists of social media warfare tactics, with groups taking 10–15 minutes to develop measures that can effectively negate the defensive measures designed by the groups. Meet as a group and discuss the offensive tactics selected by the groups and the defensive measures to counter the tactics that were developed by the groups.

References

1. U.S. Department of Health and Human Services. Bullying definition. Accessed September 22, 2016. http://www.stopbullying.gov/what-is-bullying/definition/index.html.

2. U.S. Department of Health and Human Services. What is cyberbullying? Accessed September 22, 2016. http://www.stopbullying.gov/cyberbullying/what-is-it/index.html.

3. U.S. Department of Health and Human Services. Prevent cyberbullying. Accessed September 22, 2016. http://www.stopbullying.gov/cyberbullying/prevention/index.html.

4. U.S. Department of Health and Human Services. Report cyberbullying. Accessed September 22, 2016. http://www.stopbullying.gov/cyberbullying/how-to-report/index.html.

5. U.S. Federal Bureau of Investigation. Violent crimes against children/online predators. Accessed September 22, 2016. https://www.fbi.gov/investigate/violent-crime/cac.

6. U.S. Department of Justice. 2001. Review of child pornography and obscenity crimes. Report Number I-2001-07. Accessed September 23, 2016. https://www.oig.justice.gov/reports/plus/e0107/results.htm.

7. U.S. Department of Justice. Child Exploitation and Obscenity Section (CEOS). Accessed September 23, 2016. https://www.justice.gov/criminal-ceos.

8. U.S. Department of Justice. 2010. The National Strategy for Child Exploitation Prevention and Interdiction. A Report to Congress. Accessed September 23, 2016. https://www.justice.gov/sites/default/files/criminal-ceos/legacy/2012/03/19/natstrategyreport.pdf.

Chapter 12

Adult Victims in Social Media Warfare

Adults, like children, become victims of social media warfare from several sources of attack. These can take the form of harassment, revenge actions, identity theft, fraudulent transactions, and having computers or phones hacked. Children can certainly be targets of the same sort of attacks but the major concerns about children, including cyberbullying, sexual exploitation, kidnapping, and child pornography, are covered in Chapter 11: "Child Victims in Social Media Warfare." This chapter examines some of the ways adults are harmed by other individuals who use these adverse social media warfare tactics against them.

12.1 Theft of Adult Identities

In 1998, the U.S. Congress passed the Identity Theft and Assumption Deterrence Act to address the increasing problem of *identity theft*. The act specifically amended Title 18, U.S. Code, Section 1028 to make it a federal crime to "knowingly transfer or use, without lawful authority, a means of identification of another person with the intent to commit, or to aid or abet, any unlawful activity that constitutes a violation of federal law, or that constitutes a felony under any applicable state or local law."

Congress also passed the Identity Theft Penalty Enhancement Act in 2004 establishing penalties for aggravated identity theft, which is, using the identity of another person to commit felony crimes, including immigration violations, theft of another's Social Security benefits, and acts of domestic terrorism. The act requires courts to sentence offenders to two additional years for a general offense and five years for a terrorism offense.

It is difficult to provide a precise assessment because different law enforcement agencies may classify identity theft crimes differently, and because identity theft can also involve credit card fraud, Internet fraud, or mail theft, among other crimes. The FBI has dealt with criminals faking identifications (IDs) for decades, from check forgers to fugitives on the run. Now, the threat is more pervasive and the scams include Internet and social media warfare elements. The FBI uses both its criminal investigation and cyber resources to identify and stop criminal groups in their early stages and to root out the many types of perpetrators.

Along with names, Social Security numbers (SSNs), and dates of birth, fraudsters also use Medicare numbers, addresses, birth certificates, death certificates, passport numbers, financial account numbers (e.g., bank account, credit card), passwords (e.g., mother's maiden name, father's middle name), telephone numbers, and biometric data (e.g., fingerprints, iris scans) to commit identity theft.

Some of the more prevalent schemes used by criminals to steal identities include suspicious e-mail or phishing attempts to trick victims into revealing personally identifiable information; smash and grab burglaries involving the theft of hard copy driver's licenses, credit cards, check books, and so on; and computer and network intrusions that result in the loss of *personally identifiable information (PII)* [1].

Many people do not realize how easily criminals can obtain an individual's personal data without having to break into their homes. If residents receive applications for pre-approved credit cards in the mail, but discard them without tearing up the enclosed materials, criminals may retrieve them and try to activate the cards for their use without their knowledge. Also, if personal mail is delivered to a place where others have ready access to it, criminals may simply intercept and redirect your mail to another location.

The Internet has become an easily accessible place for criminals to obtain identifying data, such as passwords or even banking information. Many people respond to spam e-mail that promises them some benefit but requests identifying data, without realizing that in many cases, the requester has no intention of keeping his promise. In some cases, criminals reportedly use computer technology to obtain large amounts of personal data.

With enough identifying information about an individual, a criminal can take over that individual's identity to conduct a wide range of crimes: false applications for loans and credit cards, fraudulent withdrawals from bank accounts, fraudulent use of telephone calling cards, or obtaining other goods or privileges that a criminal might be denied if he were to use his real name. If the criminal takes steps to ensure that bills for the falsely obtained credit cards, or bank statements showing the unauthorized withdrawals, are sent to an address other than the victim's, the victim may not become aware of what is happening until the criminal has already inflicted substantial damage on the victim's assets, credit, and reputation [2].

Once identity thieves have an individual's personal information, they can drain their bank account, run up charges on credit cards, open new utility accounts, or get medical treatment on someone else's health insurance. An identity thief can file a tax refund in their name and get your refund. In some extreme cases, a thief might even give some else's name to the police during an arrest. There are several clues that individuals can watch for that may mean an identity has been stolen:

- Withdrawals from a bank account that cannot be explained.
- Routine bills and other mail is not being delivered.
- Merchants refuse checks.
- Debt collectors call about debts that are not explainable.
- Unfamiliar accounts or charges on a credit report.
- Medical providers bill for unexplainable services.
- A health plan rejects legitimate medical claims because the records show the policy has reached its benefits limit.
- A health plan will not provide coverage because medical records show a condition an individual does not have.
- The Internal Revenue Service (IRS) notifies a taxpayer that more than one tax return was filed in a name, or that there is income from an unknown employer.
- A notice is received that information was compromised by a data breach at a company where an account is active [3].

The IRS uses an SSN to make sure the tax return form that a person is filing is accurate and complete and that the person receives any refund due. Identity theft can affect how a tax return is processed. An unexpected notice or letter from the IRS could alert people that someone else is using their SSN; however, the IRS does not start contact with a taxpayer by sending an e-mail, text, or social media message that asks for personal or financial information. If people receive an e-mail that claims to be from the IRS, they should not reply or click on any links. Instead, forward it to phishing@irs.gov. If someone uses a person's SSN to file for a tax refund before they do, the IRS might think the person already filed and received a refund. When the proper owners of the SSN file their return later, IRS records will show the first filing and refund, and the victims of identity theft will get a notice or letter from the IRS saying more than one return was filed for that SSN.

If an identity thief uses a stolen SSN to get a job, the employer may report that person's income to the IRS using the stolen SSN. When the SSN proper owner files a tax return, he or she will not include those earnings. IRS records will show he or she failed to report all their income. The agency will send a notice or letter saying the individual received wages but did not report them. Individuals should contact the IRS immediately. Specialists will help to get tax returns properly filed and individuals will get any refund they are due [4].

12.2 Protecting an Identity from Thieves

Individuals and businesses for that matter can take very simple steps to protect their identity information and avoid becoming victims of identity theft. It is essential that people stay in the know about who is getting their personal or financial information. Personal information should not be given out on the phone, through the mail, or over the Internet unless the individual has initiated the contact or absolutely knows who they are working with during any type of transaction. If a company claims that an individual has an account with them by sending e-mails asking for personal information, do not click on any links in the e-mail. Instead, type the company name into a web browser, go to their site, and contact them through customer service. Or, call the customer service number listed on the account statement and ask whether the company really sent a request. Thousands of such e-mails float around the Internet every day and many look authentic, with company logs and hijacked greetings.

There are also many basic steps that individuals should continuously take to help protect their personal information and their identity:

- Lock financial documents and records in a safe place at home, and lock wallets or purses in a safe place at work. Always keep information secure from roommates or workers who come into the home or office.
- When going out, take only the identification, credit, and debit cards needed. Leave the Social Security card at home. Make a copy of Medicare cards and black out all but the last four digits on the copy. Carry the copy instead of the original card unless specifically needed at a doctor's office or clinic.
- Before sharing information at a workplace, a business, a child's school, or a doctor's office, ask why they need it, how they will safeguard it, and the consequences of not sharing.
- Shred receipts, credit offers, credit applications, insurance forms, physician statements, checks, bank statements, expired charge cards, and similar documents when they are no longer needed.
- Destroy the labels on prescription bottles before discarding them and do not share health plan information with anyone who offers free health services or products.
- Take outgoing mail to post office collection boxes or the post office. Promptly remove mail that arrives in a residential or business mailbox. If gone from home for several days, request a vacation hold on mail.
- When ordering new checks, do not have them mailed to a residence unless there is a secure mailbox with a lock.
- Consider opting out of prescreened offers of credit and insurance by mail.
- Store and dispose of personal information securely.
- Before disposing of a computer, get rid of all personal information it stores. Use a wipe utility program to overwrite the entire hard drive.

- Before disposing of a mobile device, check the owner's manual, the service provider's website, or the device manufacturer's website for information on how to delete information permanently, and how to save or transfer information to a new device.
- Remove the memory or subscriber identity module (SIM) card from a mobile device. Remove the phone book, lists of calls made and received, voicemails, messages sent and received, organizer folders, web search history, and photos.
- Keep browsers secure and use encryption software that scrambles information sent over the Internet. A lock icon on the status bar of an Internet browser means information will be safe when it is transmitted. Look for the lock before sending personal or financial information online.
- Use strong passwords with laptops, credit cards, banks, and other accounts.
- Do not overly share personally identifiable information on social networking sites. Sharing too much information allows an identity thief to find information that can be used to answer "challenge" questions on accounts, and get access to money and personal information.
- Consider limiting access to social networking pages to a small group of people. Never post full names, Social Security numbers (SSNs), addresses, phone numbers, or account numbers in publicly accessible sites.
- The decision to share SSNs is up to an individual and a business may not provide services or benefits if individuals will not provide SSNs. Sometimes, it may be necessary to share an SSN if employers and financial institutions need it for wage and tax reporting purposes. A business may ask for an SSN to check credit for loans, rent an apartment, or sign up for utility services.
- Install anti-virus software, anti-spyware software, and a firewall. Set your preference to update these protections often.
- Protect against intrusions and infections that can compromise computer files or passwords by installing security patches for operating system and other software programs.
- Do not open files, click on links, or download programs sent by strangers. Opening a file from an unknown source could expose computer systems to a virus or spyware that captures passwords or other information as it is typed.
- Before sending personal information over a laptop or smartphone on a public wireless network in a coffee shop, library, airport, hotel, or other public place, see if the information will be protected. If using an encrypted website, it protects only the information sent to and from that site. If using a secure wireless network, all the information you send on that network is protected.
- Keep financial information on a laptop only when necessary. Do not use an automatic log-in feature that saves user names and passwords, and always log off when finished. That way, if a laptop is stolen, it will be harder for a thief to get at personal information.

■ Read privacy policies on websites to determine how the site maintains accuracy, access, security, and control of the personal information it collects; how it uses the information, and whether it provides information to third parties [5].

Many companies refer to their services as *identity theft protection services*. In fact, no service can protect an individual from having personal information stolen. What these companies offer are monitoring and recovery services. Monitoring services watch for signs that an identity thief may be using personal information. Recovery services help to deal with the effects of identity theft after it happens. Monitoring and recovery services are often sold together, and may include options like regular access to credit reports or credit scores.

There are two basic types of monitoring services: credit monitoring and identity monitoring. Credit monitoring tracks activity on credit reports at one, two, or all three of the major credit reporting agencies (CRAs)—Equifax, Experian, and TransUnion. If activity is spotted that might result from identity theft or a mistake, individuals can take steps to resolve the problem before it grows. Usually, credit monitoring will send alerts when

■ A company checks people's credit history.
■ A new loan or credit card account is opened in a person's name.
■ A creditor or debt collector says payments are late.
■ Public records show that a person has filed for bankruptcy.
■ There is a legal judgment against an individual.
■ Credit limits change unexpectedly.
■ Personal information, like name, address, or phone number, changes without authorization.

Credit monitoring only warns people about activity that shows up on their credit report. But many types of identity theft will not appear. For example, credit monitoring will not indicate if an identity thief withdraws money from a bank account, or uses an SSN to file a tax return and collect a refund. Some services only monitor credit reports at one of the CRAs. So, for example, if a service only monitors TransUnion, there will not be alerts on items that appear on Equifax or Experian reports. Prices for credit monitoring vary widely, so it pays to comparison shop. These are questions to ask credit monitoring service providers:

■ What credit reporting agencies they monitor?
■ How often do they monitor CRA reports? (Some monitor daily, others less frequently.)
■ What access do customers have to credit reports?
■ Do they show reports for all three CRAs?
■ Is there a limit to how often reports can be viewed?

- Is there a separate fee for each time reports are viewed?
- Are other services included, such as access to a credit score?

Identity monitoring provides alerts when personal information like bank account information or an SSN, driver's license, passport, or medical ID number is being used in ways that generally will not show up on a credit report. Identity monitoring services may warn when personal information shows up in

- Change of address requests
- Court or arrest records
- Orders for new utility, cable, or wireless services
- Payday loan applications
- Check cashing requests
- Social media
- Websites that identity thieves use to trade stolen information

Identity recovery services are designed to help regain control of a name and finances after identity theft occurs. Usually, trained counselors or case managers review the process of addressing identity theft problems. They may help write letters to creditors and debt collectors, place a freeze on credit reports to prevent an identity thief from opening new accounts, or explain documents that must be reviewed. Some services will represent clients in dealing with creditors or other institutions.

Identity theft insurance is offered by most of the major identity theft protection services. The insurance generally covers only out-of-pocket expenses directly associated with reclaiming an identity. Typically, these expenses are limited to things like postage, copying, and notary costs. Less often, the expenses might include lost wages or legal fees. The insurance generally does not reimburse for any stolen money or financial loss resulting from the theft. As with any insurance policy, there may be a deductible, as well as limitations and exclusions.

IdentityTheft.gov is the government's free, one-stop resource for reporting and recovering from identity theft. IdentityTheft.gov has recovery plans for more than 30 types of identity theft, including tax-related identity theft and identity theft involving a child's information. The website, available in Spanish at RobodeIdentidad.gov, provides a personal, interactive recovery plan tailored to an individual's identity theft needs. The website will

- Walk users through each recovery step
- Generate pre-filled letters, affidavits, and forms to send to credit bureaus, businesses, debt collectors, and the IRS
- Adapt to changing needs, and provide follow-up reminders, and help track progress
- Provide advice on what to do if individuals are affected by specific data breaches [6]

It is also advisable to keep up on identity theft trends to help determine if an individual or business has become more vulnerable or a more likely target for identity theft. In 2015, Utica College's Center for Identity Management and Information Protection (CIMIP) released "The new face of identity theft," a report that analyzes federal case data from 2008 to 2013 as a follow up to a similar study completed in 2007 that evaluated identity crime trends.

The study found that the five states with the largest number of offenders convicted during the study's period were Florida, California, Texas, New Jersey, and Georgia. Nearly 90% of these offenders were charged with identity theft, while the other most common charges were bank fraud, tax fraud, access device fraud and wire fraud. The 2015 report states that more identity criminals, now almost 64%, operated as part of a group rather than individually, in contrast with results from the 2007 study, which found that most identity criminals acted alone. Similarly, the use of technological devices by offenders increased to now represent 62% of all identity theft cases in the study. In an almost identical result to the 2007 study, the 2015 study found that the majority of identity thieves, 60%, target strangers.

An emerging form of identity theft, prominent in the new study, was the submission of false tax claims with the IRS using stolen identity information. Offenders used several approaches to commit these types of offenses, stealing identity information from a variety of sources, including prisons and nursing homes [7].

12.3 Revenge Porn and Sextortion

Revenge porn, the disclosure of sexually explicit images without consent and for no legitimate purpose, is now against the law in many states of the United States. There have been several high-profile cases over the last few years. Revenge porn can cause immediate, devastating, and in many cases irreversible harm. A vengeful ex-partner, opportunistic hacker, or rapist can upload an explicit image of a victim to a website where thousands of people can view it and hundreds of other websites can share it. In a matter of days, that image can dominate the first several pages of search engine results for the victim's name; it can also be e-mailed or otherwise exhibited to the victim's family, employers, coworkers, and peers.

The Internet has greatly facilitated the rise of nonconsensual pornography, as dedicated revenge porn sites and other forums openly solicit private intimate images and expose them to millions of viewers. Several thousand websites host revenge porn. Intimate material is also widely distributed without consent through social media blogs, e-mails, and texts. Victims are routinely threatened with sexual assault, stalked, harassed, fired from jobs, forced to change schools, disciplined at school, and forced to move and change their names. Some victims have even committed suicide.

The Cyber Civil Rights Initiative, Inc. (CCRI) (www.cybercivilrights.org) and Without My Consent (WMC) (withoutmyconsent.org) are two organizations leading the way in the fight against revenge porn. CCRI is a not-for-profit organization with the mission to bring awareness to and reduce the occurrence of harassment on the Internet. CCRI's End Revenge Porn (ERP) campaign specifically focuses on the problem of nonconsensual distribution of intimate images Through the ERP, CCRI advocates for technological, social, and legal innovation to fight nonconsensual pornography and provides direct support to its victims. CCRI collaborates with law firms and private attorneys to provide pro bono legal services to victims around the world. It also operates a 24-hour hotline for victims, providing them with emotional support and referrals for takedown services and lawyers. Finally, CCRI works with major social media and technology companies to develop policies to prevent the proliferation of intimate images and other forms of online harassment. CCRI provides direct services to over 1,500 victims of revenge porn every year and has almost 100,000 unique visitors from 191 countries visit its website. CCRI educates stakeholders on the drafting of criminal legislation prohibiting nonconsensual pornography.

WMC is a not-for-profit organization that provides tools and educational materials free of charge to empower victims and survivors of online harassment to combat online invasions of privacy. The WMC website is a one-stop resource for attorneys seeking substantive information about current statutes, case law, and procedure on the legal topics of personal privacy and online harassment. WMC publishes and updates practical resources for victims and advocates across the United States and provides training to law enforcement, lawyers, and victim advocates on how to effectively fight online harassment through the criminal and civil justice system [8].

In a 2015 landmark case, Craig Brittain, the operator of an alleged revenge porn website, was banned from publicly sharing any more nude videos or photographs of people without their affirmative express consent, under a settlement with the FTC. In addition, he was ordered to destroy the intimate images and personal contact information he collected while operating the site. The FTC's complaint against Craig Brittain alleged that he used deception to acquire and post intimate images of women, then referred them to another website he controlled, where they were told they could have the pictures removed if they paid hundreds of dollars [9].

According to the FTC's complaint, Brittain acquired the images in several ways, such as by posing as a woman on the advertising site Craigslist, and offering nude photos purportedly of himself in exchange for photos provided by women. When women provided him with the photos, Brittain posted them on his site without their knowledge or permission. In addition to collecting and posting the images himself, Brittain solicited viewers of his site to anonymously submit nude photos of people to his site, according to the complaint. He required submissions to include sensitive personal information about the people in the photos, including their full name, town and state, phone number, and Facebook profile. Overall,

Brittain's site included photos of more than 1000 individuals, according to the complaint.

Women whose photographs and information were posted on the site contacted Brittain to have the information removed, citing the potential harm to their careers and reputations. In addition, women cited unwelcome contact from strangers who had discovered their information on Brittain's site. The FTC complaint notes that in many cases Brittain did not respond to the women's requests to remove the information. In fact, the complaint alleges that Brittain's site advertised content removal services under the name "takedown hammer" and "takedown lawyer" that could delete consumers' images and content from the site in exchange for a payment of $200–$500. Despite presenting these as third-party services, the complaint alleges that the sites for these services were owned and operated by Brittain [10].

In 2015, a revenge porn website operator and an accomplice, Charles Evens and Hunter Moore, were sentenced to 25 months in a federal prison on computer crime and identity theft charges. Evens pleaded guilty in July to one count of unauthorized access to a protected computer to obtain information for purposes of private financial gain and one count of aggravated identity theft. Evens obtained nude pictures that were posted on the revenge porn website operated by Hunter Moore (http://isanyoneup.com) [11].

On his website, Moore posted nude and sexually explicit photos that were submitted without the permission of victims. To obtain more photos for the website, Evens hacked into Google e-mail accounts. Moore sent payments to Evens in exchange for nude photos unlawfully obtained from victims' accounts. Moore then posted the illegally obtained photos on his website without the victims' consent. Evens admitted that he hacked into e-mail accounts belonging to hundreds of victims [12].

Revenge porn cases have also been reported in Australia [13] and the United Kingdom [14]. In 2015, the technology company Google stated it planned to honor requests to remove revenge porn or unauthorized nude or sexually explicit images from its Internet search engine. Earlier in 2015, social networking site Twitter took similar action, banning intimate photos or videos that were taken or distributed without a subject's consent. The social forum Reddit also updated its privacy policy so that such content is not posted without the subject's permission [15]. In 2014, Japan enacted a new Revenge Porn Prevention Act largely because the number of cases were increasing from year to year and in 2013 there were 318 suspects arrested in Japan [16].

Sextortion is a crime closely related to revenge porn in several ways. However, with sextortion a person is being blackmailed to not have photos or videos posted on the Internet, whereas with revenge porn the dynamic is usually the opposite, victims are asked for money to remove already posted material. The Brookings Institute published an in-depth study of sextortion in 2016. Researchers at Brookings searched dockets and news stories for criminal cases in which one person used a computer network to extort another into producing pornography or engaging in sexual activity. They found nearly 80 such cases involving, by conservative estimates, more than 3000 victims [17].

Far too often, former spouses and former lovers are the perpetrators of social media warfare attacks using exposure or deception tactics like revenge porn, stalking, and harassment. *Cyberstalking* can be defined as the use of the Internet, e-mail, social media, or other electronic communications devices to stalk another person. Few research studies have examined the use of technology in partner or former partner stalking. There are relatively low rates of technology use within the context of stalking in general, but partner stalking victims have reported unwanted contact through e-mail or Internet applications. Clearly, websites or social networking sites can be used to threaten victims, encourage others to contact victims, post personal information publicly, impersonate others to gain information about or access to victims, and spread rumors about victims [18].

One study found that prior relationships between victims and stalkers included marriage (57%), cohabitation (25%), serious dating but not living together (24%), and casual dating (15%). Almost two-thirds of victims had suffered domestic violence in their prior relationship with the stalker. The length of stalking ranged between one month and 38 years, with a median of 12 months [19]. Many U.S. states have passed laws against cyberstalking.

12.4 Cybercrime and Financial Fraud

Financial fraud has long existed. The Internet and social media provide fraudsters with new tools to do the same old nasty things they have been doing for centuries. Now it is faster, easier, and safer for fraudsters to victimize people all over the world and do so from all over the world. Several common Internet fraud methods are listed in Table 12.1.

The Internet Crime Complaint Center (IC3) provides the public with a reliable and convenient reporting mechanism to submit information to the FBI concerning

Table 12.1   Common Cyber Fraud Methods

Auction fraud	Internet extortion
Counterfeit cashier's check	Investment fraud
Credit card fraud	Lotteries
Debt elimination	Nigerian letter or "419"
Parcel courier e-mail scheme	Phishing/spoofing
Employment/business opportunities	Ponzi/pyramid
Escrow services fraud	Ransomware
Identity theft	Reshipping
	Spam
	Third-party receiver of funds

suspected Internet-facilitated criminal activity. Since 2000, the IC3 has received complaints across the spectrum of cybercrime, including the many forms of online fraud related to intellectual property rights (IPRs) matters, computer intrusions (hacking), economic espionage (theft of trade secrets), online extortion, international money laundering, identity theft, and a growing list of Internet-facilitated crimes.

It is increasingly evident that, regardless of the label placed on a cybercrime matter, the potential for it to overlap with another referred matter is substantial. The IC3, formerly known as the Internet Fraud Complaint Center, was renamed in October 2003 to better reflect the broad character of Internet- or cyber-based matters that are referred to the IC3, and to minimize the need for one to distinguish Internet fraud from other potentially overlapping cybercrimes. There have been 3,463,620 complaints reported to the IC3 since its inception. Over the last five years, the IC3 received an average of nearly 300,000 complaints per year. The complaints address a wide array of Internet scams affecting victims across the globe.

For 2015, the ICS recorded over one billion dollars in losses from reported Internet fraud, with over 125,000 complainants reporting financial losses. The median dollar loss reported by complainants was $560.00 while the average loss was $8421.00. Losses by type of incident reported to IC3 are shown in Table 12.2 [20].

Many types of fraud can be found in social media, e-mail messages, and on websites:

- A Ponzi scheme is investment fraud that involves the payment of purported returns to existing investors from funds contributed by new investors. Ponzi schemes often share common characteristics, such as offering overly consistent returns, unregistered investments, high returns with little or no risk, or secretive or complex strategies. This arrangement gives investors the impression there is a legitimate, money-making enterprise behind the subject's story, but in reality unwitting investors are the only source of funding.
- Affinity fraud: Perpetrators of affinity fraud take advantage of the tendency of people to trust others with whom they share similarities—such as religion or ethnic identity—to gain their trust and money.
- Pyramid schemes: In pyramid schemes, as in Ponzi schemes, money collected from new participants is paid to earlier participants. In pyramid schemes, however, participants receive commissions for recruiting new participants into the scheme.
- Prime bank investment fraud: In these schemes, perpetrators claim to have access to a secret trading program endorsed by large financial institutions such as the Federal Reserve Bank, Treasury Department, World Bank, International Monetary Fund, and so on. Perpetrators often claim the unusually high rates of return and low risk are the result of a worldwide secret exchange open only to the world's largest financial institutions. Victims are

Table 12.2   2015 Internet Crimes by Victim Loss

Type of Crime	Dollar Loss	Type of Crime	Dollar Loss
Business e-mail compromise	$246,226,016	Harassment/threats of violence	$13,126,123
Confidence fraud/ romance	$203,390,531	Government impersonation	$12,090,159
Non-payment/ non-delivery	$121,329,122	Civil matter	$9,946,345
Investment	$119,177,899	Phishing/vishing/ smishing/pharming	$8,174,316
Identity theft	$57,294,589	Copyright and counterfeit	$7,230,803
Other	$56,153,977	Reshipping	$3,831,957
Advanced fee	$50,721,226	Malware/scareware	$2,912,628
419/overpayment	$49,217,119	Denial of service	$2,770,978
Personal data breach	$43,477,526	Ransomware	$1,620,814
Credit card fraud	$41,503,502	Charity	$1,328,153
Real estate/rental	$41,417,647	Virus	$1,230,812
Corporate data breach	$38,800,430	Gambling	$955,360
Employment	$33,890,824	Healthcare related	$906,343
Lottery/sweepstake	$19,365,223	Hacktivist	$171,601
Auction	$18,906,416	Crimes against children	$97,584
Misrepresentation	$17,974,014	Terrorism	$65,789
Extortion	$14,799,705	Criminal forums	$55,996

often drawn into prime bank investment fraud because the criminals use sophisticated terms, legal-looking documents, and claim the investments are insured against loss.

■ Advance fee fraud: Advance fee schemes require victims to advance relatively small sums of money in the hope of realizing much larger gains. Not all advance fee schemes are investment frauds. In those that are, however, victims are told that to have the opportunity to be an investor (in an initial offering of a promising security, investment, commodity, etc.), the victim must first send funds to cover taxes or processing fees and other expenses.

■ Promissory notes: These are generally short-term debt instruments issued by little-known or nonexistent companies. The notes typically promise high returns with little or no risk and are typically not registered as securities with the appropriate regulatory agency.

■ Commodities fraud: Commodities fraud is the sale or purported sale of a commodity through illegal means. Commodities are raw materials or semi-finished goods that are relatively uniform in nature and are sold on an exchange (e.g., gold, pork bellies, orange juice, and coffee). Commodities fraud usually involves illicit marketing or trading in commodities futures or options. Perpetrators often offer investment opportunities in commodities markets that falsely promise high rates of return with little or no risk.

■ Foreign currency exchange (Forex) fraud: Perpetrators of Forex fraud entice individuals into investing in the spot foreign currency market through false claims and high-pressure sales tactics. Foreign currency firms that engage in this type of fraud invest client funds into the Forex market not with the intent to conduct a profitable trade for the client, but merely to churn the client's account. Churning creates large commission charges benefiting the trading firm. In other forms of Forex fraud, the perpetrator creates artificial account statements that reflect purported investments when, in reality, no such investments have been made. Instead, the money has been diverted for the perpetrator's personal use.

■ Precious metals fraud: These fraud schemes offer investment opportunities in metals commodities such as rare earth, gold, and silver. Perpetrators of precious metals fraud entice individuals into investing in a commodity through false claims and high-pressure sales tactics. Often in these types of fraud, perpetrators create artificial account statements that reflect purported investments when, in reality, no such investments have been made. Instead, the money has been diverted for the perpetrators' personal use [21].

Mortgage fraud schemes employ some type of material misstatement, misrepresentation, or omission relating to a real estate transaction that one or more parties to the transaction relies on. These schemes include foreclosure rescue schemes; loan modification schemes; illegal property flipping; builder bailout/condo conversion; equity skimming; silent second; home equity conversion mortgage; commercial real estate loans; and air loans. The following is a more detailed explanation of these schemes:

■ Foreclosure rescue schemes: Perpetrators identify homeowners who are in foreclosure or at risk of defaulting on their mortgage loan. Perpetrators then mislead homeowners into believing they can save their homes by transferring the deed or putting the property in the name of an investor. Perpetrators profit by selling the property to an investor or straw borrower, creating equity using a fraudulent appraisal, and stealing the seller proceeds or fees paid by the homeowners. The homeowners are sometimes told they can pay rent for at least a year and repurchase the property once their credit has been re-established. However, the perpetrators fail to make the mortgage payments and usually the property goes into foreclosure.

■ Loan modification schemes: Scammers purport to assist homeowners who are delinquent in their mortgage payments and are on the verge of losing their home by offering to renegotiate the terms of the homeowners' loan with the lender. The scammers, however, demand large fees up front and often negotiate unfavorable terms for the clients, or do not negotiate at all. Usually, homeowners ultimately lose their homes. This scheme is similar to a foreclosure rescue scam.

■ Illegal property flipping: Property is purchased, falsely appraised at a higher value, and then quickly sold. What makes property flipping illegal is that the appraisal information is fraudulent. Schemes typically involve one or more of the following: fraudulent appraisals; falsified loan documentation; inflated buyer income; or kickbacks to buyers, investors, property/loan brokers, appraisers, and title company employees.

■ Builder bailout/condo conversion: Builders facing rising inventory and declining demand for newly constructed homes employ bailout schemes to offset losses. Builders find buyers who obtain loans for the properties. The buyers then allow the properties to go into foreclosure. In a condo-conversion scheme, apartment complexes purchased by developers during a housing boom are converted into condos. When the market declines, developers have excess inventory of units. Developers recruit straw buyers with cash-back incentives and inflate the value of the condos to obtain a larger sales price at closing. In addition to failing to disclose the cash-back incentives to the lender, the straw buyers' income and asset information are often inflated for them to qualify for properties that they otherwise would be ineligible or unqualified to purchase.

■ Equity skimming: An investor may use a straw buyer, false income documents, and false credit reports to obtain a mortgage loan in the straw buyer's name. After closing, the straw buyer signs the property over to the investor in a quit claim deed, which relinquishes all rights to the property and provides no guaranty to title. The investor does not make any mortgage payments and rents the property until foreclosure takes place several months later.

■ Silent second: The buyer of a property borrows the down payment from the seller through the issuance of a non-disclosed second mortgage. The primary lender believes the borrower has invested his own money in the down payment, when in fact, it is borrowed. The second mortgage may not be recorded to further conceal its status from the primary lender.

■ Home equity conversion mortgage (HECM): A HECM is a reverse mortgage loan product insured by the Federal Housing Administration to borrowers who are 62 years or older, own their own property (or have a small mortgage balance), occupy the property as their primary residence, and participate in HECM counseling. It provides homeowners access to equity in their homes, usually in a lump sum payment. Perpetrators recruit seniors through local churches, investment seminars, and television, radio, billboard, and mailer advertisements. The scammers then obtain a HECM in the name of the recruited homeowner to convert equity in the homes into cash. The scammers keep the cash and pay a fee to the senior citizen or take the full amount unbeknownst to the senior citizen. No loan payment or repayment is required until the borrower no longer uses the house as a primary residence. In the scheme, the appraisals on the home are vastly inflated and the lender does not detect the fraud until the homeowner dies and the true value of the property is discovered.

■ Commercial real estate loans: Owners of distressed commercial real estate obtain financing by creating bogus leases and using these fake leases to exaggerate the building's profitability, thus inflating their appraisal values using the income method approach. These false leases and appraisals trick lenders into extending loans to the owner. As cash flows are restricted to the borrower, property repairs are neglected. By the time the commercial loans are in default, the lender is often left with dilapidated and unusable or difficult-to-rent commercial property. Many of the methods of committing mortgage fraud that are found in residential real estate are also present in commercial loan fraud.

■ Air loans: This is a nonexistent property loan where there is usually no collateral. Air loans involve brokers who invent borrowers and properties, establish accounts for payments, and maintain custodial accounts for escrows. They may establish an office with a bank of telephones, each one used as the fake employer, appraiser, or credit agency to fraudulently deceive creditors who attempt to verify information on loan applications [21].

12.5 Conclusions

Adults and children frequently become victims of social media warfare from several sources of attack. These can take the form of harassment, revenge actions, identity theft, fraudulent transactions, and computer or phone hacking. This chapter examined some of the ways adults have been harmed by other individuals who used these adverse social media warfare tactics against them. Important conclusions can be drawn from the material presented in this chapter:

■ It is difficult to provide a precise assessment because different law enforcement agencies may classify identity theft crimes differently, and because identity theft can also involve credit card fraud, Internet fraud, or mail theft, among other crimes.

- Many people do not realize how easily criminals can obtain an individual's personal data without having to break into their homes.
- With enough identifying information about an individual, a criminal can take over that individual's identity to conduct a wide range of crimes.
- Individuals and businesses can take many very simple steps to protect their identity information and avoid becoming victims of identity theft.
- Many companies refer to their services as identity theft protection services. In fact, no service can protect an individual from having personal information stolen.
- An emerging form of identity theft that came to prominence in a new study was the submission of false tax claims with the IRS using stolen identification information.
- The Internet has greatly facilitated the rise of nonconsensual pornography, as dedicated revenge porn sites and other forums openly solicit private intimate images and expose them to millions of viewers.
- Far too often, former spouses and former lovers are the perpetrators of social media warfare attacks using exposure or deception tactics like revenge porn, stalking, and harassment.
- Over the last five years, the IC3 received an average of nearly 300,000 complaints per year. The complaints address a wide array of Internet scams affecting victims across the globe.

12.6 Agenda for Action

It has taken far too long to address vulnerabilities in cybersecurity and identity security. Research has been done and best practices developed to reduce and defend against fraud, scams, and attacks on individual privacy. There are numerous sources of education and advice on how individuals can protect themselves from such attacks. Clearly, not all have paid heed and fraud, scams, and attacks on individual privacy continue at an alarming rate. Action steps should include, but not be limited to, the following areas:

- Support and expand education programs on how individuals can protect themselves from personal attacks on the Internet
- Support and expand education programs at elementary and middle school level on how individuals can protect themselves from personal attacks on the Internet.
- Develop a series of public service advertisements to help raise awareness of the need for individuals to practice more effective Internet habits.
- Continue and expand training programs for law enforcement to investigate Internet fraud and revenge porn.

12.7 Key Terms

Credit monitoring is a service and process that warns people about activity that shows up on their credit report.

Cyberstalking is the use of the Internet, e-mail, social media, or other electronic communications devices to stalk another person.

Identity monitoring provides alerts when personal information like bank account information or social security, driver's license, passport, or medical identification number is being used in ways that generally will not show up on a credit report.

Identity recovery services are designed to help regain control of a name and finances after identity theft occurs.

Identity theft is the unauthorized use of an individual's personally identifiable information to impersonate the individual and illegally use that information to commit crimes of fraud.

Identity theft insurance is offered by most major identity theft protection services; it generally covers out-of-pocket expenses directly associated with reclaiming an identity.

Identity theft protection services are monitoring and recovery services that watch for signs that an identity thief may be using personal information and helps to deal with the effects of identity theft after it happens.

Personally identifiable information (PII) is information that can be used to distinguish or trace an individual's identity, either alone or when combined with other personal or identifying information that is linked or linkable to a specific individual.

Revenge porn is the disclosure of sexually explicit images without consent and for no legitimate purpose.

Sextortion is a crime closely related to revenge porn; however, with sextortion a person is blackmailed to not have photos or videos posted on the Internet whereas with revenge porn the dynamic is usually the opposite, victims are asked for money to remove already-posted material.

12.8 Seminar Discussion Topics

Discussion topics for graduate- or professional-level seminars:

- What experience have seminar participants had in situations where social media warfare tactics were used to commit fraud? What was done about the fraud?
- What experience have seminar participants had in situations where social media warfare tactics were used to perpetrate a revenge porn offense? What was done about the revenge porn offense?

■ What experience have seminar participants had in situations where social media warfare tactics were used to perpetrate a sextortion offense? What was done about the sextortion offense?

12.9 Seminar Group Project

Divide participants into multiple groups with each group taking 10–15 minutes to develop a list of defenses against social media warfare tactics that are used to commit fraud. Upon completion, have groups exchange their lists of social media warfare tactics, with groups taking 10–15 minutes to develop measures to effectively counter the defensive tactics. Meet as a group and discuss the offensive tactics selected by the groups and the defensive measures to counter the tactics that were developed by the groups.

References

1. U.S. Federal Bureau of Investigation. Identity theft. Accessed September 24, 2016. https://www.fbi.gov/investigate/cyber/identity-theft.
2. U.S. Department of Justice. 2015. Identity theft. Accessed September 24, 2016. https://www.justice.gov/criminal-fraud/identity-theft/identity-theft-and-identity-fraud.
3. U.S. Federal Trade Commission. 2015. Warning signs of identity theft. Accessed September 24, 2016. https://www.consumer.ftc.gov/articles/0272-how-keep-your-personal-information-secure.
4. U.S. Federal Trade Commission. 2013. Tax-related identity theft. Accessed September 24, 2016. https://www.consumer.ftc.gov/articles/0008-tax-related-identity-theft.
5. U.S. Federal Trade Commission. 2012. How to keep your personal information secure. Accessed September 24, 2016. https://www.consumer.ftc.gov/articles/0272-how-keep-your-personal-information-secure.
6. U.S. Federal Trade Commission. 2016. Identity theft protection services. Accessed September 24, 2016. https://www.consumer.ftc.gov/articles/0235-identity-theft-protection-services.
7. Filletti, Marissa. 17, 2015. UC CIMIP releases report: 'New face of identity theft.' Accessed September 24, 2016. http://www.utica.edu/academic/institutes/cimip/mediacenter/index.cfm?action=detail&id=4305.
8. U.S. Federal Trade Commission. 2015. Comments of the Cyber Civil Rights Initiative, Inc. and Without My Consent, Inc. to the Federal Trade Commission in the matter of Craig Brittain, individually. FTC File No. 132 3120. Accessed September 26, 2016. https://www.ftc.gov/system/files/documents/public_comments/2015/02/00007-93359.pdf.
9. U.S. Federal Trade Commission. 2015. Website operator banned from the 'revenge porn' business after FTC charges he unfairly posted nude photos. Accessed September 26, 2016. https://www.ftc.gov/news-events/press-releases/2015/01/website-operator-banned-revenge-porn-business-after-ftc-charges.

10. U.S. Federal Trade Commission. 2016. FTC approves final order in Craig Brittain 'revenge porn' case. Accessed September 26, 2016. https://www.ftc.gov/news-events/press-releases/2016/01/ftc-approves-final-order-craig-brittain-revenge-porn-case.

11. U.S. Federal Bureau of Investigation. 2015. L.A. man who hacked into e-mail accounts and obtained nude photos for revenge pornography website sentenced to ederal prison. Accessed September 26, 2016. https://www.fbi.gov/contact-us/field-offices/losangeles/news/press-releases/l.a.-man-who-hacked-into-e-mail-accounts-and-obtained-nude-photos-for-revenge-porn-website-sentenced-to-federal-prison.

12. U.S. Federal Bureau of Investigation. 2015. Operator of revenge pornography website sentenced to more than two years in federal prison in e-mail hacking scheme to obtain nude photos. Accessed September 26, 2016. https://www.fbi.gov/contact-us/field-offices/losangeles/news/press-releases/operator-of-revenge-pornography-website-sentenced-to-more-than-two-years-in-federal-prison-in-e-mail-hacking-scheme-to-obtain-nude-photos.

13. U.S. Library of Congress. 2015. Australia: Damages awarded in revenge porn case. *Global Legal Monitor*. Accessed September 26, 2016. http://www.loc.gov/law/foreign-news/article/australia-damages-awarded-in-revenge-porn-case/.

14. U.S. Library of Congress. 2015. England and Wales: First woman convicted under revenge porn law receives suspended sentence. *Global Legal Monitor*. Accessed September 26, 2016. https://www.loc.gov/law/foreign-news/article/england-and-wales-first-woman-convicted-under-revenge-porn-law-receives-suspended-sentence/.

15. Voice of America. 2015. Google cracks down on 'revenge porn.' *VOA News*. Accessed September 26, 2016. http://www.voanews.com/a/google-cracks-down-revenge-porn/2831137.html.

16. U.S. Library of Congress. 2014. Japan: New Revenge Porn Prevention Act. *Global Legal Monitor*. Accessed September 26, 2016. http://www.loc.gov/law/foreign-news/article/japan-new-revenge-porn-prevention-act/.

17. Wittes, Benjamin, Poplin, Cody, Jurecic, Quinta and Spera, Clara. 2016. Sextortion: Cybersecurity, teenagers, and remote sexual assault. Brookings Institute. Accessed September 27, 2016. https://www.brookings.edu/research/sextortion-cybersecurity-teenagers-and-remote-sexual-assault/.

18. National Institute of Justice. 2012. Intimate partner stalking tactics. Accessed September 27, 2016. http://nij.gov/topics/crime/intimate-partner-violence/stalking/pages/tactics.aspx.

19. National Institute of Justice. 2007. Information on stalking victims. Accessed September 27, 2016. http://www.nij.gov/topics/crime/stalking/Pages/victims.aspx.

20. U.S. Federal Bureau of Investigation. 2015 Internet crime report. Accessed September 27, 2016. https://pdf.ic3.gov/2015_IC3Report.pdf.

21. U.S. Federal Bureau of Investigation. 2009–2011. Financial crimes report 2010–2011. Accessed September 28, 2016. https://www.fbi.gov/stats-services/publications/financial-crimes-report-2010-2011.

Chapter 13

Law Enforcement Response to Social Media Warfare

Law enforcement agencies and officers are stuck right in the middle of social media warfare. Criminal activity is riddled with social media warfare tactics as are law enforcement's efforts to fight crime. Social protest and civil disobedience is organized quickly using social media and often more quickly than law enforcement can respond. Crimes of fraud and harassment are perpetrated using social media warfare tactics, which creates a challenge for law enforcement to keep abreast of tactics and criminal activity. Another challenge is policing the personal use of social media by law enforcement officers, which at times has been embarrassing and compromising for law enforcement agencies around the world. This chapter examines some of the issues and challenges that law enforcement agencies are addressing in the realm of social media warfare.

13.1 Law Enforcement Officers' Personal Use of Social Media

Given the thorough integration of social media into everyday life and the ease with which people can instantly share their thoughts, opinions, and status with family, friends, and strangers, some people, including law enforcement officers, will post items that other people may find inappropriate. This becomes particularly problematic when an employee of a public safety agency posts or is depicted in such material. Because of the significant adverse effects public safety employees' misuse of social media can have on them as witnesses, on agency operations, and on a department's relationship with the community it serves, many police agencies have addressed their employees' use of social media, whether proactively in the form of policy, reactively in the face of an incident, or both [1].

Some law enforcement employees, particularly those accustomed to using social media regularly to communicate with friends or followers, often post material with little or no consideration of who may have access to it or how it may be shared. Not surprisingly, there are many examples of the perils faced by officers or other department employees who post first and think later.

Further complicating the issue for police agencies and because of evolving generational standards of what constitutes private information, younger officers and other agency employees are more inclined to share information publicly that in the past was communicated only to family members or close acquaintances.

Because of the ever-increasing frequency of government employees' use of social media both on and off duty, many law enforcement agencies have recently adopted policies and guidelines that specifically address this issue. These policies set forth the expectations and rules governing employees' use of social media, and violation of them might subject the employee to departmental discipline. Several law enforcement agencies integrate a *cybervetting* component into the comprehensive background investigations they conduct on applicants and on-board employees.

Law enforcement always has been a dangerous profession because officers risk their lives daily. In the past, officers could take several steps to help protect themselves and their loved ones from threats. Social media has brought danger home to officers and their families because they cannot shield themselves as easily from the repercussions of their job responsibilities. More and more law enforcement agencies are beginning to understand the influence and pitfalls of social media and are adopting policies addressing the use of social media in order to protect their employees.

Information obtained from public records (e.g., birth, death, and real estate) has been available online for years. By increasing exposure of *personally identifiable information*, social media raises the threat level for law enforcement personnel and their families. There are few constraints in the use of social media and almost anyone can post anything online with little fear of repercussion. An anonymous online environment encourages inflammatory and shocking behavior and makes it easier to perpetrate the *theft of personal or financial data*. Individuals sometimes create screen names or new identities that allow them to act outside their normal inhibitions and participate in caustic and less ethical activities they would otherwise avoid. Anonymity of social media users makes it far more difficult to address these issues. Social media can create a mob mentality where one stimulus may spark a wide-scale reaction that feeds on itself and rapidly develops faster, reaches farther, and spreads more rapidly than anything law enforcement has had to deal with before.

Rapid access to personally identifiable information about law enforcement officers makes it easier for an individual to learn personal facts about an officer. This can help to eliminate any cooling off period during which individuals might reconsider their retaliatory actions. Outraged offenders easily could get to officers' doorsteps before their patrol shifts end, leaving them unable to defend their homes or families.

There have been cases of comments posted online by officers that have led to disciplinary actions. These behaviors are the key focus of social media policies currently in place. Postings by the public over which departments have no control can be even more damaging. Regardless of their level of truth, negative comments create lasting impressions.

To protect employees, law enforcement agencies are implementing internal management mechanisms to lessen this potential threat. Ongoing training on current issues, the hazards of social media, and self-protection is important, but so is having a dedicated social media manager who facilitates the elimination of employees' personally identifiable information from social networking sites and maintains consistency for all personnel.

Law enforcement agencies can also benefit from paying attention to comments about a department, its programs, and personnel that are posted on social media. Agencies can identify and mitigate negative images or potential dangers. Consistent monitoring of networking sites provides an early warning system against any threats being developed or discussed online [2].

A typical law enforcement agency will have a policy that covers employee personal use of social media that covers employee personal use of social media affecting the workplace and or the department's ability to perform its public mission. Many departments recognize the role that social media plays in the personal lives of some employees. However, since the personal use of social media can affect employees in their official capacity, law enforcement agencies are cautious about how employees use social media in their private lives.

Policies generally state that engaging in prohibited speech outlined in the policy may provide grounds for discipline and may be used to undermine or impeach an officer's testimony in legal proceedings. Many policies include the following concepts:

- Employees shall not post speech that negatively impacts the department's ability to serve the public.
- Employees may express themselves as private citizens on social media sites as long as employees do not make, share, or comment in support of any posting that includes harassment, threats of violence, or similar conduct.
- Employees will not make, share, or comment in support of any posting that ridicules, maligns, disparages, expresses bias, or disrespect toward any race, religion, sex, gender, sexual orientation, nationality, or any other protected class of individuals.

- Employees will not make, share, or comment in support of any posting that suggests that department personnel are engaged in behavior reasonably considered to be unlawful or reckless toward public safety.
- Employees shall make reasonable efforts to remove content appearing on their social media accounts that violates policy upon learning of the offensive content.
- Employees shall not post or otherwise disseminate any confidential information they have access to as a result of their employment with the department.
- Employees may not make any statements, appearances, endorsements, or publish materials that could reasonably be considered to represent the views or positions of the department.
- Employees may not use their city e-mail address to register a personal account on social media [3].

Most departments expect employees to be attentive and careful in their use of social media and are cautioned that they should be aware that their use of social media may be perceived as representing their city and city government, and should tailor their use accordingly. Many social media use policies are specific about unacceptable uses and include the following concepts:

- Using social media in a manner that does not comply with federal, state, and local laws and regulations, and with city and agency policies.
- Using social media in a manner that violates the copyright, trademark, or other intellectual property rights of any person or entity, or otherwise violates their legal ownership interests.
- Using social media in a manner that includes ethnic slurs, profanity, personal insults; material that is harassing, defamatory, fraudulent, or discriminatory; or other content or communications that would not be acceptable in a city workplace under city or agency policy or practice.
- Using social media in a manner that violates the terms of contracts governing the use of any social media content, including but not limited to, software and other intellectual property licenses; displays sexually explicit images, cartoons, jokes, messages, or other material in violation of City Policy Preventing Sexual Harassment in city government [4,5].

13.2 Social Media Warfare in Intelligence and Investigative Activities

Social media warfare tactics are increasingly being used to instigate or conduct criminal activity, and law enforcement personnel should understand the concept and function of these sites and know how social media tools and resources can be used to prevent, mitigate, respond to, and investigate criminal activity. To ensure that information obtained from social media sites for investigative and criminal intelligence–related activity is used lawfully while also ensuring that individuals' and groups' privacy, civil rights, and civil liberties are protected, law enforcement agencies should have a policy on how such social media research is used and managed. This policy should communicate the differing levels of engagement with subjects, such as apparent, overt, discrete, or covert, that law enforcement personnel are involved in when accessing social media sites, and specify the authorization requirements, if any, associated with each level of engagement.

These levels of engagement range from law enforcement personnel viewing information that is publicly available on social media sites to the creation of an undercover profile to directly interact with an identified criminal online. Articulating the agency's levels of engagement and authorization requirements is critical to agency personnel's understanding of how information from social media sites can be used by law enforcement and is a key aspect of a social media use policy.

Social media sites and resources should be viewed as another tool in the law enforcement investigative toolbox and should be used in a manner that adheres to the same principles that govern all law enforcement activity. Such actions must be lawful and personnel must have a defined objective and a valid law enforcement purpose for gathering, maintaining, or sharing personally identifiable information. In addition, any law enforcement action involving undercover activity (including developing an undercover profile on a social media site) should address supervisory approval, required documentation of activity, periodic reviews of activity, and the audit of undercover processes and behavior. Law enforcement agencies should also not collect or maintain the political, religious, or social views, associations, or activities of any individual or group, association, corporation, business, partnership, or organization unless there is a legitimate public safety purpose.

These principles help define and place limitations on law enforcement actions and ensure that individuals' and groups' privacy, civil rights, and civil liberties are diligently protected. When law enforcement personnel adhere to these principles, they are ensuring that their actions are performed with the highest respect for the law.

The Bureau of Justice Assistance (BJA) with the support of the Global Justice Information Sharing Initiative Global Advisory Committee (GAC), a Federal Advisory Committee (FAC) to the U.S. Attorney General on justice-related information sharing, and the Criminal Intelligence Coordinating Council (CICC) have developed the resource "Developing a Policy on the Use of Social Media in Intelligence and Investigative Activities: Guidance and Recommendations," which provides law enforcement leadership and policymakers with recommendations and issues to consider when developing policy related to the use of social media information for criminal intelligence and investigative activities. A social media–related policy (or a policy that includes procedures on the use of social media information) will help protect law enforcement agencies and agency personnel and will also help ensure the continued protection of privacy, civil rights, and civil liberties of individuals and groups in the community.

"The Developing a Policy on the Use of Social Media in Intelligence and Investigative Activities: Guidance and Recommendations" publication is designed to guide law enforcement agency personnel through the development of a social media policy by identifying elements that should be considered when drafting a policy, as well as issues to consider when developing a policy, focusing on privacy, civil rights, and civil liberties protections. All law enforcement agencies, regardless of size and jurisdiction, can benefit from the guidance [6]. The guidance on social media policy recommends that a policy address several key elements, which are shown in Table 13.1.

In May 2016, the Director of National Intelligence, James Clapper, signed "Security Executive Agent Directive Five," codifying federal background investigative authority to incorporate publicly available social media information in the security clearance process. The new policy comes into effect after a long, deliberative process recognizing the ubiquity of social media and the importance of maintaining privacy and civil liberties. The policy does not require security investigations to consider social media information. Instead, it permits the collection of publicly available social media information if an agency head determines it is an

Table 13.1 Social Media Investigatory Policy Key Elements

- Articulate that the use of social media resources will be consistent with applicable laws, regulations, and other agency policies.
- Define if and when the use of social media sites or tools is authorized (as well as use of information on these sites pursuant to the agency's legal authorities and mission requirements).
- Articulate and define the authorization levels needed to use information from social media sites.
- Specify that information obtained from social media resources will undergo evaluation to determine confidence levels (source reliability and content validity).
- Specify the documentation, storage, and retention requirements related to information obtained from social media resources.
- Identify the reasons and purpose, if any, for off-duty personnel to use social media information in connection with their law enforcement responsibilities, as well as how and when personal equipment may be used for an authorized law enforcement purpose.
- Identify dissemination procedures for criminal intelligence and investigative products that contain information obtained from social media sites, including appropriate limitations on the dissemination of personally identifiable information [6].

appropriate investigative tool. This opens possibilities for the U.S. federal government to tap an important open source in efforts to safeguard national security.

This policy places important restrictions that limit the federal government's reach into the private lives of clearance applicants and holders. Absent a national security concern, or criminal reporting requirement, information pertaining to individuals other than the individual being investigated, even information collected inadvertently, will not be pursued. In addition, investigators may not request or require individuals to provide social media passwords, log into a private account, or take any action that would disclose non-publicly available social media information [7].

13.3 Government Training of Social Media Warfare Intelligence and Investigative Professionals

There are several U.S. federal government initiatives and programs for training intelligence and investigative professionals on the use of social media warfare tactics to support their efforts. There are also several agencies involved in providing this training, each for different types of intelligence and investigative professionals.

The U.S. Department of Homeland Security manages the National Initiative for Cybersecurity Careers and Studies (NICCS). The vision of the NICCS is to provide the United States with the tools necessary to ensure citizens and the workforce have more dynamic cybersecurity skills. The NICCS directly focuses on enhancing awareness, expanding the pipeline, and evolving the field of study and practice of cybersecurity skills. NICCS is a national resource available to anyone from government, industry, academia, and the public who seeks to learn more about cybersecurity and opportunities in the field. NICCS is managed by the Cybersecurity Education and Awareness Branch (CEA) within the Department of Homeland Security Office of Cybersecurity and Communications [8]. The following paragraphs describe training programs provided through the MacAfee Institute.

Certified Cyber Intelligence Investigator (CCII)™ program contains 26 modules of self-study learning opportunities. Learning objectives include a cyber intelligence overview, e-crime investigation methodologies, advanced e-crime investigations, classified investigation methodologies, exploring the deep web, *open source intelligence*, and documenting social media evidence. A more advanced program in the same area is the Certified Cyber Intelligence Professional (CCIP)™.

Certified Cyber Investigations Expert's (CCIE's)™ program is designed to train elite cyber investigators in advanced and state-of-the-art methodologies to identify, investigate, and resolve the most complex cybercrimes. This is a 6-month online professional board certification focused on enhancing skill sets that takes a blended learning approach of self-study, live interactions, and instructor-led investigative exercises. The program contains over 500 video-based lectures resulting in hundreds of hours of online training, online prep review quizzes to prepare for a final exam, and the necessary study manuals. Learning objectives include conducting cyber investigations and intelligence gathering, cyber intelligence methodologies, e-crime investigations, social media investigations, deep web investigations, digital evidence collection, and setting up a cyber lab [9]. Other training courses in the curriculum include

- Certified Cyber Threat Analyst (CCTA)
- Certified Cyber Threat Forensic Investigator (CTFI)
- Certified eCommerce Fraud Investigator (CEFI)
- Certified Forensic HiTech Investigator (CFHI)
- Certified Human Trafficking Investigator (CHTI)
- Certified Organized Retail Crime Investigator (CORCI)
- Certified Social Media Intelligence Expert (CSMIE)

The U.S. Federal Law Enforcement Training Centers (FLETC) provide career-long training to law enforcement professionals to help them fulfill their responsibilities safely and proficiently. FLETC has grown into the nation's largest provider of law enforcement training. Under a collaborative training model, FLETC's federal partner organizations deliver training unique to their missions, while FLETC provides training in areas common to all law enforcement officers, such as firearms, driving, tactics, investigations, and legal training. Partner agencies realize quantitative and qualitative benefits from this model, including the efficiencies inherent in shared services, higher quality training, and improved interoperability. FLETC's mission is to train all those who protect the homeland, and therefore, its training audience also includes state, local, and tribal departments throughout the United States [10].

FLETC provide the Internet Investigations Training Program which is designed to give investigators, analysts, and individuals serving as direct law enforcement support personnel the basic understanding they need to conduct Internet-based investigations. The program focuses on investigations and operations centered on the use of the Internet and its many communities that are being exploited for criminal activity on a day-to-day basis.

The program is delivered in two instructional modules: investigating Internet crimes and conducting online investigations. The Internet investigations module focuses on the examination of historical Internet data such as e-mails and website posting to identify the author or originator of the Internet activity by looking at system artifacts and attributes. The online investigations segment focuses on the live and active interrogation of online data, such as investigating websites and attempting to determine their physical location. Participants are instructed on how to properly configure their investigative computer and how to setup investigative profiles and personas and on the use of system archival and interrogation tools. Modules include federal court procedures, electronic law and evidence, conducting investigations online, investigating Internet crimes, and the Internet environment [11].

The National White Collar Crime Center (NW3C) supports state and local law enforcement efforts to prevent, investigate, and prosecute economic and high-tech crime. NW3C began its existence in 1978 as the Leviticus Project and was created to conduct a formally structured and centrally coordinated multi-state investigation of a variety of crimes affecting the coal industry in the United States. Funding was provided by the U.S. federal government through a central funding pool, the so-called multi-state projects, which are now known as the Regional Information Sharing System (RISS). In 1991, the project expanded its membership to include all traditional law enforcement agencies in all 50 states and it expanded mission scope. The project shifted its focus from facilitating information sharing to providing training, creating databases, and providing analytical services to assist the membership. In November 1992, the project's name was changed to the National White Collar Crime Center (NW3C). NW3C links criminal justice agencies across jurisdictional borders and provides support for the prevention, investigation, and prosecution of economic and high-tech crime through a combination of research, training, and investigative support services. NW3C now has more than 4000 member agencies in the United States and its territories as well as 15 other countries throughout the world.

The cybercrime section offers free courses to law enforcement personnel that provide training for successful criminal prosecutions [12]. Course topics include the following:

- Advanced Wireless Network Investigations (AWNI)
- Apple® iDevice Forensics (iDF)
- Basic Computer Skills for Law Enforcement (BCS-WB)
- Basic Data Recovery and Acquisition (BDRA)
- Basic Network Intrusion Investigations (BNII)
- Cell Phone Mapping and Analysis (Formerly BCPI) (CPMA)
- Cell Phone Seizure and Acquisition (Formerly CPI) (CPSA)
- Encryption (ENC-WB)
- Fast Track Program (STOP, BDRA, and IDRA) (ICAC-FT - Basic)
- Fast Track Program Advanced (WinArt, INET, MTI, and iDevices) (ICAC-FT—Advanced)
- First Responders and Digital Evidence (LC1-WB)
- GPS Interrogation (GPSI-WB)
- Identifying and Seizing Electronic Evidence—Web Based (ISEE-WB)
- Identifying and Seizing Electronic Evidence (ISEE)
- Intermediate Data Recovery and Analysis (IDRA)
- Introduction to Cell Phone Investigations (ICPI-WB)

- Introduction to Computer Networks (ICN-WB)
- Linux Open Source Forensics (LOSF)
- Macintosh® Forensic Analysis (MFA)
- Macintosh® Triage and Imaging (MTI)
- Mobile Digital Devices and GPS (LC7-WB)
- Online Undercover (LC5-WB)
- Post-Seizure Evidentiary Concerns (LC6-WB)
- Search Warrants and Digital Evidence (LC2-WB)
- Searching Without a Warrant (LC3-WB)
- Secure Techniques for Onsite Previewing (STOP)
- Social Media and Technical Skills (ICAC-SMTS)
- Social Media and Technical Skills (SMTS)
- Social Media Basics (SMB-WB)
- The Stored Communications Act (LC4-WB)
- Windows Artifacts (WinArt)
- Windows Internet Trace Evidence (INET)

The U.S. Department of Defense (DOD) Cyber Crime Center (DC3) provides training for the military, is designated as a national cyber center and DoD center of excellence, and serves as the operational focal point for the Defense Industrial Base Cybersecurity Program. DC3 operates under the executive agency of the secretary of the Air Force. The DC3 mission is to deliver digital forensics and multimedia (D/MM) lab services, cyber technical training, technical solutions development, and cyber analytics for DoD mission areas, including information assurance (IA) and critical infrastructure protection (CIP), law enforcement and counterintelligence (LE/CI), document and media exploitation (DOMEX), and counterterrorism (CT) [13]. Courses offered online or in residence by DC3 include the following:

- ICIT+ Introduction to Cyber Insider Threat
- CTTS+ Cyber Threats and Techniques Seminar
- DDP+ Digital Data Protection
- CITA+ Cyber Insider Threat Analysis
- CAC+ Cyber Analyst Course
- OUT+ Online Undercover Techniques

In March 2016, the U.S. Department of Homeland Security (DHS) executed Cyber Storm V, the fifth iteration of Cyber Storm, DHS's capstone national-level cyber exercise series. Mandated by Congress, these biennial exercises are part of DHS's ongoing efforts to assess and strengthen cyber preparedness, examine incident response processes, and enhance information sharing among federal, state, international, and private sector partners. Each Cyber Storm event builds on lessons learned from previous exercises and real world incidents, ensuring that participants face more sophisticated and challenging exercises every 2 years.

Cyber Storm exercises give the cyber incident response community a safe venue to coordinate and practice plans, response mechanisms and recovery tasks, and build and maintain relationships. Most importantly, the exercises provide the community with the opportunity to identify strengths and areas for improvement, incorporating those lessons into operations to help reduce cyber risks to the nation. Cyber Storm V focused on the main objectives that are shown in Table 13.2.

Cyber Storm V was a distributed exercise that allowed players around the world to participate from their normal work locations. The Exercise Control (EXCON) cell was located at a DHS facility in the Washington, D.C. metropolitan area. The scenario progressed as players received injects through e-mail, phone, in person, and via exercise websites from EXCON. Exercise play simulated adverse effects through which the participants executed their cyber crisis response systems, policies, and procedures.

The significance of the Cyber Storm exercise series has grown since its inception with Cyber Storm I. As cyber-based threats continue to increase, more government agencies, private sector companies, and critical infrastructure organizations have acknowledged the benefits of good cyber hygiene. Cyber Storm V communities include

■ Federal partners
■ Law enforcement/intelligence/Department of Defense
■ State governments
■ International
■ Information technology (IT)/communications
■ Commercial retail facilities
■ Healthcare and public health
■ Public affairs

Table 13.2   Cyber Storm V Main Objectives

• Continue exercising coordination mechanisms, information sharing efforts, development of shared situational awareness, and decision-making procedures of the cyber incident response community.
• Evaluate relevant policy, statutory, and fiscal issues that govern cyber incident response authorities and resource prioritization.
• Provide a forum for exercise participants to exercise, evaluate, and improve the processes, procedures, interactions, and information sharing mechanisms within their organization or community of interest; and
• Assess the role, functions, and capabilities of DHS and other government entities in a cyber event.

The Cyber Storm V scenario introduced participants to multiple adversaries, some working together and others working independently. These adversaries distributed complex new malware that resulted in crippling effects throughout several critical infrastructure sectors. This challenging scenario gave partners the opportunity to practice and assess their policies and procedures for responding to cyber attacks, and required them to cooperate and share information about cyber threats [14].

Some state governments in the United States have also established training programs. The state of California, for example offers a course on Computer Crime Investigation of Internet Crimes. The 40-hour course is designed to provide investigators with the necessary training, skills, knowledge, and practical experience to conduct a variety of online crime investigations. Instruction is also provided on using the Internet as an investigative tool, including Internet protocols; LAN/WAN/GAN operations; e-mail tracing; and using social networking sites as investigative resources. The course is designed for law enforcement personnel assigned to high-technology crime investigation units, white collar crime units, fraud or forgery units, sex and vice crimes units. Additionally, any law enforcement officers with an interest in Internet crime investigations may attend. Upon course completion, students will understand crimes committed on the Internet, use of the Internet as an investigative tool, be able to conduct reactive and proactive investigations on the Internet, and be able to use basic tools to gather evidence on the Internet. Additionally, students will learn state and federal laws applicable to Internet crimes and who to contact for additional resources to aid their investigations [15].

The National Computer Forensic Institute (NCFI) is a federally funded training center dedicated to instructing state and local officials in digital evidence and cybercrime investigations. The NCFI was opened in 2008 with a mandate to provide state and local law enforcement, legal and judicial professionals with a free, comprehensive education on current cybercrime trends, investigative methods, and prosecutorial and judicial challenges.

Run by the U.S. Secret Service's Criminal Investigative Division and the Alabama Office of Prosecution Services, the training model is based upon the Secret Service's successful cyber investigative strategy, which relies on partnering with and sharing information between academia, private industry, and law enforcement/legal communities to combat the ever-evolving threat of cybercrime. Prior to 2008, training for state and local law enforcement in cybercrime was difficult to find. local departments could find occasional training slots in courses taught to federal agents or could acquire the skills and equipment at great cost to their respective agencies.

In 2007, the State of Alabama approached the Secret Service and DHS with a proposal. The State of Alabama agreed to provide the property and funds to construct a state-of-the-art facility if the federal government would fund the training and allow the Secret Service to operate it. An accord was struck, between the DHS, the State of Alabama, the U.S. Secret Service, the Alabama District Attorneys Association, and the City of Hoover. In March of 2007, U.S. Secretary

of Homeland Security, Michael Chertoff went to Hoover to announce the foundation of the National Computer Forensics Institute.

The NCFI's 32,000 square foot facility is located in Hoover, Alabama, a sub-
urb of Birmingham. The NCFI boasts three multi-purpose classrooms, two network investigation classrooms, a mock courtroom, administrative work areas, and
an operational forensics lab dedicated to the Birmingham Electronics Crimes Task
Force. The style and technological features in the classrooms are distinct from any
within the U.S. federal government.

The full-time staff of the NCFI includes a Secret Service member who serves as NCFI
Director, a Special Agent from the Electronic Crimes Special Agent program (ECSAP),
an Administrative Officer, an Alabama state prosecutor, and a course administrator.
Instruction is provided by both Secret Service employees and contract instructors.

State and local agencies benefit from a tuition-free education. In addition, all
travel costs, hotel, and per diem are covered by the NCFI. In some of the forensic
courses and intrusion courses, students are issued with all the hardware, software,
and licenses necessary to conduct these investigations. NCFI students receive the
same equipment and software as the special agents trained by the Secret Service; a
considerable benefit as it allows both the local officer and the federal agent to operate on common systems [16]. The following is a list of courses offered:

■ Basic Mobile Device Investigations (BMDI)
■ Basic Network Investigation Training (BNIT)
■ Online Social Networking (OSN)
■ Basic Computer Evidence Recovery Training (BCERT)
■ Mobile Device Examiner (MDE)
■ Network Intrusion Response Program (NITRO)
■ Advanced Mobile Device Examiner (AMDE)
■ Mac Forensics Training (MFT)
■ Computer Forensics in Court—Judges (CFC-J)
■ Computer Forensics in Court—Prosecutors (CFC-P)
■ Mobile Devices in Court—Prosecutors (MDC-P) [16]

Other training opportunities are available from colleges and universities as
well as state police academies. There are numerous programs geared toward particular states and large municipalities. The best way to find such programs is to
review local education offerings.

13.4 Social Media Warfare Analysts Qualifications, Training, and Functions

One of the most important functions in social media warfare is data collection and
analysis that can help determine the defensive and offensive social media warfare

tactics necessary to achieve a specific goal. Whether an organization is chasing criminals or combating terrorists, to succeed in the use of social media warfare tactics an understanding of the enemy, or the target, is required.

Open source data gathering and analytical skills are a must for the social media warfare analyst. These tools collect data from multiple sources, including websites, social media, broadcast media, gray literature sources, the *dark web*, and traditional press sources, and combine that information with that of geospatial analysts, cyber specialists, librarians, data scientists, and other subject matter experts to identify trends, patterns, and relationships that provide unique insights into specific issues or areas of activity.

A social media warfare analyst usually comes equipped with skills and knowledge in one or more fields, such as military operations, law enforcement, terrorism, cyber security, science, and so on. Social media warfare analysts also need strong writing and analytic skills; foreign language proficiency; well-developed Internet research skills; excellent communication and English-language skills, excellent analytical ability, solid interpersonal skills; the capacity to think clearly and creatively; and the ability to work under tight deadlines.

Social media warfare analysts that specialize in counterterrorism, for example, assess the leadership, motivations, capabilities, plans, and intentions of foreign terrorist groups and their state and non-state sponsors. Their key mission is to identify specific threats, warn of and preempt attacks, disrupt their networks, and eventually defeat terrorist organizations. Counterterrorism analysts analyze a variety of information to gain a comprehensive understanding of a complex analytic issue and produce a range of written intelligence products. Counterterrorism analysts may also be responsible for briefing policy makers and foreign partners, military officials, and intelligence and law enforcement agencies. They highlight targeting opportunities to support intelligence operations designed to counter terrorism. Analysts generally maintain and broaden their professional ties through academic study, contacts, and attendance at professional meetings. They may also choose to pursue additional studies in fields relevant to their areas of responsibility.

Intelligence collection analysts apply their expertise on intelligence collection systems, capabilities, processes, and policies to inform intelligence consumers about collection developments and their effect on analysis through a range of written products and briefings. They collaborate with other analysts and collectors across the intelligence community (IC) to identify intelligence gaps and develop strategies to overcome collection challenges. Collection analysts provide insight that informs decisions on the acquisition and development of current and future collection systems [17].

Investigating the Internet criminal can be one of the most complex tasks facing law enforcement professionals and requires a multi-disciplinary approach supported by technical expertise that was not needed with traditional crime. Internet investigations can focus on the examination of historical Internet data such as e-mails, social media *consumer-generated content*, and website postings to identify the author or originator of the Internet activity by looking at system artifacts and attributes. Online investigations focus on the live and active interrogation of online data, such as investigating websites and attempting to determine their physical location. Investigators must be able to successfully seize and acquire digital evidence whether online or from seized computers, which requires comprehensive digital forensics techniques [18].

Criminal investigators as well as counterterrorism agents need the training necessary to complete a forensically sound, logical acquisition of digital evidence from mobile devices. This requires an understanding of cell technologies (GSM, CDMA, and iDEN), practical application of historical tracking, and the skills to frame an investigation from evidence obtained through call detail records from cellular service providers to map and track the mobile device's movement by using standard mapping programs such as Google Earth™. Evidence must also be correctly extracted from mobile devices.

Criminal investigators may also be confronted with network-related crimes that might include network intrusions and hacking attacks. To be successful, investigators must be familiar with hacking methodologies and popular hacking tools, but they must also utilize proper evidence handling in the investigative processes to assist with network forensic investigations. These investigations can become very technical when trying to determine what security measures were in place at the time of the incident and the types of logs that were maintained. This can help determine if unauthorized user accounts were added; files were added, modified, copied, or deleted; security settings were reconfigured or a *backdoor* added; intrusion and sniffer tools were copied to the network; and services were stopped or started [19].

13.5 Conclusions

Law enforcement agencies and officers are stuck right in the middle of social media warfare. Criminal activity is riddled with social media warfare tactics as are law enforcement's efforts to fight crime. Crimes of fraud create a challenge for law enforcement to keep abreast of criminal social media warfare tactics and activity. This chapter examined some of the issues and challenges that law enforcement agencies address in the realm of social media warfare. Important conclusions can be drawn from the material presented in this chapter:

- Because of the significant adverse effects that public safety employees' misuse of social media can have on them as witnesses, on agency operations, and on a department's relationship with the community it serves, many police agencies have addressed their employees' use of social media in the form of policy.
- Several law enforcement agencies have integrated a cybervetting component into the comprehensive background investigations they conduct on applicants and on-board employees.

- By increasing exposure of personally identifiable information, social media has raised the threat level for law enforcement personnel and their families.
- Social media sites are increasingly being used to instigate or conduct criminal activity, and law enforcement personnel should understand the concept and function of these websites.
- Social media sites and resources are another tool in the law enforcement investigative toolbox and should be used in a manner that adheres to the same principles that govern all law enforcement activity and such actions must be lawful.
- Among the most important tasks in social media warfare is data collection and analysis which can help determine defensive as well as offensive social media warfare tactics necessary to achieve a specific goal.
- Investigating the Internet criminal can be one of the most complex tasks facing law enforcement professionals and requires a multi-disciplinary approach supported by technical expertise that has not been needed with traditional crime.

13.6 Agenda for Action

Research on social media warfare is well advanced in some areas but lags in others. Since social media warfare is in its infancy and it is time to get ahead of it and not flounder as has been done in the face of cyber threats whether they are criminal, military, or terrorist in nature. Action steps should include, but not be limited to, the following areas:

- Establish and support research efforts addressing the threats inherent in social media warfare
- Expand training for criminal investigators and intelligence analysts on online discovery and preservation of evidence and intelligence materials
- Add training modules for all law enforcement officers that educates them on what not to do with electronic sources of evidence to ensure that only officers well trained in extraction and preservation handle electronic sources of evidence
- Add training modules for all law enforcement officers that educates them on what not to do with online sources of evidence to ensure that only officers well trained in discovery and preservation handle online sources of evidence
- Expand social media vetting efforts for law enforcement officers and potential new hires for law enforcement positions.
- Expand training for law enforcement personnel and their families on how to control personally identifiable information in their use of social media to reduce the potential threat level for law enforcement personnel and their families

13.7 Key Terms

Backdoor a backdoor generally circumvents security programs and provides access to a program, an online service, or an entire computer system. It can be authorized or unauthorized, documented or undocumented.

Consumer-generated content is digital content that is produced by self-publishers and sometimes picked up or referenced in traditional media.

Cybervetting is the process of reviewing and evaluating an employee's or potential employee's use of social media to determine if they have made posts that can harm law enforcement officers or agencies or compromise the prosecutorial process.

Open source intelligence is data and information that can be found in multiple sources including social media, websites, databases, libraries, and archives.

Personally identifiable information (PII) is information that can be used to distinguish or trace an individual's identity, either alone or when combined with other personal or identifying information that is linked or linkable to a specific individual.

Theft of personal or financial data is the illegal obtaining of information that potentially allows someone to use or create accounts under another name (individual, business, or some other entity). Personal information includes names, dates of birth, social security numbers, or other personal information. Financial information includes credit, debit, or automated teller machine (ATM) card account numbers or personal identification number (PIN).

13.8 Seminar Discussion Topics

Discussion topics for graduate- or professional-level seminars:

- What experience have seminar participants had in situations where social media warfare strategies or tactics were deployed by law enforcement officers?
- What experience have seminar participants had in situations where social media warfare strategies or tactics were deployed by intelligence analysts?
- What experience have seminar participants had in situations where social media warfare strategies or tactics were used to investigate any type of crime?
- What experience have seminar participants had in situations where social media warfare strategies or tactics were deployed to counter or investigate terrorism?

13.9 Seminar Group Project

Divide participants into multiple groups with each group taking 10–15 minutes to develop a list of offensive social media warfare tactics that law enforcement officers may need to investigate. Upon completion, have groups exchange their lists of social media warfare tactics, with groups taking 10–15 minutes to develop defensive measures to effectively counter the offensive tactics used by criminals. Meet as a group and discuss the offensive tactics selected by the groups and the defensive measures to counter the tactics that were developed by the groups.

References

1. Pettry, Michael T. 2012. Social media: Legal challenges and pitfalls for law enforcement agencies. *FBI Law Enforcement Bulletin*. Accessed September 28, 2016. https://leb.fbi.gov/2014/december/legal-digest-social-media-legal-challenges-and-pitfalls-for-law-enforcement.
2. Waters, Gwendolyn. 2012. Social media and law enforcement potential risks. *FBI Law Enforcement Bulletin*. Accessed September 28, 2016. https://leb.fbi.gov/2012/november/social-media-and-law-enforcement-potential-risks.
3. Seattle Government. 2015. Social media. *Seattle Police Department Manual*. Accessed September 28, 2016. http://www.seattle.gov/police-manual/title-5---employee-conduct/5125---social-media.
4. City of Philadelphia. Social media use policy. (no date provided). Accessed September 28, 2016. http://www.phila.gov/pdfs/Social%20Media%20Policy.pdf.
5. Stuart, Robert D. 2013. Social media: Establishing criteria for law enforcement use. *FBI Law Enforcement Bulletin*. Accessed September 28, 2016. https://leb.fbi.gov/2013/february/social-media-establishing-criteria-for-law-enforcement-use.
6. U.S. Department of Justice Office of Justice Programs. 2013. Developing a policy on the use of social media in intelligence and investigative activities: Guidance and recommendations." Accessed September 28, 2016. https://it.ojp.gov/documents/d/Developing%20a%20Policy%20on%20the%20Use%20of%20Social%20Media%20in%20Intelligence%20and%20Inves....pdf.
7. Office of the Director of National Intelligence. 2016. DNI Clapper signs new policy on social media for federal background investigations for security clearances. Accessed September 28, 2016. https://www.dni.gov/index.php/newsroom/press-releases/215-press-releases-2016/1374-dni-clapper-signs-new-policy-on-social-media-for-federal-background-investigations-for-security-clearances-1.
8. U.S. Department of Homeland Security. National Initiative for Cybersecurity Careers and Studies (NICCS). (no date provided). Accessed September 28, 2016. https://niccs.us-cert.gov/home/about-niccs.
9. United States Department of Homeland Security. National Initiative for Cybersecurity careers and studies (NICCS) education and training catalog. Accessed September 28, 2016. https://niccs.us-cert.gov/training/training-home/mcafee-institute.
10. Federal Law Enforcement Training Centers. Learn about FLETC. Accessed September 28, 2016. https://www.fletc.gov/learn-about-fletc.
11. Federal Law Enforcement Training Centers. Internet Investigations Training Program. Accessed September 28, 2016. https://www.fletc.gov/training-program/internet-investigations-training-program.
12. National White Collar Crime Center (NW3C). Cybercrime courses. Accessed September 29, 2016. http://nw3c.org/training/cybercrime.

13. Department of Defense Cyber Crime Center (DC3), Air Force Office of Special Investigations. Defense Cyber Investigations Training Academy (DCITA). Accessed September 29, 2016. http://www.dc3.mil/cyber-training.
14. U.S. Department of Homeland Security. Cyber Storm V: National cyber exercise. Accessed September 29, 2016. https://www.dhs.gov/cyber-storm-v.
15. State of California Department of Justice, Office of the Attorney General. Computer crime/investigation of Internet crimes. Accessed September 28, 2016. https://oag.ca.gov/atc/courses/cc-investigation-internet-crimes.
16. National Computer Forensic Institute. About the National Computer Forensic Institute (NCFI). Accessed September 29, 2016. https://www.ncfi.usss.gov/ncfi/pages/about.jsf;jsessionid=Nx6uLFtatjKvdDsgy0wWdA+e.
17. U.S. Central Intelligence Agency. 2016. Careers and internships, career opportunities. Accessed September 29, 2016. https://www.cia.gov/careers/opportunities/analytical/view-jobs.html.
18. U.S. Department of Homeland Security Federal Law Enforcement Training Centers. Training at FLETC. Accessed September 30, 2016. https://www.fletc.gov/training-catalog.
19. National Institute of Justice, Office of Justice Programs. 2007. Investigations involving the Internet and computer networks. Accessed September 30, 2016. https://www.ncjrs.gov/pdffiles1/nij/210798.pdf.

Chapter 14

Educational Institutions' Response to Social Media Warfare

Social media warfare has an impact on educational institutions at all levels. This chapter examines many of the issues that schools face because of social media warfare. All schools face the need to develop social media use policies for students, staff, and faculty that address a number of issues, including appropriate use, cyberbullying, and students using social media to organize protests against schools. Primary and secondary schools face the challenge of teaching students about being secure online as well as teachers and counselors to better enable them to identify potential issues students have with social media. Colleges and universities have had to develop new curriculums to address the quickly changing world of social media and its impact on governments, criminal justice, business, and social and cultural life. Colleges and universities also have new research opportunities to examine the impact of social media warfare on contemporary society.

14.1 Developing Social Media Guidelines for Students

Young people are using *personal technologies* including media technology, cell phones, personal data assistants, and the Internet to communicate with others in the United States and throughout the world. Communication avenues, such as text messaging, chat rooms, and social networking websites, such as Twitter and Facebook, allow youths to easily develop relationships, some with people they have never met in person. One of the things that schools must do is to prevent their students becoming victims in social media warfare.

Social media technology has many potential benefits for youths. It allows young people to communicate with family and friends on a regular basis. This technology also provides opportunities to make rewarding social connections for those teens and pre-teens that have difficulty developing friendships in traditional social settings or because of limited contact with same-aged peers. In addition, regular Internet access allows young people to quickly increase their knowledge on a wide variety of topics.

The explosion in communication tools and avenues does not come without possible risks. Parents and educators are both concerned about how primary and secondary students can be exposed to inappropriate online content, unwanted adult interactions, and bullying from peers. There is also concern over students at all levels revealing too much *personally identifiable information (PII)* when they use social media. Youths can use electronic media to embarrass, harass, or threaten their peers. Increasing numbers of teens and pre-teens are becoming victims of this new form of violence. Although many different terms, such as cyberbullying, Internet harassment, and Internet bullying, are used to describe this type of violence, *electronic aggression* is the term that most accurately captures all types of violence that occur electronically. Like traditional forms of youth violence, electronic aggression is associated with emotional distress and conduct problems at school. In fact, recent research suggests that youths who are victimized electronically are also very likely to also be victimized offline [1].

The *2013–2014 School Crime Supplement* (National Center for Education Statistics and Bureau of Justice Statistics) indicates that 7% of students in Grades 6–12 experienced *cyberbullying*. The *2013 Youth Risk Behavior Surveillance Survey* finds that 15% of high school students (Grades 9–12) were electronically bullied in the past year [2]. More detail on how children can be victimized through social media and other Internet applications is provided in Chapter 11, "Child Victims in Social Media Warfare."

Writing complex social media use guidelines or policies for young people and giving them a 20-page document of rules that they should follow is a relatively worthless endeavor. All such material must be developed in *plain language*. Young people need guidance that they can understand and apply. This means that developing, communicating, and implementing social media use policies for a primary or secondary students takes time and patience.

Teaching the behaviors that reflect those policies is far more important than creating a lengthy policy document that is not readable. This all, however, is very worthwhile because the younger people learn about proper and acceptable social media use the better off they will be as they pursue their education and later their careers. The New York City Department of Education published *Student Social Media Guidelines* in the fall 2013 that are very straightforward and are easily translated into behaviors, including

- Create the digital image you want and align your online image with your goals.
- Your online reputation includes material posted on blogs and mentions on websites.
- Be thoughtful about what you share online and consider how it would appear to others.
- Stand behind your words and always take responsibility for what you post in social media.
- Post responsibly and be mindful of your audience.
- Put your best foot forward and be responsible when acting online.
- Pause before you post and take a few extra minutes to think whether a post will be hurtful or embarrassing.
- Consider the consequences of your online actions.
- Protect yourself and only accept friend requests from people you know.
- Do not to post too many identifying details (such as where you live or your social security number) because revealing that information can be potentially dangerous and compromise your identity.
- Do not share passwords with friends and be sure that computers do not automatically save passwords.
- Adjust your privacy settings appropriately.
- Take threats of cyberbullying seriously.
- De-friend, block, or remove people who send inappropriate content [3].

College and university students need the same type of guidance as well as a bit of parenting on their use of social media. Colleges and universities tend to take the approach of advising students to be cautious when using social media and addressing a number of concerns with social networking sites of which students should be aware. This is especially true when it comes to privacy, and students are reminded to use appropriate privacy settings on social media websites and be cautious about who is added as a friend to a personal site. Students are also cautioned about infringing on the privacy of others, to not post personal information about others that could be embarrassing to them, and to ask permission of those involved in photographs before posting.

A unique challenge that colleges and universities face is dealing with student organizations and the necessity to set strong policies on how those organizations use social media. The social media accounts of student organizations are often monitored to ensure that comments are absent of expletives, obscenity, and vulgarity. Comments threatening in tone or evolving into personal attacks are required to be deleted by account administrators.

College and university faculty, staff, and student employees are required to follow the same laws and rules on social media as they are required to in real life. This includes following the guidelines of the Family Educational Rights and Privacy Act (FERPA), the Health Insurance Portability and Accountability Act (HIPAA), and the National Collegiate Athletic Association (NCAA).

Table 14.1   Social Media Policy Core Elements for Colleges and Universities

- The endorsement of commercial products or services is prohibited unless approved via the Office of Business and Finance in accordance with university policies and procedures.
- Public universities do not endorse one single religious belief and comments on religion are best avoided.
- Endorsing political candidates is not permitted on university social media sites. The use of university resources to support individuals or parties in a political campaign is prohibited.

Athletic related posts must be handled with caution and be mindful of NCAA sanctions and good sportsmanship conduct. University employees are warned that it is best to avoid commentary on athletic related topics other than game outcomes and general comments concerning attending or watching upcoming game and athletic activities. Per NCAA guidelines, employees and university accounts are prohibited from commenting or sharing any information on social media platforms regarding recruiting or the recruitment of specific student-athletes. Inappropriate postings and comments on athletic events and activities, student-athletes, coaches, or the possible recruitment of student-athletes and coaches can have serious implications both for employees involved and for the university [4]. Other core policy elements are shown in Table 14.1.

14.2 Training Students on Social Media Use

There are many areas in which schools can help train students to help prevent them from becoming victims in social media warfare. Many of the threats children face are covered in Chapter 11: "Child Victims in Social Media Warfare." These can take the form of cyberbullying, slander and exposure campaigns, revenge actions such as revenge pornography, and sexual harassment. Chapter 11 examines some of the ways individuals are harmed by other individuals who use these adverse social media warfare tactics and how social media warfare tactics are used to fight back against perpetrators. Areas covered include cyberbullying, responding to cyberbullying, the threat of online predators to children, social media warfare to rescue missing and exploited children, and child pornography.

Adults, like children, become victims of social media warfare from several sources of attack. These can take the form of harassment, revenge actions, identity theft, fraudulent transactions, and hacking of computers or phones. Chapter 12, "Adult Victims in Social Media Warfare," discussed how adults have been harmed by other individuals who use adverse social media warfare tactics, such as revenge porn and sextortion, Internet fraud, and identity theft. There are several online resources that can help in educating children of all ages about social media.

Kids.gov is the official kids' portal for the U.S. federal government it links kids, parents, and teachers to information and services on the Web from government agencies, schools, and educational organizations, all geared to the learning level and interest of kids. Kids.gov is organized according to four audiences: kids (Grades K-5), teens (Ggrades 6–8), teachers, and parents. Each audience tab is divided into educational subjects like arts, math, and history [5]. The website list and links to several online resources to help teach young people about good social media practices are summarized here:

Cyberbullying, sometimes referred to as online social cruelty or electronic bullying, can involve sending mean, vulgar, or threatening messages or images, or pretending to be someone else. (www.StopBullying.gov) StopBullying.gov provides information from various government agencies on what bullying is, what cyberbullying is, who is at risk, and how one can prevent and respond to bullying. The site includes games, videos, and lessons.

Cyberbullying prevention (http://www.ncpc.org/topics/cyberbullying): Cyberbullying happens when kids use the Internet, cell phones, or other devices to send or post text or images intended to hurt or embarrass another person. The National Crime Prevention Council's mission helps people keep themselves, their families, and their communities safe from crime. The website provides information and training material for several areas, as shown in Table 14.2.

The website provides numerous products and publications on cyberbullying including "Helping Kids Handle Conflict," a book for teaching children nonviolent ways to settle arguments, deal with bullies, and avoid fights; cyberbullying banners for websites; a cyberbullying crime flyer; cyberbullying crime palm card; a cyberbullying crime poster; and a cyberbullying research brief.

There are also a series of podcasts on cyberbullying: "The Basic Facts on Cyberbullying" discusses basic facts on cyberbullying; "Taking Action" explores different ways to prevent and manage cyberbullying; "Creating Change" is a podcast on creating change in schools and bystander empowerment; and "Students Speak Out" is a podcast where teens weigh in on how they feel about cyberbullying.

The FBI provides "Cyber Surf Islands," a presentation on how to stay safe online, including protecting personal identifiable information, cell phone safety, and more (sos.fbi.gov) (Flash required). Finally, the U.S. Federal Trade Commission provided Online Safety for Kids Lessons, which cover topics such as posting or sending a

Table 14.2 Cyberbullying Prevention Training Topics

- What is cyberbullying?
- What parents can do about cyberbullying.
- Cyberbullying frequently asked questions (FAQs) for teens.
- Cyberbullying public service announcement (PSA) contest.
- Training on cyberbullying.

message or a photo, downloading a file, game, or program, and shopping for something (www.consumer.ftc.gov/articles/0012-kids-and-socializing-online) [5].

14.3 Developing Social Media Policies for Faculty and Staff

Schools and school districts are developing guidelines as reference points for faculty and staff personal use of social media. Guidelines frequently reiterate state laws and school policies relating to faculty conduct and responsibilities while reminding employees social media is not without risk, both personally and professionally, if used in the absence of an appropriate level of discretion and intent.

Many schools do not take a position on an employee's decision to participate in blogs, wikis, and social media pages for personal use on personal time. Many schools do ask that staff not communicate with students and families regarding topics pertaining to school business and to not friend, follow, or otherwise interact with students from their personal social media accounts. Some schools have district-provided devices or district-supported technology that staff should use to communicate with students or parents, and thus avoid giving out their personal phone numbers, especially cell phone numbers.

The purpose of the policies and regulations on social media use is to prevent unauthorized access and other inappropriate activities by staff online, to prevent unauthorized disclosure of or access to sensitive information, and to comply with the Children's Internet Protection Act (CIPA) and other applicable laws. When social media postings violate the law or school policies or create a substantial disruption to the educational community and environment, administrators usually have an obligation to respond and take appropriate action, including but not limited to investigation, removal of posts, discipline, or referral to law enforcement.

Social media use policies serve as a reminder that all existing policies and behavior guidelines that cover employee conduct on school premises and at school-related activities similarly apply to the online environment in those same venues. Schools often warn that they reserve the right to monitor users' official online activities and to access, review, copy, and store or delete any electronic communication or files and/or disclose them to others as deemed necessary. Typical policy statements cover a wide range of circumstances, including

- Keeping personal social network accounts separate from work related accounts.
- Not accepting invitations to non-school-related social networking sites from parents, students, or alumni under the age of 18 years old.
- Not posting threatening, harassing, racist, biased, derogatory, disparaging, or bullying comments toward or about any student, faculty, or staff members.

- Not posting any identifying student information including names, videos, and photographs on any school-based, personal or professional online forum or social networking website, without the written, informed consent of the child's parent/legal guardian and the principal.
- Not sharing confidential or privileged information about students or personnel (e.g., grades, attendance records, or other pupil/personnel record information).
- Take any threats seriously that may be subject to law enforcement intervention, including but not limited to formal threat assessments or injunctive relief.
- School employees are responsible for the information they post, share, or respond to online, and they should post a disclaimer on their website or social media pages stating that the views on the page are personal and do not reflect the views of the school where they are employed.
- School employees should use privacy settings to control access to personal networks, web pages, profiles, posts, digital media, forums, fan pages, and so on.
- Employees should think twice about the value of the content and consider whether or not it may potentially malign or polarize any person or group.

14.4 Programs for Social Media Warfare Education

Social media warfare troops will need cyber skills, military intelligence and civilian intelligence skills, language skills, cultural knowledge, and propaganda skills. Developing these skills and knowledge will take considerable training and time. Cyber skills are certainly something that people can be trained in but intelligence analysis skills take longer to develop and requires technical knowledge, cultural knowledge, and multi-lingual skills. Propaganda skills can also be learned but not everyone will have a natural propensity for becoming a propagandist. Military academies have been a part of educating military leaders and specialists for a long time. Training military and law enforcement in social media warfare tactics is covered in Chapter 3, "Military Applications of Social Media Warfare" and Chapter 13, "Law Enforcement Response to Social Media Warfare."

A review of various course offerings in social media from colleges and universities shows that many disciplines have incorporated courses on social media. There are hundreds of short courses provided through continuing education programs and extension services. There are also courses being launched that are part of formal degree programs that address social media, including

- Social Media in the Healthcare Setting: This course introduces the healthcare student to concepts related to social media channels available today as they apply to communications in the field of healthcare. The course explores basic concepts in sociology and online privacy, how to investigate and use specific social media channels, as well as reviews of the Health Insurance Portability and Accountability Act (HIPAA) and the legal aspects of social media. Using specific examples, students are exposed to how businesses in healthcare adopt social media strategies and develop policies for responsible social media use by staff and patients [6].

■ Social Media Marketing: This course focuses on new digital and social media tools in the world of business and provides students with a foundation and skill set in the evolving world of social media tools and strategies. Topics covered include what social media is and why it is important; how to use social media tools to build relationships and increase productivity; the importance of building an online community; creating and executing social media campaigns; trends in mobile applications; and real world case studies of the effective use of social media within business-to-business and business-to-consumer settings [7].

■ Social Media Masters of Arts: This program covers social media as culture, online enterprise and innovation, and social media as practice; it includes work in a production lab, and it requires a master's dissertation [8].

■ Social Media Management Certificate: This course covers using social media tools effectively, writing for social media, social media strategies and tactics, measuring and calculating return on investment (ROI), strategic communication planning, policies and procedures to manage risk, and a capstone course in social media [9].

■ Social Media Certificate: This course is designed for individuals who aspire to work with social media as content creators, marketers, analysts or administrators in the business, non-profit, governmental, or educational sector. Learning outcomes include a working knowledge of current social media platforms as they are used in workplace, consumer, and informal setting; familiarity with strategies of social media deployment; a command of quantitative and qualitative measures of social networks; the ability to analyze patterns in social media, and a portfolio of work demonstrating these capabilities as applied to real-world social media [10].

■ Social Media Marketing Certificate: This is a nine-module certificate program. Topics covered include constructing a strategy; leveraging listening channels; crises and landmines; content development; measurement and ROI; social media platforms; mobile opportunities; engaging influencers and change management; analyzing social media marketing opportunities; exploring the behavioral and psychological factors that drive social media, and designing effective communication strategies of social networks [11].

■ MS in Social Media and Mobile Marketing: This program is designed for marketing, advertising, information technology (IT), and management professionals who seek to meet the challenges presented by new media's impact on the marketplace. The program integrates digital and traditional media skills and offers specialized training in segment and target markets for social media and mobile strategies; understanding the interaction of key media elements in the advertising industry; effective strategies for integrated communications using traditional and new media; setting objectives; brand strategy; media plans; and tracking and measuring campaigns using industry-standard metrics and techniques [12].

14.5 Social Media Warfare Presents a New Field of Academic Research

Several academic disciplines can make considerable contributions to the study of the use of the Internet and social media. However, academic disciplines are often slow to initiate research streams in new areas primarily because of a lack of funding for such research. The lack of funding is unfortunate because there is much to be researched. It is unlikely that funding will increase in the near future given the increasing feeling of disdain for science and academia that the conservative electorate has brought to the legislative process.

As discussed in Chapter 1, "A Framework to Analyze Emerging Social Media Warfare Strategies," a review of academic programs listed by the National Center for Education Statistics in its 2000 edition of *Classification of Instructional Programs* shows several academic disciplines that can and will eventually provide more insight into social media warfare. Academic disciplines that can contribute to the understanding of social media warfare include mass communication/media studies; political communication programs; social psychology and sociology.

The small amount of research on social media that was reviewed for this project indicates that there is an interest in developing methods to mine social media content to explore how people use social media to interact about specific subjects. It will take time for academic disciplines to develop reliable data collection methods that take the research beyond just discovering and compiling anecdotal data.

One hint on the future directions of social media warfare research is that the Defense Advance Research Project Agency (DARPA) has an interest in understanding how social network communication affects events on the ground as part of its mission to prevent strategic surprise. The general goal of DARPA's social media in strategic communication (SMISC) program is to develop a new science of social networks built on an emerging technology base. Through the program, DARPA seeks to develop tools to help identify misinformation or deception campaigns and counter them with truthful information, reducing adversaries' ability to manipulate events [13].

There are multiple forms of Internet research, some of which may include elements conducted through the Internet, for example, using a social media application as a recruitment tool combined with traditional research methods and spaces;

Table 14.3   Internet Research Where Human Subjects May Be Involved

> - Research studying information that is already available on or via the Internet without direct interaction with human subjects (harvesting, mining, profiling)
> - Research that uses the Internet as a vehicle for recruiting or interacting, directly or indirectly, with subjects (self-testing websites and survey tools)
> - Research about the Internet itself and its effects. which could include use patterns or effects of social media, search engines, e-mail, evolution of privacy issues, information contagion, and so on
> - Research about Internet users, what they do, and how the Internet affects individuals and their behaviors
> - Research that utilizes the Internet as an interventional tool, for example, interventions that influence subjects' behavior.
> - Recruitment in or through Internet locales or tools, for example social media, push technologies [14]

some research can only be conducted on the Internet, for example, an ethnography of an online-only forum that has no corresponding geo-physical location; or, the Internet may be a tool underlying data collection. The range of Internet research involving human subjects is shown in Table 14.3.

14.6 Threats from Campus Protest Organization

The popularity of campus protest has come and gone many times over the last century. Chapter 7, "Social Media Warfare for Support of Social Causes," covered non-campus social action. This section examines the impact of social media warfare tactics in organizing socially motivated campus protest.

In the fall of 2015, racial tensions at the University of Missouri helped to bring attention to issues that have been simmering on college campuses for a very long time; and this time, there was the backdrop of a national discussion on race relations and treatment of blacks in the United States. The issues varied between campuses, but many students stated that there was a common atmosphere in the various campuses that was inhospitable to students from racial minorities. Students were calling for more diversity among faculty and more spending on scholarships for minorities, and for resources such as cultural centers.

Tensions flared at the Columbia, Missouri, campus, where black students said school officials were not addressing racial slurs and incidents at the school. Under public scrutiny, the university president and chancellor resigned. Soon after, a Missouri college student was arrested for making death threats against black students at the school. Driven by social media warfare tactics, the protest quickly spread to universities and colleges across the country. Nationally, students said the protests in Missouri emboldened them to take a harder line. Citizen journalists were on the scene in Missouri as well as across the country to record police involvement or school representative actions and disseminate that information to the community at large and to interested activists.

Campus unrest spread beyond the University of Missouri, with students nationwide rallying in solidarity with their counterparts at the University of Missouri. The Black Student Assembly (BSA) hosted a rally at the campus of the University of California–Los Angeles; this was part of a nationwide effort by student activists who wore black in solidarity with black students at Missouri. Within a week thousands of students participated in protests at dozens of universities [15].

A consensus rapidly emerged that the problem is much larger than the events in Missouri alone; this led other schools to address similar concerns on their campuses. Some students, faculty, and alumni said the protests and academic institution leaders' resignations are the culmination of years of racial tension at the University of Missouri and that the university has promised changes. Social media warfare drove the rapid organization and deployment of protesters.

Outrage was trending on Twitter as tens of thousands of black and other minority students tweeted their personal experiences with racism on college campuses in the United States. Other tweets noted the small percentage of black students relative to the student body, or detected hypocrisy when white students complain about affirmative action and minority scholarships, but do not complain about legacy admissions.

Consumer-generated content was rapidly filling social media platforms. The Twitter hashtag #blackoncampus was created and within a couple of days quickly went national. In less than 48 hours, over 70,000 tweets with that hashtag had been sent. Together, the tweets sent a searing and largely unheard message that reached at least one presidential candidate. "I am listening," tweeted Senator Bernie Sanders in response, "It's time to address structural racism on college campuses."

As tensions grew, a 19-year-old white Missouri man was charged with making terrorist threats and posting *hate messages* on social media threatening to shoot black students at the University of Missouri campus. His bond was denied. Court documents said the white male expressed a "deep interest" in a recent Oregon school massacre. Police said the 19-year-old's threats had circulated on social media, including a favorite student messaging application called Yik Yak. Another student, at Northwest Missouri State University in Maryville, was charged with two counts of making a terrorist threat for sentiments he allegedly posted on Yik Yak [16].

Bear in mind that the University of Missouri controversy arose amid ongoing nationwide racial tensions surrounding instances of police violence against unarmed black men. The University of Missouri is about 120 miles west of where 18-year-old Michael Brown was shot after a confrontation with a white police officer in Ferguson, Missouri in 2014. The police officer was not charged. Chapter 7, "Social Media Warfare for Support of Social Causes," discusses the Ferguson case and Michael Brown.

14.7 Conclusions

This chapter examined many of the issues that schools face as a result of social media warfare. All schools must develop social media use policies for students, staff, and faculty that address a number of issues, including appropriate use, cyberbullying, and students using social media to organize protests against schools. Colleges and universities have had to develop new curriculums to address the quickly changing world of social media and its impact on governments, criminal justice, business, and social and cultural life. Important conclusions can be drawn from the material presented in this chapter:

- The explosion in communication tools and avenues does not come without possible risks. Parents and educators are both concerned about how primary and secondary students might be exposed to inappropriate online content, unwanted adult interactions, and bullying from peers.
- Like traditional forms of youth violence, electronic aggression is associated with emotional distress and conduct problems at school.
- Developing, communicating, and implementing social media use policies for a primary or secondary students is just the beginning, teaching the behaviors that reflect those policies is far more important than creating a lengthy policy document.
- Colleges and universities tend to take the approach of advising students to be cautious when using social media and addressing a number of concerns pertaining to social networking sites of which students should be aware.
- One challenge that colleges and universities uniquely face is the presence of student organizations and the necessity to set strong policies on how those organizations use social media.
- Many schools ask that staff not communicate with students and families regarding topics pertaining to school business and that staff not friend, follow, or otherwise interact with students from their personal social media accounts.
- DARPA has an interest in understanding how social network communication affects events on the ground as part of its mission to prevent strategic surprise.
- Driven by social media warfare tactics, the protests at the University of Missouri in 2015 quickly spread to universities and colleges across the country. Nationally, students said the protests in Missouri emboldened them to take a harder line on issues on their campus.

14.8 Agenda for Action

Social media warfare has an impact on educational institutions at all levels. Colleges and universities have new research opportunities to examine the impact of social media warfare on contemporary society. But social media warfare is in its infancy and it is time to get ahead of it and not flounder as was done in the face of cyber threats. Action steps should include, but not be limited to, the following areas:

- Establish and support academic research efforts addressing the threats and opportunities inherent in social media warfare.
- Publish school policies and guidelines on social media use in multiple languages to meet the diversity needs of the educational system.
- Publish training and educational material on social media use in multiple languages to meet the diversity needs of the educational system.
- Produce podcast and other video material used for education and training on social media use in American sign language.
- Establish and support academic research efforts addressing electronic violence especially on minors inflict harm on other minors.

14.9 Key Terms

Citizen journalist is an individual who uses technology such as smartphones to record police or government representative actions and disseminate that evidence to the community at large and to interested activists.

Consumer-generated content is digital content that is produced by self-publishers and sometimes picked up or referenced in traditional media.

Cyberbullying is bullying that takes place using electronic technology including devices and equipment such as cell phones, computers, and tablets as well as communication tools including social media sites, text messages, chat, and websites.

Electronic aggression is the use of any electronic device to commit such acts as cyberbullying, Internet harassment, and Internet bullying.

Hate messages are social media posts that use obnoxious language to ridicule or discriminate against minority or ethnic groups.

Personal technologies include individually owned devices such as cell phones, tablets, laptops, and digital media.

Personally identifiable information (PII) is information that can be used to distinguish or trace an individual's identity, either alone or when combined with other personal or identifying information that is linked or linkable to a specific individual.

Plain language is the straightforward writing that enables readers of all types and levels of education to better understand written content in any media through which it is delivered.

14.10 Seminar Discussion Topics

Discussion topics for graduate- or professional-level seminars:

- What experience have seminar participants had in situations where social media warfare strategies or tactics were used in a campus protest?
- What experience have seminar participants had in developing social media guidelines for students or faculty?
- What courses on social media have seminar participants taken in the past? What courses on social media do seminar participants plan to take in the future?

14.11 Seminar Group Project

Divide participants into multiple groups with each group taking 10–15 minutes to develop a list of social media warfare research topics. Upon completion, have groups exchange their lists of social media warfare research topics, with groups taking 10–15 minutes to review the lists and expand upon them. Meet as a group and discuss what research topics are the most important and should be addressed with the highest priority.

References

1. U.S. Centers for Disease Control and Prevention. 2016. Electronic aggression: Technology and youth violence. Accessed September 22, 2016. http://www.cdc.gov/violenceprevention/youthviolence/electronicaggression/index.html.
2. U.S. Department of Health and Human Services. What is cyberbullying. Accessed September 22, 2016. http://www.stopbullying.gov/cyberbullying/what-is-it/index.html.
3. New York City Department of Education. 2013. Student social media guidelines. Accessed October 2, 2016. http://schools.nyc.gov/NR/rdonlyres/9765B2DF-9BD5-42AA-8D85-005D0FC8AA23/0/Student_Social_MediaGuidelines_finalv3_20140128.pdf.
4. University of Memphis. 2014. Social media handbook. November 12. Accessed October 3, 2016. http://www.memphis.edu/communications/socialmedia/index.php.
5. U.S. Government, kids.gov. About us. Accessed October 3, 2016. https://kids.usa.gov/about-us/index.shtml.

6. Maryland Higher Education Commission. 2016. Academic program proposal. Accessed October 3, 2016. http://mhec.maryland.gov/institutions_training/documents/acadaff/acadproginstitapprovals/Proposals/PP15332.pdf.
7. Utah State Board of Education. 2012. Social media marketing. Accessed October 3, 2016. http://www.schools.utah.gov/CTE/marketing/DOCS/resources/social/SocialMediaCurriculum.aspx.
8. Birmingham City University, Birmingham School of Media. Courses. Accessed October 3, 2016. http://www.bcu.ac.uk/courses/social-media.
9. Georgetown University. Social Media Management. Accessed October 3, 2016. http://scs.georgetown.edu/programs/395/social-media-management/.
10. University of Maine at Augusta. The Social Media Certificate. Accessed October 3, 2016. http://www.uma.edu/academics/programs/social-sciences/concentrations/social-media/
11. Rutgers University, Rutgers Business School. Social Media Marketing. Accessed October 3, 2016. http://www.business.rutgers.edu/executive-education/programs/mini-mba-social-media-marketing.
12. Pace University. MS in Social Media and Mobile Marketing. Accessed October 3, 2016. http://www.pace.edu/lubin/ms-in-social-media-mobile-marketing.
13. Hsieh, Michael. Social media in strategic communication (SMISC). The Defense Advance Research Project Agency (DARPA). Accessed October 4, 2016. http://www.darpa.mil/program/social-media-in-strategic-communication.
14. U.S. Department of Health and Human Services. Considerations and recommendations concerning Internet research and human subjects research regulations. Accessed October 4, 2016. http://www.hhs.gov/ohrp/sites/default/files/ohrp/sachrp/mtgings/2013%20March%20Mtg/internet_research.pdf.
15. Voice of America News. 2015. Missouri protests embolden minorities on other U.S. campuses. Accessed October 4, 2016. http://www.voanews.com/a/missouri-protests-embolden-minorities-on-other-us-campuses/3056726.html.
16. McKitterick, Molly. 2015. Mizzou unrest spreads to other campuses. Accessed October 4, 2016. http://www.voanews.com/a/mizzou-unrest-spreads-to-other-campuses/3056105.html.

Chapter 15

Monitoring Social Media Warfare Threats

Security agencies and criminal justice investigators in the United States and several countries around the world monitor social media under specific circumstances. In addition, political campaigns, corporations, and special interest groups monitor social media regarding issues that threaten them. They also monitor their known adversaries' use of social media. This chapter reviews some monitoring trends and tools to monitor social media warfare activities.

15.1 Monitoring Social Media for Security and Intelligence Purposes

The Department of Homeland Security (DHS) Office of Operations Coordination and Planning (OPS), including the National Operations Center (NOC), launched the Social Networking/Media Capability (SNMC) to assist DHS and its components involved in the response, recovery, and rebuilding effort resulting from the earthquake and after-effects in Haiti as well as the security, safety, and border control associated with the 2010 Winter Olympics. These limited purposes were expanded in June 2013 to meet the operational needs of DHS. Since then, and to meet its statutory requirements, OPS, through SNMC analysts, monitors publicly available online forums, blogs, public websites, and message boards to collect information used in providing *situational awareness* and establishing a *common operating picture*.

The DHS Privacy Office (PRIV) and OPS/NOC decided to further broaden the program's capability to collect additional information, including limited instances of *personally identifiable information (PII)*. As such, a Publicly Available Social Media Monitoring and Situational Awareness Initiative Privacy Impact Assessment (PIA) Update and new DHS/OPS-004 Publicly Available Social Media Monitoring and Situational Awareness Initiative System of Records Notice (SORN) were issued on January 6, 2011 and February 1, 2011, respectively.

The OPS/NOC will only monitor publicly available online forums, blogs, public websites, and message boards to collect information used in providing situational awareness and a common operating picture. OPS/NOC is permitted to collect PII on the following categories of individuals when it lends credibility to the report or facilitates coordination with federal, state, local, tribal, territorial, foreign, or international government partners:

- U.S. and foreign individuals *in extremis* situations involving potential life or death circumstances
- Senior U.S. and foreign government officials who make public statements or provide public updates
- U.S. and foreign government spokespersons who make public statements or provide public updates
- U.S. and foreign private sector officials and spokespersons who make public statements or provide public updates
- Names of anchors, newscasters, or on-scene reporters who are known or identified as reporters in their post or article or who use traditional and/ or social media in real time to keep their audience aware and informed of situations
- Current and former public officials who are victims of incidents or activities related to homeland security
- Terrorists, drug cartel leaders, or other persons known to have been involved in major crimes of homeland security interest

According to policy, PII inadvertently or incidentally collected outside the scope of these discrete set of categories of individuals shall be redacted immediately before further use and sharing. In accordance with the retention schedule and disposal policy that was established and approved by the OPS/NOC records officer and NARA (NARA: N1-563-08-23), the NOC will retain information for no more than five years. OPS/NOC will share Media Monitoring Reports (MMRs) with departmental and component leadership, private sector, and international partners where necessary, appropriate, and authorized by law to ensure that critical disaster-related information reaches government decision makers.

OPS/NOC must maintain a log of social media monitoring Internet-based platforms and information technology infrastructure that SNMC analysts visit under this initiative. Additionally, OPS/NOC will implement auditing at the router level for all outbound http(s) traffic and generate audit reports that will be available for each compliance review and upon request. SNMC analysts are required to take annual privacy training and specific PII training [1].

Several foreign governments have been known to monitor social media, websites, and e-mails for security and legal purposes. Those countries are identified annually by the U.S. Department of State. A summary of the worst offenders is provided in Chapter 2: "Civilian Government Use of Social Media to Attack, Defend, or Control."

The U.S. Department of State sought to hire social media warfare monitors for the Iraqi Political and Social Media Monitoring Project. The project sought a Virtual Fellow to serve with the Office of Iraq Affairs, Bureau of Near Eastern Affairs (NEA/I) as a consultant on Iraqi press and social media coverage of Iraqi political, economic, and security developments. The Virtual Fellow was to monitor Iraqi media and social media outlets in order to provide up-to-the-moment summaries of important developments to NEA/I decision makers. The Virtual Fellow was to be responsible for combing Iraqi media and social media outlets for breaking political, military, and economic news. In particular, the Fellow would closely follow news related to important Iraqi figures, political parties, militias, as well as government ministries and agencies in Baghdad and the Iraqi provinces in order to provide a summary of the most relevant information and, where appropriate, analysis based on the Fellow's own knowledge and experience related to Iraq and Iraqi politics. The position required native fluency in Arabic (preferably Iraqi), along with an in-depth knowledge and understanding of Iraqi politics, history, culture, and society [2]. Restrictions on the use of personally identifiable information of those being monitored were not discussed in the announcement.

15.2 Monitoring Social Media for Disaster Response Purposes

U.S. Federal Emergency Management Agency (FEMA) Watch Center analysts typically monitor and review publicly available Internet social media and use a set of key words to find and retrieve content relevant to FEMA for situational awareness purposes. FEMA aggregates information to share with internal and external partners as appropriate using this social media content and other publicly available content. This may include a FEMA-written narrative of the situation being described through various media or social media outlets, as well as links or uniform record locators (URL) to the publicly available open source resources that FEMA references. FEMA's social media monitoring under this initiative is neither designed nor intended to collect PII from members of the public; however, given the unpredictable nature of disasters coupled with the voluntary and unrestricted nature of social media, it is possible during *in extremis* situations for FEMA to collect a limited amount of PII from the public through its monitoring of Internet social media [2]. Publicly available sites monitored by FEMA Watch Centers include

- ABCNews Blotter http://abcnews.go.com/Blotter/
- Al Sahwa http://al-sahwa.blogspot.com/
- allAfrica http://allafrica.com/
- Avian Flu Diary http://afludiary.blogspot.com/
- BNOnews http://www.bnonews.com/
- Borderfire http://www.borderfirereport.net/
- Collecta http://collecta.com
- Counter-Terrorism Blog http://www.counterterrorismblog.com/
- Crisisblogger http://crisisblogger.wordpress.com/
- Cryptome http://cryptome.org/
- Danger Room http://www.wired.com/dangerroom/
- El Blog Del Narco http://elblogdelnarco.blogspot.com/
- Facebook http://www.facebook.com
- Flickr http://www.flickr.com/
- Global Incident Map http://globalincidentmap.com/
- Global Security Newswire http://gsn.nti.org/gsn/
- Global Terror Alert http://www.globalterroralert.com/
- Global Voices Network http://globalvoicesonline.org/-/world/americas/haiti/
- Google Blog Search http://blogsearch.google.com
- Google Flu Trends http://www.google.org/flutrends/
- Guerra Contra El Narco http://guerracontraelnarco.blogspot.com/
- H5N1 Blog http://crofsblogs.typepad.com/h5n1/
- Hulu http://www.hulu.com
- IBISEYE http://www.ibiseye.com/
- InciWeb http://www.inciweb.org/
- Informed Comment http://www.juancole.com/
- iReport.com http://www.ireport.com/
- It's Trending http://www.itstrending.com/news/
- Jihad Watch http://www.jihadwatch.org/
- Krebs on Security http://krebsonsecurity.com/
- Live Leak http://www.liveleak.com/
- LongWarJournal http://www.longwarjournal.org/
- Magma http://mag.ma/
- Malware Intelligence Blog http://malwareint.blogspot.com/
- MEMRI http://www.memri.org/
- MexiData.info http://mexidata.info/
- Monitter http://www.monitter.com/
- MySpace (limited search) http://www.myspace.com
- MySpace http://www.myspace.com
- MySpace Video http://vids.myspace.com/

- Narcotrafico en Mexico http://narcotraficoenmexico.blogspot.com/
- National Terror Alert http://www.nationalterroralert.com/
- Newspapers on Twitter http://www.newspapersontwitter.com/
- Picfog http://picfog.com/
- Public Intelligence http://publicintelligence.net/
- Radio on Twitter http://www.radioontwitter.com/
- ReliefWeb http://www.reliefweb.int
- RigZone http://www.rigzone.com/
- RSSOwl http://www.rssowl.org/
- Shrook RSS reader http://www.utsire.com/shrook/
- Social Mention http://socialmention.com/
- Spy http://www.spy.appspot.com
- Stormpulse http://www.stormpulse.com/
- Technorati http://technorati.com/
- Terror Finance Blog http://www.terrorfinance.org/the_terror_finance_blog/
- Threat Level http://www.wired.com/threatlevel/
- Threat Matrix http://www.longwarjournal.org/threat-matrix/
- Tickle the Wire http://www.ticklethewire.com/
- Time Tube http://www.dipity.com/mashups/timetube
- Trendistic http://trendistic.com/
- Trendrr http://www.trendrr.com/
- Trends Map http://www.trendsmap.com
- Tribuna Regional http://latribunaregional.blogspot.com/
- TV on Twitter http://www.tvontwitter.com/
- Twazzup http://www.twazzup.com
- Tweefind http://www.tweefind.com/
- Tweet Meme http://tweetmeme.com/
- Tweetgrid http://tweetgrid.com/
- TweetStats http://tweetstats.com/
- Tweetzi http://tweetzi.com/
- Twellow http://www.twellow.com/
- Twendz http://twendz.waggeneredstrom.com/
- Twicsy http://www.twicsy.com
- Twitcaps http://www.twitcaps.com
- Twitoaster http://twitoaster.com/
- Twitscoop http://www.twitscoop.com/
- Twitter Search http://search.twitter.com/advanced
- Twitter/API http://www.twitter.com
- Twitturly http://twitturly.com/
- Ushahidi Haiti http://haiti.ushahidi.org/
- Vimeo http://www.vimeo.com
- War on Terrorism http://terrorism-online.blogspot.com/
- We Follow http://wefollow.com/

- Who's Talkin http://www.whostalkin.com/
- WikiLeaks http://wikileaks.org/
- YouTube http://www.youtube.com [3]

In addition to following the social media feeds of numerous organizations around the world, FEMA Watch Centers use a number of key words to search various social media sources. These key words are shown in Table 15.1.

Table 15.1 FEMA Watch Center Key Words for Search

Agro Terror	E. Coli/Ebola	Nuclear facility/threat
Airport	Earthquake	Port Authority
Anthrax	Electric	Powder (white)
Antiviral	Emergency response	Power lines/outage
Assassination	Epidemic	Quarantine
Attack	Erosion	Radiation/Radioactive
Avalanche	Evacuation	Recovery/Relief
Avian	Exposure	Response
Bacteria	Extreme weather	Ricin
Biological infection	Failure or outage	Salmonella
Black out	First responder	Sarin
Blister agent	Flood	Service disruption
Blizzard	Food Poisoning	Shelter-in-place
Body scanner	Forest fire	Sleet
Bridge	Gas	Small Pox
Brown out	Grid	Smart
Brush fire	H1N1/H5N1	Snow
Burn	Hacker	Spammer
Burst	Hail	Spillover
Cancelled	Hazardous/incident	Storm
Chemical agent/spill	Hazardous material	Strain
Chemical burn/fire	Hazmat/spill	Stranded/Stuck
Closure	Human to animal	Subway
Collapse	Human to human	Suspicious package
Contamination	Hurricane	Symptoms
Cops	Infection	Tamiflu
Critical infrastructure	Influenza/flu	Tornado
Cyber attack/terror	Law enforcement	Toxic
Cyber security	authorities	Transportation security
Denial of service	Leak	Tremor
Dirty bomb	Lightening	Tsunami
Disaster assistance	Listeria	Tuberculosis (TB)
Disaster management	Magnitude	Twister
DNDO (Domestic Nuclear	Malware	Typhoon
Detection Office)	Mitigation	Vaccine
Dock	Mudslide	Viral hemorrhagic fever
Domestic nuclear detection	Mutation	Virus
Domestic security	MySQL injection	Water/air borne
	Nerve agent	Wildfire
	Norovirus	

15.3 Monitoring Social Media for Law Enforcement Purposes

Another U.S. federal agency that uses social media monitoring to fight crime is the U.S. National Park Service Investigative Services Branch (Investigative Services Branch). Most investigations supported in 2015 focused on a series of auto burglaries in various parks. Other investigations included arson, homicide, vandalism, sexual assault, and sexual exploitation. During the summer of 2014, social media brought national attention to a female graffiti artist who vandalized several parks. Photos obtained from the perpetrator's social media accounts enabled intelligence analysts to provide the U.S. Attorney with a timeline of the illegal activity.

Intelligence services cover cell phone mapping, financial analysis, link analysis, telephone toll analysis, social media monitoring/analysis, timelines, and organizational charts. The Investigative Services Branch relies on several resources including Thompson Reuters CP CLEAR, Geofeedia, Google Earth Pro, El Paso Intelligence Center (EPIC), Analyst Notebook, Parcel Quest, Transaction Record Analysis Center (TRAC), TLO, Crimedex Online Law Enforcement Community, Regional Information Sharing System (RISS Network), Nuance Omniscan, Vigilant License Plate Reader, and facial recognition applications [4].

Social media sites and resources should be viewed as another tool in the law enforcement investigative toolbox and should be used in a manner that adheres to the same principles that govern all law enforcement activity. That is, actions must be lawful and personnel must have a defined objective and a valid law enforcement purpose for gathering, maintaining, or sharing PII. In addition, any law enforcement action involving undercover activity (including developing an undercover profile on a social media site) should address supervisory approval, required documentation of activity, periodic reviews of activity, and the audit of undercover processes and behavior. Law enforcement agencies should also not collect or maintain the political, religious, or social views, associations, or activities of any individual or group, association, corporation, business, partnership, or organization unless there is a legitimate public safety purpose [5]. Law enforcement use of social media warfare tactics to conduct investigations and identify criminals, such as child predators and pornographers, is discussed in greater depth in Chapter 13: "Law Enforcement Response to Social Media Warfare."

A private social media investigator or consultant does not face as many restrictions as law enforcement officers do. A new breed of private investigator will look into the social media posts, status updates, photos, and conversations of an individual or group. Social media investigations are reportedly being used more and more in custody cases, divorces, and even criminal trials.

Private investigators and social media consultants search for key terms and posts to discover information required to support a client's need. The process is similar to what was discussed previously in reference to homeland security and disaster response management. The process might include looking at the location tags for Facebook, Twitter, and Instagram posts, authenticating the posts, and determining what other individuals are associated with a case. Such an investigation often includes searching and setting up alerts for specific terms relating to the case under investigation.

In addition, corporations and investors hire private investigators or consultants to search and monitor social media sites for intelligence about competitors and to monitor potential insider leaks or evidence of employee misconduct.

15.4 Developing Monitoring Technology for Social Media Warfare

Law enforcement, emergency management agencies, intelligence gathering and analysis agencies, the U.S. Department of State, and national security agencies such as the DHS all have a need to monitor and mine publicly available online forums, blogs, public websites, message boards, and social media platforms to collect information used in providing situational awareness and to fight domestic and international terrorism. The U.S. Congress has made it clear that publicly available social media monitoring of current and former public officials who are victims of incidents or activities related to homeland security and of terrorists, drug cartel leaders, or other persons known to have been involved in major crimes of homeland security interest is a legal and prudent activity. Social media warfare monitors are employed by these agencies as well as probably many others around the world. The social nature of open-source information suggests that significant investments need to be made in mapping and mining these sources [6].

Advances in science and technology provide a unique opportunity to transform intelligence applying expanded analytic, collection, and processing capabilities, and to improve cross-component collaboration through the intelligence community system for information sharing. Innovative programs such as In-Q-Tel provide the CIA and the intelligence community with effective reach into the cutting-edge creativity of the U.S. private sector [7].

The CIA has supported the development of technology since the 1960s when it supported the development of lithium-ion batteries because certain operational missions required long-lasting batteries of various shapes and sizes. The lithium-ion battery improved the performance of surveillance equipment and prolonged the operation of reconnaissance satellites. In the early 1970s, the CIA passed the technology to the medical community where it was used in heart pacemakers.

In February 2003, the CIA-funded strategic investor In-Q-Tel made an investment in Keyhole, Inc. Keyhole was a pioneer of interactive 3D Earth visualization and creator of the Earth viewer 3D system. The CIA worked closely with other intelligence community organizations to tailor Keyhole's systems to meet operational needs. The technology was also useful to multiple TV networks using Earthviewer 3D: to fly over Iraqi cities during news coverage of Operation Iraqi Freedom. The popularity of this technology eventually caught the attention of Google, which acquired Keyhole in 2004. This technology is now known as Google Earth [8].

To keep up with the boom in innovations in the private sector, especially in information technology (IT), the CIA assembled a team of senior staff and outside consultants and lawyers in 1998 to design an entity to partner with industry in accelerated solutions to IT problems facing the intelligence community. After meeting with investment bankers, venture capitalists, entrepreneurs, and members of Congress and staff, the team conceived what is now known as In-Q-Tel.

In-Q-Tel is a congressionally created, government-funded non-profit venture capital firm that seeks to accelerate market introduction of products that could benefit U.S. intelligence efforts. In-Q-Tel was created in 1998 but did not get fully underway until later. In-Q-Tel generally does not get involved in technologies until they are well on their way to development or in the prototype stage. It does not yet have much of a track record and no one has analyzed how it might function in the energy market. Moreover, the expanding use of government-funded firms with equity in private companies could raise questions about the appropriate role of government in the financial marketplace. In-Q-Tel started off making investments primarily in IT, including Internet security, data integration, imagery analysis, and language translation. These investments have helped government agencies to keep up with technology developments in the commercial marketplace, and helped the intelligence community to mold, develop, and deploy crucial technologies in a timely manner.

Small or newer companies often do not to target the U.S. federal government market because it can be difficult to target or slow to access. Because those companies often need to penetrate their markets quickly to generate cash flow, government customers can miss the chance to influence product development. Moreover, private venture capital firms sometimes discourage small companies they invest in from doing business with the government because of the complexity of the procurement process and long lead time on procurement decisions. This means that agencies are often two to three years behind the commercial market for technology, especially in areas like IT where there is rapid innovation.

A Board of Trustees oversees In-Q-Tel's direction, strategy, and policies. In-Q-Tel offers the CIA a mechanism by which to involve industry in solving the specific technology problems faced by its one customer, the intelligence community [9]. In-Q-Tel has funded, in part, several technology companies developing social media mining and monitoring capabilities, including Platfora, Dataminr, Geofeedia, Pathar, Basis Technology, and TransVoyant.

In-Q-Tel's 2015 revenue was $91.8 million and its 2014 revenue was $130.6 million. It had 121 employees in 2014 with a salary expenditure of $30.0 million. Net assets were $326.8 million. In 2014, the CEO was paid $1.5 million and the executive vice president and managing partner was paid $1.8 million. In-Q-Tel received $93.8 million in government grants in 2014 and held publicly traded securities valued at $211 million. Since 1999, In-Q-Tel has invested in over 250 companies and raised $8.9 billion in private sector funds [10].

In 2014, In-Q-Tel invested $1.9 million in Platfora, a data analytics company that has since been acquired by Workday. Platfora provides several analytic capabilities including the analysis of IT system security attacks. Another $1.5 million was invested in Protonex, which develops portable power solutions for the military. Expect Labs, the creator of the MindMeld app, which is an intelligent assistant that understands conversations and finds information one needs before one has to search for it, received a $1.5 million investment from In-Q-Tel in 2014 [10].

15.5 Social Media Monitoring Tools

Selecting social media marketing tools can take some time, depending on the user's mission. Fortunately, there are dozens of social media monitoring tools on the market each with slightly different basic capabilities, and the top tier tools have considerable functionality but will cost money. Many social media sites have some sort of tool that allows users to conduct a search of the site by subject and they offer those limited services for free. More sophisticated tools are available but they have fees attached to them, and the more sophisticated the tool the higher the fees. There are several sources of information and comparison websites for social media monitoring tools:

■ The Top 25 Social Media Monitoring Tools: http://keyhole.co/blog/the-top-25-social-media-monitoring-tools/
■ Social Media Monitoring Reviews 2016 Best: http://www.toptenreviews.com/services/internet/best-social-media-monitoring/
■ Six Social Media Monitoring Tools to Track Your Brand: http://www.social-mediaexaminer.com/6-social-media-monitoring-tools/
■ 46 Free Social Media Monitoring Tools to Improve Your Results: http://www.dreamgrow.com/69-free-social-media-monitoring-tools/
■ Never Miss a Thing: 11 Powerful Social Media Monitoring Tools: https://blog.hootsuite.com/social-media-monitoring-tools/
■ Marketing: Top 15 Free Social Media Monitoring Tools: https://www.brandwatch.com/2013/08/top-10-free-social-media-monitoring-tools/
■ Ten Free Social Media Monitoring Tools: http://www.procommunicator.com/free-monitoring-tools/
■ Best Social Media Monitoring Software: https://www.g2crowd.com/categories/social-media-monitoring

Review websites each have a slightly different approach so reading several of the reviews can provide more insight into the product. Reviews can be found using

Table 15.2 Social Media Monitoring Tools Not in Top Tier

76Insigh	Icerocket	ReviewInc
Addictomatic	Infegy atlas,	Sendible
Adobe Social	Klear	Shoutlet
AgoraPulse	Klout	Social response
Audiense Sprinklr	MarketMeSuite	Socialbakers
BackTweets	MediaMiser	Spredfast
BlitzMetrics	MediaVantage	Sprout Social
BoardTracker	Meltwater	SWIX
Bottlenose	Meltwater Buzz	Technorati
BrandsEye	Mention	Topsy
Buffer for business	Monitter	Trackur
CARMA	NetBase	Tracx
Collective intellect	Oktopost	TweetBeep
Crowd analyzer	OutboundEngine	TweetDeck
CyberAlert	Pinterest Web	Twitalyzer
Cyfe	Analytics	Ubermetrics Delta
Falcon.io	Plugg.io	UberVU
Fliptop	Radarly	Union Metrics
Geofeedia	Reddit Keywo	Vocus
Geopiq for Instagram	Monitor Pro	Web2express
Google alerts	Reputology	Monitoring
Gorkana		Workstreamer

most search engines. The list presented earlier was generated using Yahoo search. Many of these tools will evolve over time, so it is wise to read the latest reviews before making a purchasing decision. The tools that charge a fee, have consistently good reviews, and are rather popular include Brand24, Brandwatch Analytics, Crimson Hexagon, Digimind Social, Hootsuite, NetBase, NUVI, Social Studio, Synthesio, Sysomos, Talkwalker, and Zoho Social.

There are many popular social media monitoring tools, some are free, some have a basic service that is free and an advanced service for which there is a fee, and some charge a fee but do not offer any free service. Tools that are not in the top tier of reviews are shown in Table 15.2.

15.6 Conclusions

To fight crime and terrorism it is necessary for security agencies and criminal justice investigators in countries around the world to monitor social media. Other groups such as political campaigns, corporations, and special interest groups monitor social media to track their known adversaries' use of social media. This chapter reviewed monitoring trends and tools to monitor social media warfare activities. Important conclusions can be drawn from the material presented in this chapter:

- Government agencies routinely monitor social media to track terrorists, drug cartel leaders, or other persons known to have been involved in major crimes.
- Several foreign governments have been known to monitor social media, websites, and e-mails for security and legal purposes.
- Government agencies recruit social media analysts for a variety of monitoring purposes, including fighting crime and terrorism but also to help respond to disasters.
- Social media sites and resources should be viewed as another tool in the law enforcement investigative toolbox and should be used in a manner that adheres to the same principles that govern all law enforcement activity.
- A new breed of private investigator will look into the social media posts, status updates, photos, and conversations of an individual or group. Social media investigations are reportedly being used more and more in custody cases, divorces, and even criminal trials.
- Corporations and investors hire private investigators or consultants to search and monitor social media sites for intelligence about competitors or to monitor potential insider leaks or evidence of employee misconduct.
- The CIA has supported the development of technology to monitor social media and collect data and information from social media websites.
- Selecting social media marketing tools can take time depending on the user's mission.

15.7 Agenda for Action

The fight against crime and terrorism has been going on for a long time and there is no end in sight. Social media warfare, on the other hand, is in its infancy and it is time to get ahead of it and not flounder as has been the case in the face of cyber threats. Action steps should include, but not be limited to, the following areas:

- Establish and support research efforts focusing on social media monitoring and data mining.
- Support further research efforts focusing on data visualization and information mined from social media monitoring.
- Support further research efforts focusing on data and information mining from social media.
- Expand research efforts focusing on situational awareness and establish a common operating picture using social media warfare tactics.

15.8 Key Terms

Common operating picture is the mutual understanding and common vision of what actions all players will take to address a situation.

Personally identifiable information (PII) is information that can be used to distinguish or trace an individual's identity, either alone or when combined with other personal or identifying information that is linked or linkable to a specific individual.

Privacy impact assessment (PIA) is an analysis of how information is handled by ensuring handling conforms to applicable legal, regulatory, and policy requirements regarding privacy, determining the risks and effects of collecting, maintaining, and disseminating information in identifiable form in an electronic information system, and examining and evaluating protections and alternative processes for handling information to mitigate potential privacy risks.

Publicly available social media is social media applications and content that can be accessed and viewed by a general public without restrictions.

Situational awareness is the level of current knowledge and understanding of a social condition, anomaly, environmental condition, or conflict situation.

15.9 Seminar Discussion Topics

Discussion topics for graduate- or professional-level seminars:

- What experience have seminar participants had in situations where social media was being monitored? What was the purpose of the monitoring?
- What experience have seminar participants had using social media monitoring tools? What tools were used?
- What experience have seminar participants had using data visualization tools to analyze monitored social media? What tools were used?

15.10 Seminar Group Project

Divide participants into multiple groups with each group taking 10–15 minutes to develop a list of methods to monitor social media content. Upon completion, have groups exchange their lists of methods, with groups taking 10–15 minutes to develop measures that an adversary might use to reduce the effectiveness of the identified monitoring methods. Meet as a group and discuss the offensive tactics selected by the groups and the defensive measures to counter the tactics that were developed by the groups.

References

1. Department of Homeland Security. 2011. Privacy compliance review of the NOC Media Monitoring Initiative. Accessed September 30, 2016. https://www.dhs.gov/xlibrary/assets/privacy/privacy_privcomrev_ops_monitoring_initiative.pdf.
2. U.S. Department of State. 2014. NEA/I. Iraqi Political and Social Media Monitoring Project. Accessed October 4, 2016. http://www.state.gov/m/irm/vfp/253330.htm.
3. U.S. Department of Homeland Security. 2016. Privacy impact assessment for the FEMA operational use of publicly available social media for situational awareness. Accessed October 4, 2016. https://www.dhs.gov/sites/default/files/publications/privacy-pia-FEMA-OUSM-April2016.pdf.
4. U.S. National Park Service. Investigative services. Accessed October 4, 2016. https://www.nps.gov/orgs/1563/intelligence-analysis.htm.
5. U.S. Department of Justice, Office of Justice Programs. 2013. Developing a policy on the use of social media in intelligence and investigative activities: Guidance and recommendations. Accessed September 28, 2016. https://it.ojp.gov/documents/d/Developing%20a%20Policy%20on%20the%20Use%20of%20Social%20Media%20in%20Intelligence%20and%20Inves....pdf.
6. Kringen, John A. 2015. Keeping watch on the world: Rethinking the concept of global coverage in the U.S. intelligence community. *Studies in Intelligence* 59, no. 3. Accessed September 28, 2016. https://www.cia.gov/library/center-for-the-study-of-intelligence/csi-publications/csi-studies/studies/vol-59-no-3/pdfs/Keeping-Watch-on-the-World.pdf.
7. U.S. Central Intelligence Agency. 2012. Looking ahead. Accessed October 5, 2016. https://www.cia.gov/library/reports/archived-reports-1/Ann_Rpt_2002/looking.html
8. U.S. Central Intelligence Agency. 2014. The CIA and you: CIA's contributions to modern technology. Accessed October 5, 2016. https://www.cia.gov/news-information/featured-story-archive/2014-featured-story-archive/the-cia-and-you-cia2019s-contributions-to-modern-technology.html.
9. U.S. Congress Committee on Science, Space, and Technology. 2006. Should Congress establish "ARPA–E," the Advanced Research Projects Agency–Energy? Hearing before the Committee on Science, House of Representatives. Accessed October 5, 2016. http://commdocs.house.gov/committees/science/hsy26480.000/hsy26480_0.HTM
10. TaxExemptWorld.com. In-Q-Tel IRS form 990 return of organization exempt from income tax 2014. Accessed October 5, 2016. http://www.TaxExemptWorld.com.

Glossary of Key Terms

active deception: measures designed to mislead by causing an object or situation to seem threatening when a threat does not exist; it normally involves a calculated policy of disclosing half-truths supported by appropriate "proof" signals or other material evidence.

advance fee fraud: are fee schemes that require victims to advance relatively small sums of money in the hope of realizing much larger gains. Not all advance fee schemes are investment frauds. In those that are, however, victims are told that in order to have the opportunity to be an investor (in an initial offering of a promising security, investment, or commodity, for example), the victim must first send funds to cover taxes or processing fees, and so on.

affinity fraud: perpetrators of affinity fraud take advantage of people's tendency to trust others with whom they share similarities, such as religion or ethnic identity, to gain their trust and money.

alternative master narratives: are designed to replace violent extremist narrative by offering an entire cultural, political, or social philosophy that eliminates the appeal of the extremist narrative.

alternative narratives: are narratives that are designed to replace radical or extremist narratives, and which are intended to provide viable alternatives to radicalization.

asymmetric warfare: is warfare in which belligerents are mismatched in their military capabilities or their accustomed methods of engagement.

A-team, B-team: is an experimental method developed within the intelligence community in the mid-1970s to improve the quality of national intelligence estimates on important warning problems through competitive and alternative analysis. The "A-team" usually includes U.S. intelligence analysts, while the "B-team" consists of members outside of the intelligence community. Both teams look at identical warning problems and take different sides of an issue.

backdoor: a backdoor generally circumvents security programs and provides access to a program, an online service, or an entire computer system. It can be authorized or unauthorized, documented or undocumented.

best practices: are techniques or methodologies that, through experience and research, have reliably led to a desired or optimum result.

bias-free police and court practices: are criminal justice practices that do not discriminate against any type of minority and treat all citizens equally.

biometrics: is the science of using one or more unique physical characteristic or behavioral trait to identify individuals.

chain of custody: is a process used to maintain and document the chronological history of evidence. Documents should include name or initials of the individual collecting the evidence, each person or entity subsequently having custody of it, dates the items were collected or transferred, agency and case number, victim's or suspect's name, and a brief description of the item.

chaos factor: is a condition that occurs as a result of the unsettled and disrupted routine operations of an organization's or a facility, and an atmosphere of disorder and confusion prevails.

chat group: is an Internet site that allows users to engage in large group conversation.

child pornography: is sexually explicit or themed images or recordings involving minors less than 18 years of age.

child sexual exploitation: is the recruiting or involvement of minors less than 18 years of age in any sexual capacity.

citizen diplomacy: is diplomacy performed by non-professional diplomats to promote specific cultural or political agendas on behalf of their country.

citizen journalist: is an individual that uses technology such as smartphones to record police or government representative actions and disseminate that evidence to the community at large and to interested activists.

civil society leaders: are individuals who hold government, business, or religious positions that enable them to influence their societies, communities, and individuals.

civilian oversight boards: are independent boards not comprised of police officials or officers that review and examine complaints of police misconduct.

common operating picture: is the mutual understanding and common vision of what actions all players will take to address a situation.

community engagement strategy: is a policing strategy that brings citizens and civic groups into a partnership with policing practices and public safety concerns.

community resilience: is the social beliefs and norms of a local population that enables the community to resist radicalization and neutralizes the impact of the radical narrative.

community-targeted approach: is a set of methods and techniques designed to engage individuals or groups in the communities where they live to diminish the possibility of radicalization and to identify radicalized individuals or groups.

compromise: is a violation of the security policy of a system such that unauthorized disclosure of sensitive information may have occurred.

computer fraud: is crime involving deliberate misrepresentation, alteration, or disclosure of data in order to obtain something of value (usually for monetary gain).

computer use surveillance: is a process that tracks and records what users do or attempt to do when using corporate computer systems.

consolidated registry: is a mechanism the U.S. military services use to inventory, approve, and authenticate social media use throughout all levels of the services.

constitutional and effective policing: is the use of policing practices that simultaneously protect the constitutional rights of citizens while effectively addressing public safety concerns.

consumer-generated content: is digital content that is produced by self-publishers and sometimes picked up or referenced in traditional media.

corroborating evidence: is evidence that tends to support a proposition that is already supported by some evidence.

counter messaging: is the process of matching radical extremist messages on a head-to-head basis in order mitigate the recruitment and radicalization to violent extremism.

countermeasure: is any action, device, procedure, technique, or other measure that reduces the vulnerability of or threat to a system.

counter narrative to radicalization: is a narrative that neutralizes or invalidates the narrative designed to radicalize individuals or groups.

credible voices: are those voices of trusted community leaders, religious leaders, and intellectuals that can provide a positive influence on a society or community.

credit monitoring: is a service and process that warns people about activity that shows up on their credit report.

crime analysis and situational assessment reports: record and communicate analytic activities to enable law enforcement agencies to identify and understand trends, causes, and potential indicia of criminal activity, including terrorism.

criminal enterprise: the FBI defines a criminal enterprise as a group of individuals with an identified hierarchy, or comparable structure, engaged in significant criminal activity.

criminal groups: are comprised of people who are organized for the purpose of committing criminal activity for economic gain or political clout or dominance in a specific geographical area.

criminal intelligence information: is data that meets criminal intelligence collection criteria and that has been evaluated and determined to be relevant to the identification of criminal activity engaged in by individuals who or organizations that are reasonably suspected of involvement in criminal activity.

critical industry sectors: are those industries and business sectors that provide essential infrastructure support for the economic activity that enables a country to function economically, politically, and socially.

critical intelligence: is intelligence that requires immediate attention by a commander or policy maker and that may enhance or refute previously held beliefs about hostilities or actions, leading to a change of policy.

cross-deputization agreements: allow law enforcement personnel from state and tribal entities to cross jurisdictions in criminal cases. Such agreements have been used to enhance law enforcement capabilities in areas were state and tribal lands were contiguous and intermingled. Under some agreements, federal, state, county/local, and/or tribal law enforcement officers have the power to arrest Indian and non-Indian wrongdoers wherever the violation of law occurs.

crowdsourcing: is soliciting data related to a specific topic, idea, or issue from a large population of public users, traditionally an online community, who have knowledge of that topic, idea, or issue.

culinary diplomacy: is the process of using culinary celebrities and a culinary context and agenda to promote improved relations and cultural exchanges between nations.

culture of security: is an organization culture in which security pervades every aspect of daily life and in all operational situations.

custom offers: are exclusive proposals that a seller can create in response to the specific requirements of a buyer on Fiverr.

custom orders: are requests made by a buyer to receive a custom offer from a seller on Fiverr.

customer-centric approach: means that agencies respond to customers' needs and make it easy to find and share information and accomplish important tasks through the delivery of timely data, informative content, simple transactions, and seamless interactions that are easily accessible anytime, anywhere, and from any device.

cyberbullying: is bullying that takes place using electronic technology including devices and equipment such as cell phones, computers, and tablets as well as communication tools including social media sites, text messages, chat, and websites.

cyberstalking: is the use of the Internet, e-mail, social media, or other electronic communications devices to stalk another person.

damages: Monetary compensation or indemnity for wrong or injury caused by the violation of a legal right. Compensatory damages are a reimbursement for actual loss or injury. Exemplary damages are a monetary award by way of punishment for injury caused by aggravated circumstances or malice, in addition to compensation for the injury. Punitive damages are monetary compensation awarded in excess of ordinary damages, as punishment for a gross wrong.

digital government: is a system of electronically accessible utilities and applications that provides access to government services and information.

disaster fraud: is often committed by individuals who seek to profit via false claims of damages. There are also non-insurance-related disaster frauds where organizations and individuals solicit contributions for victims of disaster. Victims may be approached through unsolicited e-mails asking for donations to a legitimate-sounding organization. The schemer will instruct the victim to send a donation via a money transfer.

discriminatory policing practices: are those practices that target specific segments of the population including minorities of any type.

disinformation: is false or irrelevant information made available to deceive.

domestic anti-social groups: are groups of people or mini-societies that oppose the larger society in which they live and/or work.

domestic fanatics: are radical groups that are residents or citizens of the countries in which they kill, sabotage, or spread hate and fear.

economic exploitation: in this context is the excessive fining and penalizing of citizens for minor offenses in order to raise revenue for a governmental entity.

eco-terrorists: are individuals or groups that oppose environmental policies or actions of governments and private companies and who use a variety of methods to hinder or halt projects or operations.

effective prosecution: is the successful prosecution of intellectual crime perpetrators while simultaneously protecting the trade secrets and other intellectual property of the victim organization.

electronic aggression: is the use of any electronic device to commit such acts as cyberbullying, Internet harassment, and Internet bullying.

exposure tactics: most often involve the unauthorized release of information that might embarrass or otherwise jeopardize the owner or creator of the information exposed.

facial recognition technologies: are technologies that enable the identification of human subjects in an idle position or while in motion; the identification and images are used to improve security and security officer safety.

family child abductions: are abductions of a child by a family member that does not have legal custody of the child.

freedom of information law: is a law defining the public's right to access the records of government.

gaps in security: are security measures or mitigation methods that are inadequate to protect an asset or do not thoroughly protect the asset that they were deployed to protect.

geocoding: a process and system of assigning locational values (e.g., latitude and longitude coordinates) to attribute data, such as an event or an address, that results in a feature being able to be mapped.

geographic information system (GIS): is a set of computer tools and procedures used to collect, manage, analyze, and display information associated with a specific location; a computerized mapping and database management application.

geotagging: is the process of embedding global positioning system (GPS) coordinates in photographs taken using a smartphone or other GPS-capable device.

Gigs: are services offered on Fiverr.

Gig Extras: are additional services offered on top of the seller's Gig for an additional fee defined by the seller on Fiverr.

Gig Packages: on Fiverr allow sellers to offer services in different formats and prices, including upgrades that allow sellers to price their service for an amount over the initial basic $5.00 fee.

Gig page: a Gig page on Fiverr is where the seller describes their Gig and the Gig's terms, and the buyer can purchase the Gig.

hackathon: is an event in which computer programmers and others have a specific focus, which may include the programming language used, the operating system, an application, an application programming interface (API), the subject, or the demographic group of the programmers. In other cases, there is no restriction on the type of software being created.

hate messages: are social media posts that use obnoxious language to ridicule or discriminate against minority or ethnic groups.

identity intelligence: is the intelligence resulting from the processing of identity attributes concerning individuals, groups, networks, or populations of interest.

identity monitoring: provides alerts when personal information like bank account information or social security, driver's license, passport, or medical identification (ID) number is being used in ways that generally will not show up on a credit report.

identity recovery services: are designed to help regain control of a name and finances after identity theft occurs.

identity theft: is the unauthorized use of an individual's personally identifiable information to impersonate the individual and illegally use that information to commit crimes of fraud.

identity theft insurance: is offered by most of the major identity theft protection services and generally covers out-of-pocket expenses directly associated with reclaiming an identity.

identity theft protection: services are monitoring and recovery services that watch for signs that an identity thief may be using personal information and helps to deal with the effects of identity theft after it happens.

ideological conflict: is the conflict perpetuated by radicalized groups against mainstream society and minority groups.

incident report: is a document that describes an occurrence of a security incident, or a violation or imminent threat of violation of computer security policies, acceptable use of policies, or standard security practices (NIST SP800-61).

indicator: is a measurement that reflects the status of a system that reveals the direction of a system (a community, the economy, the environment), whether it is going forward or backward, increasing or decreasing, improving or deteriorating, or staying the same.

indigenous group: is a group or class of people who live in their area of origin.

industry leader: is a company or organization that performs better than its competitors, bringing innovations to its field of endeavor, and whose products or services become the industry standard to match or beat in open market competition.

influencing aligned entities: is the process of convincing allies of the validity and legitimacy of a position or action.

information-centric approach: decouples information from its presentation by beginning with the data or content and describing that information clearly, and then exposing it to other computers in a machine-readable format commonly known as providing web APIs.

information operations: is the integrated employment, during military operations, of information-related capabilities in concert with other lines of operation to influence, disrupt, corrupt, or usurp the decision making of adversaries and potential adversaries while protecting our own.

infringement of intellectual property: can be the unauthorized reproduction or distribution of copyrighted material, the misappropriation of trade secrets for commercial gain, or the unauthorized use of a trademarked name or logo.

insider misconduct: conduct by an employee that is against organization policies or procedures or that otherwise can harm the employing organization.

insider-outsider team: is two or more people who jointly conspire to act maliciously against an organization where one of them (the insider) is employed or has privileged access.

insider-outsider threat: is a threat that emerges as a result of a relationship between an employee and a person working for an outside organization or who is otherwise not related to the employee's organization.

intelligence operations: is the variety of intelligence and counterintelligence tasks that are carried out by various intelligence organizations and activities within the intelligence process.

international fanatics: International fanatics are individuals, groups of people, or mini-societies that are greatly differentiated from the world around them by a belief system that is totally disconnected from larger realities in which they live and have a tendency to act out those differences in violent ways or politically or economically disruptive manners. They are members of radical groups that cross borders or influence individuals or groups in other countries to kill, sabotage, or spread hate and fear.

lessons learned process: is a structured method of evaluating incidents or events and determining what individuals or organizations could have done better to deal with the situation and transforming those lessons into positive actions through employee training, improving procedures, or improving mitigation methods or technology.

location tracking: is a process that employs technology such as GPS trackers of radio-frequency identification (RFID) chips to monitor the movement and/or location of assets or people.

mailing lists: are topic-oriented, e-mail-based message bases that can be read and posted to. Users subscribe to the lists they want to read and receive messages via e-mail.

mailing list moderator: is a person who looks over the messages sent to a particular mailing list, sometimes choosing not to include inappropriate messages, before sending them out. Some mailing lists are moderated, others are not.

media convergence: is the melding of different media types into multi-faceted streams of information and entertainment including video, text, photos, sound, and graphics, which were at one time all delivered from separate platforms and applications.

multi-generational challenge: describes a long-term approach of assimilating and socializing individuals and groups.

need-to-know: is the necessity for access to, knowledge of, or possession of specific information required to carry out official duties.

netiquette: is a group of principles and concepts that encourage the socially proper use of social media and other Internet applications.

nullifying opponents: is the effort to discredit or disable opponents.

online alias: is an online identity encompassing identifiers, such as name and date of birth, differing from an employee's actual identifiers and that use a non-governmental Internet protocol (IP) address. An online alias may be used to monitor activity on social media websites or to engage in authorized online undercover activity.

online undercover activity: is the use of an online alias to engage in interactions with a person via social media sites that may or may not be in the public domain (i.e., "friending" a person on Facebook).

parental control filtering software: is designed to allow parents to electronically control how their children use the Internet and social media and to monitor and generate reports on a child's computer usage.

passive deception: are measures designed to mislead a foreign power, organization, or person by causing an object or situation to appear non-threatening, when a threat does exist, by downplaying capabilities or intentions to look less threatening.

personally identifiable information (PII): is information that can be used to distinguish or trace an individual's identity, either alone or when combined with other personal or identifying information that is linked or linkable to a specific individual.

personal technologies: include individually owned devices such as cell phones, tablets, laptops, and digital media.

personal use: means using a service or an item only for personal reasons and goals that do not have any relationship to the organization employing the individual using the item or service.

persuasion of non-aligned entities: is the process of convincing non-allies of the validity and legitimacy of a position or action.

plain language: is the straightforward writing that enables readers of all types and levels of education to better understand written content in any media through which it is delivered.

platform of security and privacy: means securing how data is stored, processed, or transmitted.

policing style: is the manner and procedural conduct by which policing is managed in a community.

positive message promotional activities: are those that promote positive social behavior and counter negative messaging.

positive narratives: are designed to negate violent extremist messages and provide powerful incentives for positive action.

predatory policing methods: are policing methods that are not designed to protect life or property but are geared toward raising revenue for a governmental entity.

privacy impact assessment (PIA): is an analysis of how information is handled by ensuring handling conforms to applicable legal, regulatory, and policy requirements regarding privacy; determining the risks and effects of collecting, maintaining, and disseminating information in identifiable form in an electronic information system; and examining and evaluating protections and alternative processes for handling information to mitigate potential privacy risks.

public safety issues: encompass actions or conditions that impede the everyday functioning of a community and the protection of life and property.

publicly available social media: is social media applications and content that can be accessed and viewed by a general public without restrictions.

radicalization: is the process of indoctrinating previously non-violent individuals or groups into anti-social violent ideologies and actions.

rangers: are rather secretive groups of people with special talents that often work and live on the fringes of society and stay secluded but in touch with the world around them.

recruiting and indoctrination: is the process of drawing people into a cause and teaching cause-related doctrine.

reinforcing alliance partners: is showing support of an allies' position or action.

relationship building: is the process of establishing cooperative efforts with like-minded people or organizations.

revenge porn: is the disclosure of sexually explicit images without consent and for no legitimate purpose.

security awareness: is the basic level of understanding of security and recognition of the importance of security.

security threats: are conditions, people, or events that can jeopardize the security of a nation, organization, a facility, or any asset belonging to the threatened entity.

security vigilance: is the constant attention given to security during day-to-day operations; it contributes to security by encouraging the reporting of security violations and makes suggestions on how to improve security when weaknesses are observed.

self-validation: is the process of assuring the world of the validity and legitimacy of a position or action.

sensitive information: is information held by or created by an organization that if revealed to the wrong party would cause harm to the organization owning or creating the information.

sextortion: is a crime closely related to revenge porn, however, with sextortion a person is blackmailed to not have photos or videos posted on the Internet whereas with revenge porn the dynamic is usually the opposite, victims are asked for money to remove already posted material.

shared platform approach: is the use of a common computer system or architecture used by all government agencies to reduce inefficiencies created by fragmented procurement and development practices that waste money and result in inconsistent adoption of new technologies and approaches.

situational awareness: is the level of current knowledge and understanding of a social condition, anomaly, environmental condition, or conflict situation.

social capital: is a composite measure that reflects the breadth and depth of civic community (staying informed about community life and participating in its associations) as well as the public's participation in political life.

social media applications: are any existing or future networked computer program that facilitates communication between individuals or individuals and groups.

social media policies: specify who in an organization is responsible for social media operations, specify when, why, where, and how social media can be used on behalf of an organization, and provide guidance on the inappropriate use of social media by corporate media staff and employees.

social media presence: is an organization's use of social media accounts and applications to communicate to individuals or groups as well as the mention, comments, discussions, and display of any material on any social media application that relates to or depicts an organization.

social media warfare mercenaries: are individuals or groups that perform social media tasks as agents or imposters on behalf of organizations that desire to have a social media presence or disrupt the social media activities of other people or organizations.

sociocultural analysis: is the analysis of adversaries and other relevant actors that integrates concepts, knowledge, and understanding of societies, populations, and other groups of people, including their activities, relationships, and perspectives across time and space at varying scales.

sovereign citizens: are anti-government extremists who believe that even though they physically reside in the country, they are separate or "sovereign" from the United States. Thus, they believe they don't have to answer to any government authority, including courts, taxing entities, motor vehicle departments, or law enforcement.

special interest terrorism: are acts of violence or destruction by extremist special interest groups seeking to resolve specific issues and influence segments of society, including the general public, to change attitudes about issues considered important to their causes.

spoofing: is an attempt to gain access to a system by posing as an authorized user; it is synonymous with impersonating, masquerading, or mimicking.

sports diplomacy: is the process of using sport celebrities and a sports context and agenda to promote improved relations and cultural exchanges between nations.

sustainability: is the long-term health and vitality—cultural, economic, environmental, and social—of a community. Sustainable thinking considers the connections between various elements of a healthy society, and implies a longer time span (i.e., decades, instead of years).

tactical intelligence: is the intelligence required for the planning and conduct of tactical operations.

The Code of Federal Regulations (CFR): is the legal code formed by rules published in the *Federal Register* by executive departments and agencies of the federal government. A CFR citation number is used to reference each rule.

theft of intellectual property: is the illegal obtaining of copyrighted or patented material, trade secrets, or trademarks (including designs, plans, blueprints, codes, computer programs, software, formulas, recipes, graphics), usually by electronic copying.

theft of personal or financial data: is the illegal obtaining of information that potentially allows someone to use or create accounts under another name (individual, business, or some other entity). Personal information includes names, dates of birth, Social Security numbers, or other personal information. Financial information includes credit, debit, or automated teller machine (ATM) card accounts or personal identification numbers (PIN).

trade secrets: are any form or type of business process, scientific formula, technical specification, economic data, or engineering designs that an owner has taken measures to protect and from which economic value can be derived.

Trojan horse: is a computer program with an apparently or actually useful function that contains additional (hidden) functions that surreptitiously exploit the legitimate authorizations of the invoking process to the detriment of security or integrity.

unauthorized use: is the reading, recording, transmitting, or storing of data that belongs to a specific party and is meant for a specific and restricted use by an owning or custodial organization or its designees.

unstructured data: is data that is more free-form, such as multimedia files, images, sound files, or unstructured text. Unstructured data does not necessarily follow any format or hierarchical sequence, nor does it follow any relational rules; it is usually computerized information that does not have a data structure that is easily readable by a machine.

Usenet newsgroups: there are more than 29,000 topic-oriented message bases that can be read and posted to (also called newsgroups).

valid law enforcement purpose: is the purpose for information/intelligence gathering, collection, use, retention, or sharing that furthers the authorized functions and activities of a law enforcement agency, which may include the prevention of crime, ensuring the safety of the public, furthering officer safety, and homeland and national security, while adhering to law and agency policy designed to protect the privacy, civil rights, and civil liberties.

vetting: is a generic term to describe the full spectrum of asset evaluation for authenticity, reliability, and hostile control. It includes ops testing, case officer and psychological assessment, polygraph, security, counterintelligence interview, production review and personal record questionnaires.

vulnerability assessment: is a structured process by which to evaluate how secure a nation, organization, or individual is based on the perception of threats and security needs.

warning intelligence: are those intelligence activities intended to detect and report time-sensitive intelligence information on foreign developments that forewarn of hostile actions or intention against U.S. entities, partners, or interests.

Western-based extremists: are citizens or residents of Western countries that engage or who want to engage in violence against the governments or residents in the countries in which they reside.

wiki: is a Web environment that allows visitors to openly edit the content, used primarily for collaborative content development and publishing, for example, Wikipedia.

Index